FROM BOOT MONEY TO *BOSMAN*: FOOTBALL, SOCIETY AND THE LAW

David McArdle, PhD

Research Fellow
De Montfort University

Cavendish
Publishing
Limited

London • Sydney

First published in Great Britain 2000 by Cavendish Publishing Limited,
The Glass House, Wharton Street, London WC1X 9PX, United Kingdom
Telephone: + 44 (0)20 7278 8000   Facsimile: + 44 (0)20 7278 8080
Email: info@cavendishpublishing.com
Website: www.cavendishpublishing.com

British Library Cataloguing in Publication Data

McArdle, David
Football, Society and the Law
1 Sports – Law and legislation – Great Britain   2 Soccer – Law and
legislation – Great Britain   3 Soccer – Social aspects – Great Britain
I Title
344.4'1'09

ISBN 1 85941 437 0

Cover photographs by Ravi Deepres
Printed and bound in Great Britain

Books are to be returned on or before
the last date below.

LIBREX—

FROM BOOT MONEY TO *BOSMAN*: FOOTBALL, SOCIETY AND THE LAW

Cavendish
Publishing
Limited

London • Sydney

WITHDRAWN

For Leo Alexander Daniel.
But don't eat it all at once.

ACKNOWLEDGMENTS

The biggest professional debts of gratitude I owe are to the photographer Ravi Deepres and Mark James of Manchester Metropolitan University. Ravi kindly allowed me to use his work for the cover – those interested in his work can contact him via me or by getting in touch with the Vivid Gallery in Birmingham. Mark agreed to write the chapter on on-field violence and player injuries. He has forgotten more about those areas than I will ever know and I would like to acknowledge his contribution. My sincere thanks to both of you.

Thanks are also due to Professor Trevor Slack, who gave me the opportunity to work on this project at De Montfort University. Professor David Lewis took the lead on the research into hotlines, taskforces and codes of practice during my time as a Research Fellow at Middlesex University Business School, and I'd like to acknowledge both his support and his generosity of spirit. Colleagues at Anglia University have provided a wealth of information on various aspects of this book, notably via their Sports Law Bulletin, while Liverpool's Football Research Unit gave me the opportunity to explore some of these issues with the students on their Football Studies MBA. Special thanks to Geoff Pearson, Adam Brown, Fiona Miller, Richard Giulianotti and Gary Armstrong. Thanks also to all at Cavendish, especially to Ruth Massey for her professionalism. Thanks to Steve Redhead for all sorts of things and to Guy Osborn and Steve Greenfield for inspiration and witty banter. The influence of all those people means those expecting *The Boys' Book of Football Law* will, I hope, be disappointed. Sport matters, like it or not, and perhaps this book will go a little way towards undermining legal academia's misplaced intellectual snobbery.

Some of the material discussed in this book received its first public airing in various academic journals. It is reproduced here with the permission of those journals. Thanks, then, to the editors and referees of Culture, Sport, Society, the Cambrian Law Review, the European Journal of Sports Management, the Nottingham Law Journal and the Web Journal of Current Legal Issues.

My biggest personal debts are to Anne and Tony McArdle for support beyond the call of parental duty and to Charity Smith for her love and inspiration. This book is dedicated to her and to our darling, beautiful, extraordinary little boy.

David McArdle
East London
October 2000

CONTENTS

TABLE OF CASES

TABLE OF STATUTES

TABLE OF STATUTORY INSTRUMENTS

INTRODUCTION

In 1998, the income of English football clubs was in the region of £700 million. Since 1990, clubs have spent £600 million in upgrading grounds. The net asset value of the 92 clubs is around £200 million, rising to over £1 billion if the players in whose contracts the clubs invest are regarded as assets. The current Premier League TV deal alone is worth £670 million over five years (Szymanski and Kuypers, 2000, p 1).

The first football club to be listed on the stock market was Tottenham Hotspur, back in 1983, when Irving Scholar was chairman. Spurs diversified into sportswear, fashion and computerised ticketing systems, but these diversions performed no more successfully than the team did, and it fell into debt. In 1991, when Spurs won its first trophy (the FA Cup) since 1984, Alan Sugar (whose computer company, Amstrad, manufactured many of Sky TV's satellite dishes) purchased a controlling interest, although the club continues to be quoted on the stock market. In the summer of 1998, just months before its bid for Manchester United, it was rumoured that News International was trying to buy a controlling interest in Tottenham.

Spurs' experience did little to persuade other clubs to follow the flotation route – with the obvious exception of Manchester United, whose flotation in 1991 raised £7 million. However, even after United had taken the plunge, it was not until 1996 – after the European Championships had confirmed football's media friendly image and its place within the firmament of acceptable entertainment for the middle class family – that other owners and the stock market came to believe that football clubs could be a viable investment. Several hundred million pounds were spent on shares in the newly floated football clubs of Chelsea, Newcastle, Aston Villa and Queen's Park Rangers (as Loftus Road plc). Over a dozen others were involved in takeovers or capital raising ventures between 1996 and 1999. These included West Ham United, Leeds United, Manchester City and Leicester City. None of these clubs have come anywhere near matching what Manchester United have achieved.

'You're so rich it's unbelievable'

The achievements of Manchester United since its flotation have been due in no small measure to a simple, but devastatingly successful, business strategy. When the club floated in 1991, it decided to transfer its fixed assets and non-footballing businesses to a company so that the company, not the club, would receive a 'substantial part' of future advertising, sponsorship and promotional income as well as the rental income from the use of the ground. As Manchester United plc, the company, is not affiliated to the Football Association (FA), it is not bound by the FA's restrictions on the payment of dividends. Consequently, it can make payments to its shareholders. The company owns the football club, Manchester United Ltd, which is affiliated to the FA and which, accordingly, is not able to pay a dividend.

At the time of the 1991 flotation, the controlling interest in the club was owned by the recently departed Chief Executive, Martin Edwards (who had inherited his father Louis' shares in 1981). Edwards *minimis* is a man best described as 'profit conscious'. United spent heavily in the transfer market during the early 1980s in a failed attempt to compete consistently with the great Liverpool teams of that time. However, after Alex Ferguson was appointed in 1986, Edwards – having got his fingers burned by Ron Atkinson's questionable transfer dealings (Arnold Muerhen, Remi Moses) – was unwilling to give Ferguson similar freedom to pursue players. For example, in 1988, Edwards refused Ferguson permission to sign Paul Gascoigne from Newcastle United. However, in the summer of 1989, a demob-happy Edwards, convinced that he was about to offload his interest in the club to Michael Knighton, relented and allowed Ferguson to spend £8 million on five new players. The Knighton deal famously fell through in October of that year, but Ferguson's new players – Paul Ince and Gary Pallister among them – helped United to victory in the FA Cup in 1989/90. That success offset a disastrous League campaign, for at one stage the club was a serious candidate for relegation and, in retrospect, the most crucial match of Alex Ferguson's managerial career at Manchester United was probably the FA Cup third round tie against Nottingham Forest that year. Had United lost, there is little doubt that Ferguson would have been sacked.

The rest, Brian, is history. In 1991/92, United won the championship of the old First Division and, in the first eight years of the Premiership's existence, they won that title on six occasions. During the 1990s, they won the FA Cup four times and, on the last occasion, in 1998/99, their success represented the second leg of their hat-trick of the Premier League, the FA Cup and the European Champions' League. The club has not fared too badly financially, either. Between 1991 and 1997, Manchester United plc's cumulative profit was almost £82 million; the total dividend payout was around £20 million. This meant that an investor who had paid 385 p for a share upon flotation in 1991 would, by the middle of 1998, have seen its value rise to the equivalent of £24.75.

However, it is fair to say that not all United fans, and certainly not all football supporters in general, were enamoured of the financial success story that Manchester United had become. In discussing 'the overt attempt to re-engineer the social make-up of the game' that took place after the publication of the FA's *Blueprint for Football* in 1991, Brown and Walsh comment upon how:

> United's board had gone about the task (of re-packaging the game) with a single minded zeal. Redevelopment, first at the Stretford End and then at the United Road stand, had seen traditional areas of support uprooted and replaced with corporate hospitality and executive seats. The displaced were scattered around the ground, which had a devastating effect on the atmosphere. This was exacerbated in 1994/95 when United's security firm,

Special Projects Security, tried to intimidate those few who were attempting to create a better atmosphere into a silent and passive role at football matches [Brown and Walsh, 1999, p 19].

United's preferential treatment of the neophytes at the expense of its traditional fans led to the foundation, in the spring of 1995, of the Independent Manchester United Supporters' Association. IMUSA was to play a pivotal role in thwarting Murdoch's takeover bid when, in September 1998, BSkyB picked out Manchester United as the 'jewel in the crown' of English football and made a bid of £575 million for the whole company as it sought to capitalise on the game's appeal to a new breed of consumer. The offer price worked out at approximately £36 per share – 50% more than the market price had been in the summer of that year. The more astute City analysts, *au fait* with the globalisation and commodification of football, thought that it still represented a bargain for BSkyB. Analyses of how the relationship between television and football developed in the 1990s, and how it might progress in the near future, suggest that they were right.

'Oooh, you old mogul'

Football was first transmitted live in 1937, when that year's Cup Final between Sunderland and Preston North End was broadcast by the BBC, although the transmission could only be received by those in the immediate vicinity of the television centre at Alexandra Palace. The first game other than the Cup Final to be transmitted live was a Cup tie between Charlton Athletic and Bristol Rovers in 1947; it was not until 1960 that the Football League allowed its matches to be televised. In fact, at that time, the League was actually willing to sanction live broadcasts but the clubs resisted such a move because they were fearful of losing paying spectators. Consequently, with the exception of the FA Cup Final and, occasionally, other ties, only recorded highlights of games were broadcast. 'Match of the Day' first went out in 1964 and, in 1968, ITV began to broadcast 'The Big Match' on Sunday afternoons. The first live broadcasts of Football League games did not take place until 1983 and the total value of the first television contract was the princely sum of £2.6 million – or £28,000 to each of the 92 League clubs.

The creation of the Premiership was a direct consequence of the emergence of satellite television and a realisation that, for years, football had been fleeced by the BBC/ITV duopoly. Even back in the darkest days of the mid-1980s, Robert Maxwell, then Chairman of Derby County and a director of Central Television, had famously opined that football was worth at least £90 million to the television companies. But, prior to the formation of the Premier League in 1992, no more than 20 live League games were broadcast each season – the clubs were still fearful that attendances would suffer if too many live games were shown, although there was no evidence that this was the case. The current deal between the Premier League and the television companies, which expires at the end of the 2000/01 season, allows for the live broadcast of 60 Premiership games. The deal is now worth a total of £180 million to the Premiership clubs alone.

Szymanski and Kuypers (2000) explain that this phenomenal increase in the value of television rights is, in large part, a response to the rise in the game's popularity ('as evidenced by growing attendances'). This increases the value of the game to commercial broadcasters such as BSkyB and the ITV companies, because they can attract more advertising revenue from companies desirous of advertising their products during the innumerable commercial breaks. Before the satellite companies entered the fray, the game's authorities had no option but to deal with the terrestrial companies, which had duly carved up the market on their own terms: 'ITV and BBC did not have to offer prices close to their valuation of the rights, but just enough to make it worthwhile for the football authorities to sell them' (Szymanski and Kuypers, 2000, p 58). Only in 1985/86, when Maxwell had influence over football's authorities, did those authorities refuse to sell on the television companies' terms, and, for the first half of that season, there was no televised football. An agreement was eventually reached under which the TV companies paid £3.1 million for the television rights – a 20% increase in the value of the previous deal, but still a drop in the ocean. In 1988, a new deal was negotiated, but by this time British Satellite Broadcasting (BSB) was already attempting to establish a foothold within broadcasting in the UK. Although its presence was too small to enable it to compete with the terrestrial companies on this occasion, the reality of competition obliged the BBC and ITV to eschew their previous approach and bid for the television rights independently. ITV won the right to broadcast 18 live matches at a cost of £11 million per season, but this new four year deal would expire in 1992. By that time, satellite television would be a major player

In 1989, one year after BSB's foray, Sky Broadcasting launched its own satellite service in the UK. By 1992, Sky and BSB had merged to form BSkyB and this new company, 40% of which is owned by Rupert Murdoch's company, News International, was in a position to challenge the television companies for the television rights when the 1988 deal expired. More pertinently, BSkyB had more to gain from a successful bid than the terrestrial companies had and, consequently, it was willing to bid far more in order to secure them. As Szymanski and Kuypers explain:

> ... the rights were more valuable to [BSkyB] ... as they were able to charge viewers directly for watching and did not have to rely solely on advertising revenue. Football was the vehicle by which BSkyB aimed to penetrate aimed to penetrate the broadcast market [Szymanski and Kuypers, 2000, p 59].

All changed utterly after Hillsborough, and it changed at speed. Implementing Lord Taylor's recommendations that the stadia of the old First and Second Division clubs should be all-seated within five years required money and, although assistance was available from the Football Grounds Improvement Trust and elsewhere, other sources of funding had to be sought. Getting more money from the paying fans ought not to have been one of them, however. Taylor had said that the pricing structures for all-seater stadia should 'suit the cheapest seats to the pockets of those presently paying to stand' (Taylor Report, 1990, para 72). He cited the £6 and £4 then paid at Glasgow Rangers' Ibrox stadium as a reasonable price for the cheapest seats. But the clubs had always made money from committed fans, who would continue to turn up and pay up in sufficient numbers regardless of the admission fee, and they were too soft a target to miss. In the 1990s, a new, more affluent breed of supporter would replace those who were priced out of attending the more illustrious clubs' matches: at Manchester United, 'prices have increased 400–500% in the nine years since the [Taylor] Report' (Brown and Walsh, 2000, p 38), and the same story can be told of most other clubs. Furthermore, the new supporter expected football grounds to provide suitable accoutrements – quality merchandise, edible food, humane toilet facilities and a degree of comfort – and was willing to pay accordingly. Providing all this would cost a substantial sum, but the satellite television companies, buoyed by the commercial possibilities that Italia 90 had brought to their attention, were willing to finance it.

None of this was lost on the Football Association. Its *Blueprint for Football* (1991) proposed the formation of the Premier League so that more power would be concentrated in the hands of these bigger clubs. Rupert Murdoch himself was closely involved in the document's preparation and held a number of meetings with Rick Parry, then the FA's Chief Executive, before its publication. Murdoch and Parry knew that the BBC provided no threat to their plans – funded as it was by the licence fee and with commitments under its Royal Charter to public service broadcasting, the BBC, acting on its own, would be simply unable to match any bid that BSkyB put together. However, if the BBC was to work in cohoots with ITV, there was a possibility that BSkyB would be defeated – or, at least, that it would have to pay considerably more than it wanted to in order to secure the TV rights. Accordingly, the BBC was brought onside through being assured that the 'Match of the Day' Saturday evening highlights package could continue.

Inevitably, the creation of the Premier League was a move that the Football League strongly resisted, culminating in a failed judicial review application, *R v FA ex p Football League Ltd* (1993). The clubs from the old First Division resigned from the Football League and the creation of the Premier League went ahead, although ITV tried to obtain an injunction preventing the TV deal on the basis of the collusion between BSkyB and the FA. The BSkyB/BBC package was well in excess of anything ITV would have been able to offer and the deal netted the Premier League £49 million per season.

However, when the deal was renegotiated at the start of the 1996/97 season, BSkyB paid £150 million, with no increase in the number of live fixtures (60) shown per season. It was reported that two other 'pay TV' companies – Carlton and MAI – submitted rival bids and, under the terms of that 1997 deal, the fee received by the Premier League has increased by £10 million year on year. The Premier League's relationship with Murdoch has been mutually beneficial, though. In 1997, on a turnover of £1.2 billion, BSkyB made profits of £374 million – an increase of over 25% on the previous year. Whatever Premiership football costs BSkyB, the price will be one worth paying – live football is the only reason why BSkyB still exists. But when the details of the next television deal were announced in June 2000, BSkyB was revealed to have paid a massive £1.1 billion to secure the right to televise 66 live Premiership games per season over three years, from August 2001. NTL stumped up £328 million to show 40 matches per season on a pay-per-view basis, while ITV paid £183 million for the weekend highlights package. The emergence of NTL and other companies eager to explore the potential of digital television and pay-per-view explains why BSkyB was so keen to purchase Manchester United, and why it, and other media companies, has been buying stakes of 10% or less in Glasgow Rangers, Leeds United and a host of other top clubs.

This media feeding frenzy, the breast beating over 'hooliganism' and drug use and UEFA's latest attempts to wheedle their way out of the *Bosman* ruling ensure that barely a week passes without the breaking of a high profile football story in which a significant legal issue arises. 'Football and the law' will dwarf any other 'sports law' story – no mean feat when one considers that, over the last five years, 'sports law' has spawned ridiculously overpriced conferences (who on earth attends these things?), niche departments in solicitors' firms, a proliferation of undergraduate and masters' courses, postgraduate theses and more learned tomes than one knows what to do with. 'Sports law' epitomises Redhead's (1995) concept of 'panic law' ('the frenzied-but-simulated state of the law and justice at the end of the century'), but 'football and the law' is panic law careering out of control.

For we have reached the stage where just about every controversial incident in the game of football attracts a clamour for 'a new law' to deal with it, as if the ordinary law of the land is no longer an adequate means of dealing with the hoi polloi's shenanigans. In the new Football (Disorder) Act 2000, Parliament has enacted yet more ill-penned legislation to deal with the drunken, racist violence that is the *raison d'être* of many young Englishmen – in Charlerois this time, and no worse than that which occurs away from the cameras in many town centres of a Friday night. The good news is that the activities of racially abusive payers and managers have finally received some attention, if not yet the realisation that existing employment law provides eminently suitable remedies, if only the clubs were willing to use them. Players, agents, administrators, governing bodies and the like have no excuses for not appreciating the extent to which the law impinges upon their activities. Inaccessibility of information is not a problem, for worthwhile and substantive texts on sports law which serve the needs of practitioners and sports workers are available. But this book does not attempt to help lawyers make more money from sports. Its rationale is that the sport has a long and colourful legal history; one which reveals a dishonourable past and which forms the basis of an uncertain future. I have attempted to explore some – but by no means all – of these issues.

CHAPTER 1

LAW, LEISURE AND THE DEVELOPMENT OF MODERN FOOTBALL

INTRODUCTION

In the summer of 1999, the House of Lords gave judgment in *R v Oxfordshire CC ex p Sunningwell PC* (1999). The case concerned an application by the parish council of Sunningwell, Oxfordshire, to register an open space as a village green under s 13 of the Commons Registration Act 1965. A successful application would prevent the owners of the open space from building two executive homes upon it. At the non-statutory public inquiry, the inspector recommended refusal of the application. The villagers had failed to show that the open space had been used by the villagers 'as of right' for 'lawful sports and pastimes' for at least 20 years, as required under s 22(1) of the 1965 Act. The local authority followed his recommendation, the Court of Appeal refused the parish council's application for judicial review of the local authority's decision and the parish council appealed that decision before the House of Lords.

The House of Lords allowed the appeal and directed the county council to register the open space as a village green. It held that 'as of right' did not require the villagers to evince a subjective belief that they believed the right of user was confined to villagers alone, thereby overruling *R v Suffolk CC ex p Steed* (1996). Furthermore, the requirements of s 22(1) would be met if the parish council could show that the open space had been used predominantly by the villagers – it did not have to be used *exclusively* by them.

Section 22(1) of the 1965 Act provides that applications for registration may be made in respect of land which falls within one of three categories, namely: (a) land which has been allotted by or under any Act for the exercise or recreation of the inhabitants of any locality; (b) land on which the inhabitants of any locality have a customary right to engage in lawful sports and pastimes; or (c) land on which the inhabitants of any locality have indulged in such sports and pastimes as of right for not less than 20 years.

Although in *ex p Sunningwell PC* the council relied exclusively on head (c), Lord Hoffmann mentioned in passing that applications made under heads (a) and (b) were utilising rights that have been long established. Head (b) applications rely on the notion of immemorial custom – in theory, a custom 'which predates the accession of Richard I in 1189' and which conjures up pastoral visions of 'the traditional village green with its images of maypole dancing, cricket and warm beer'. Similarly, applications under head (a) could include land 'which was allotted for exercise and recreation by Act of

Parliament or the Inclosure Commissioners when making an order for inclosure of a common under the Inclosure Act 1845'. Lord Hoffmann went on to say that, 'before 1845, when commons were enclosed under private Acts of Parliament, it was common for the Act itself to set aside some land for this purpose'.

With this case in mind, the purpose of this chapter is to consider how those early laws on enclosure which were the predecessors of the 1965 Act – and particularly those private Acts of Parliament which Lord Hoffmann mentioned – contributed to changing leisure pursuits during the 18th and 19th centuries. The relationship between enclosure and leisure during the Industrial Revolution shows how landowners' and the courts' approach to the enclosure of land, especially their castigation of certain leisure pursuits and the privileging of other, 'lawful' sports and pastimes within the enclosure process, has helped to shape the contemporary leisure industry. In particular, this chapter explains how enclosure contributed to the demise of most animal sports, prize fighting and mass participation games of football while, directly or indirectly, assisting in the development of boxing, fox hunting and – crucially – 'modern' football.

LEISURE AND THE CIVILISING PROCESS

This research has its roots in Norbert Elias' exploration of the concentration of physical force in the hands of the State and the virtual monopoly in the use of physical force as a means of discipline and social control which States enjoy (Elias and Dunning, 1986). The development of sophisticated legal systems under the auspices of government was fundamental to the creation and maintenance of this disciplinary State (Hunt, 1995), but greater self-control and a reduced tendency to engage in violence and warfare were also vital to the successful concentration of power in the State's hands. For Elias, a widespread acceptance among individuals of the need to exercise self-control to this extent would be the hallmark of a 'civilised society'. This move towards a heightened awareness of the need for self-restraint is an ongoing process with a long history. Elias believed that it had its roots in 'that series of political, legal, social, economic and military developments which together formed ... the "feudal regime"' (Davies, 1996, p 311), epitomised by the development of such chivalric activities as jousting and archery in court circles (Birley, 1993). The pursuits that we might broadly call 'modern sports' developed as a consequence of the civilising process. The drawing up of rules, the existence of acceptable norms of behaviour, the demarcation of boundaries and (in team games) an equality of numbers may be termed 'pseudo-chivalric' and reflect a heightened degree of self-restraint, under which 'society regard[ed] offences against the prevailing pattern of drive and affect control, any "letting go" by their members, with greater or lesser disapproval' (Elias, 1982, p 254). Sports were thus one of the few outlets through which pleasure could legitimately be obtained by watching or participating in violent or exciting acts. Proponents of the 'civilising process' argue that sports have played a highly significant role in influencing individuals' behaviour, primarily through their function in the expression and control of physical violence.

The ways in which this theory has been developed in the two decades since Elias' death have not been without their critics. Some point to its disregard for feminist perspectives (Hargreaves, 1994), its ethnocentric tendencies and its general inability to accommodate gender and class differences. Others are critical of Elias' tendency 'to assume a "natural" pre-civilised aggressiveness, spontaneity and lack of inhibition ... [Elias] makes too much of the gradual withdrawal of the civilised classes from everyday cruelty to animals and the animal baiting sports' (Hunt, 1995, pp 7, 8). There are myriad examples of situations where this heightened self-restraint has proved exceedingly fragile, and, as Hunt says:

> ... highly sophisticated and refined preoccupations with the exercise of physical and emotional self-restraint can and do go hand in hand with physical and emotional violence against slaves, servants, women and employees. Similarly, collective relations of restraint and co-operation can break down into the kind of barbarism epitomised in the break-up of Yugoslavia [p 11].

Murphy *et al* (1990) counter this by asserting that:

> ... whilst violence is probably increasing in many countries at the moment, the majority at least of Western societies are today considerably more 'civilised' internally, considerably less violent than they used to be, say, 100 years ago [p 27].

The arguments as to the relative merits of the Elisian approach will continue, for they seem to be driven by personal enmity as much as by scholarly rigour, but they do illustrate why, in the 18th and 19th centuries, certain sports attracted considerable hostility from legislators and the judiciary.

They attracted hostility because they excited greater degrees of violence or unruly behaviour on the part of participants or spectators than was deemed tolerable by civilised society. Some of those practices, including most animal sports, had all but disappeared by the end of the 19th century. They fell outside the limits of civilised society as defined by parliamentarians and the other wealthy members of society who 'were instrumental in the greater pacification and regulation of [the lower classes'] pastimes' (Elias and Dunning, 1986, p 40). In contrast, sports such as football and boxing flourished, partly as a result of their being able to adapt to societal pressures and accommodate them, rather than operating in opposition to them as a counter-hegemonic subculture. But it was also the case the people who helped to popularise them were from the same social classes as the judges, parliamentarians and landowners and shared the same ethos, so far as the role of sport in society was concerned.

Elias and Dunning (1986, p 151) counselled against the tendency to see every development that occurred in the 19th century as inevitably being a product of the Industrial Revolution. But, by the middle of the century, urbanisation, industrialisation and capital accumulation had helped to shape the idea of the 'masculine achiever' – the family man who incorporated the ideals of physical courage, chivalry and patriotic virtue that the upper orders espoused (Mangan and Walvin, 1987). In the same way that some members of the aristocracy used prize fights to bind the lower orders into society, others attempted to do the same by extending these ideals of respectable masculinity to the working classes. They did so through the medium of other sports and pastimes, such as track and field athletics events, Highland Games and their English equivalents (Birley, 1993, p 240). In doing so, they encountered 'the antipathy of the poor, ill-educated and aggressive urban youths who remained the perennial but hostile targets of the proponents of this middle class ideal' (Mangan and Walvin, 1987, p 5). These were the individuals who represented 'the irresponsible and sexually licentious "dangerous classes"' and who haunted the imagination of genteel 19th century England (Collier, 1996, p 221). They presented a particular challenge to those who espoused 'Muscular Christianity', or – in more secular terms – the 'cult of muscularity', which had it roots in the writings of Charles Kingsley (Bloomfield, 1994).

Kingsley believed that sport could help to transform middle class public school boys into possessors of the qualities sought of future Empire builders and leaders. The many hours per week devoted to the sporting ritual and physical exercise in boys' (public) schools taught the need for sustained effort and spirited determination in the face of adversity. It also taught the benefits of 'self-denial and control over one's egoistic impulses, the acceptance of authority, how to fit in with one's peers, how to take decisions and confidently to lead subordinates, and to accept responsibility' (Hargreaves, 1986, p 143).

This exclusively male cult of muscularity, which stood in opposition to O'Donovan's (1985) 'cult of domesticity', not only reinforced (and continues to reinforce) gender distinctions, but also reinforced distinctions between males on the basis of class. The successful spread of Muscular Christianity through the male members of the upper classes persuaded many within that group that sport could similarly be used to 'improve' the working classes, come the second half of the 19th century. The health of the working man was the subject of much consternation, initial concern being raised by frequent outbreaks of cholera and typhoid and the lamentable physical attributes of those who volunteered for the Crimean War in 1850. There was a growing perception among the upper orders that a rational, disciplining athletic programme was needed to counteract the existence of an independent, plebeian, disreputable sporting tradition, epitomised by the attraction that prize fighting continued to hold for the most feckless members of the labouring poor. A great deal of emphasis was placed upon sexual probity and body imagery in these attempts to civilise the lower orders:

> Active participation in organised sport, frequent and regular physical exercise, fitness and good health, and above all, a 'hard' body constituted the God-fearing, obedient, hard working, respectable individual [Hargreaves, 1986, p 146].

Football and boxing would find their niche as sports in late 19th century England because they were able to respond to this changing social landscape, eventually epitomising the application of the cult of muscularity to the wider sporting domain. The formation of voluntary associations in other sports had provided the model for fledgling football clubs and for bodies such as the Football Association, which oversaw the implementation of formalised rules governing the conduct of member clubs and their players. Prize fighting never had the same degree of formalised organisation that football was to have by the 1870s, but written rules governing the sport had been introduced as early as 1743 – preceding the introduction of formal rules in more genteel sports such as racing and cricket. Less formally, notions of what was and was not acceptable conduct so far as particular sports practices were concerned – what it meant to 'play the game' – existed in most sports from the middle of the 18th century and were generally adhered to. But these written rules and unwritten conventions were accepted not only because they made 'the game' more straightforward to participate in or easier to understand, but because the rationale behind them was to prolong the excitement, tension and emotional pleasure of victory in the mock battles of sport.

Fox hunting is the prime example of a highly specialised pursuit which is governed not by written rules, but by conventions that the participants strictly adhere to. Elias and Dunning point out that, 'While hunting the fox, gentlemen strictly refrained from pursuing and killing any other animal which came their way ... even though it might have served as a most desirable delicacy' (Elias and Dunning, 1986, p 160), and the hunters would not actually engage in the killing themselves. This was 'killing by proxy', with the actual death-dealing task being delegated to the hounds and the honour code governing the chase being augmented by the organisation of the event and the whole aurora of sociability surrounding such occasions (Sassoon, 1972). The rules of the hunt had been designed to make an easily achieved objective (killing a fox) less easy, 'not because it was felt to be immoral or unfair to kill a fox outright, but because the excitement of the hunt itself had become increasingly the main source of enjoyment for the human participants' (Elias and Dunning, 1986, p 166).

But the lower thresholds of tolerance which had precipitated the introduction of rules and the acceptance of conventions permeated through society only gradually, and the history of sports law reveals frequent conflicts between those who supported activities of the lower orders and those who opposed them. Judicial records from the 16th century show how the civil and ecclesiastical courts dealt with dancers, bowlers, cricket players and, of course, football players. But legal intervention was supposed to police these pursuits out of existence and, in this respect, its impact was decidedly limited. Sports were not immune to such pressures from without, but, in the 19th century, aristocratic individuals could still complain that 'the more common sort divert themselves at football, wrestling, cudgels, ninepins, shovel-board, cricket, stow-ball, ringing of bells, throwing at cocks and lying at Ale houses' (Malcolmson, 1973, p 34).

This should not be taken as an indication that there was anything approaching a rigid, class-based distinction between the sporting pastimes of the various social classes. Neither did the leisure pursuits of the lower orders meet with hostility from all those in the higher social groups. Sabbatarians and the middle class social reformers found allies among the respectable working classes in their campaign against the licentiousness of the feckless undeserving poor and, similarly, the feckless poor found sufficient support among the aristocracy to keep their pursuits going. The two extremities of the social scale 'were never closer together than at the prize fight, the cock pit, the rat catching [and] the race track' (Cunningham, 1980, p 11), and many believed that sports contributed to a cohesive and patriotic society by acting as a bond of patronage, linking men of all social classes. Whatever the reasons for their involvement, there were always enough members of the aristocracy who would give positive assistance, such as the provision of ale or a winner's purse or the loaning of land upon which a fair or race meeting could be held. But their support could take on more subtle forms, too. Landowners and industrialists might acquiesce to the continuation of a long established tradition or custom, such as Shrove Tuesday football matches which spilled onto privately owned land, or the holding of a well-dressing on a work day. Their willingness to acquiesce was vital to the continuation of such practices in many rural communities.

On occasion, balances had to be struck between this 'bread and circuses' paternalism and the need to impose religious probity or social control. Hostility on the part of those in positions of power and influence could be engendered by many factors. Some believed that these pursuits constituted a threat to public order. Others based their antipathy on the fact that participation in sports often occurred at those times when a God-fearing citizen should be attending church. This insistence upon a strict observance of the Sabbath attracted widespread support among those who believed that any recreational practices on the part of the lower orders inevitably encouraged licentiousness and an idle, ill-disciplined way of life that was an affront to the Lord. The opinion that any enjoyment of leisure activities by the labouring poor was at odds with the lifestyle which they ought to follow was widely held among those for whom the conspicuous enjoyment of such leisure activities as gaming and horseracing was, literally, a God-given right. Industry was a virtue sanctioned by God and the State, and the divine duty of the labouring poor was to labour.

> 'The Rules of Religion and the Rules of Industry do perfectly harmonise,' opined [the early industrialist] Josiah Tucker, and 'all things hurtful to the latter are indeed a violation of the former. In short, the same good Being who formed the religious system also formed the commercial' [Malcolmson, 1973, p 91].

But the balance could be tipped by straightforward economic considerations, too. From the late 17th century, there were occasions when the death-knell for leisure pursuits in rural areas was heralded by landowners maximising the economic utility of their property – or limiting access to it for their own gaming and leisure interests – through an Act of Enclosure.

THE ENCLOSURE LAWS

There are many examples of sports practices that suffered from landowners' use of enclosure, with recourse to parliament and the courts providing the means of reinforcing their decisions. The rigour of the earliest private Enclosure Acts was reinforced by the Waltham Black Act 1723 and several Gaming Acts, for these had introduced murderously repressive legislation against poachers. Just 27 days had been needed for the Black Act to pass through all of its parliamentary stages, from first reading to royal assent, and at no time was there a debate on the proposals or a formal division on the legislation. Under the Act, which had been precipitated by a surge in the incidence of deer poaching in Windsor and the other royal parks in 1720, it had become a capital offence for persons who were:

> Armed with swords, fire-arms or other offensive weapons, and having his or their faces blacked [to] appear in any forest, chase, park, paddock or grounds enclosed ... wherein any deer have been or shall be usually kept. Or in any warren or place where hares or conies have been or shall be usually kept, or in any high road, open heath, common or down ... shall unlawfully and wilfully hunt, wound, kill, destroy or steal any red or fallow deer, or unlawfully rob any warren ... or shall unlawfully steal or take away any fish out of any river or pond [s 1 of the Black Act 1723].

One hundred years previously, Coke had condemned earlier legislation which contained similar provisions as 'an affront to the established principle that no one should lose either life or limb for killing a wild beast' (Birley, 1993, p 16). But this savage Act heralded 'the onset of the flood tide of 18th century retributive justice' (Thompson, 1980, p 23). The number of capital offences exploded from 50 to over 200 by 1820 – a period when the power of peers and the gentry was little hindered by the monarch or the general populace. Enclosure Acts were merely one more weapon in the armoury of oppressive laws, which were primarily designed for use against poachers but also had a severely detrimental effect on leisure activities. And most of these also escaped the scrutiny of a parliament whose members had reason to question neither the merit nor their severity of those laws.

> Sir William Meredith (MP) observed ... that he once passed a committee room where only one member was holding a committee, with a clerk's boy, and he happened to hear something of hanging. He immediately had the curiosity to ask what was going forward in that small committee that could merit such a punishment. He was answered that it was an enclosing Bill, in which a great many poor people were concerned and who opposed it; that they feared these people would obstruct the execution of the Act. And therefore this clause was to make it a capital felony in anyone who did so [Hay, 1974, p 114].

These laws effectively prevented access to enclosed land for many of those whose customary leisure pursuits had taken place on the downs, on the common lands or in the forests that were suddenly enclosed. Enclosure was responsible for the demise of 'common land and its privileges, restricting opportunities for ordinary folk to catch coneys or woodcock and to play games' (Birley, 1993, p 83).

The Black Act 1723 was used regularly (although not particularly frequently) against deer poachers in the 20 years after its enactment. But its deployment thereafter tended to be limited to situations where there had been aggravating circumstances, such as malicious shooting or the accompaniment of threatening letters (Thompson, 1980). The taking of 'one for the pot' or the playing of games on enclosed land did not attract the full severity of the law, and there are several instances of humane judgments on the part of the judiciary. In *R v Davis* (1783), for example, the court invoked the doctrine of implied repeal in respect of the Black Act's provisions on deer poaching. Here, the defendant had been charged with two offences – stealing a deer and killing it – under the Black Act. The court noted that the preamble to a later Act (16 Geo III (1775)) had stated that 'the statutes in force for the discovery and punishment of deer-stealers are numerous, and many of them ineffectual'. It specifically repealed the capital provisions on dear stealing contained in nine earlier Acts and replaced them with a maximum penalty of a £30 fine, except in those cases where the accused had been armed or disguised. The Black Act 1723 was not one of the statutes that had been expressly repealed in salient part. But the court decided that the 1775 Act was the only appropriate legislation to use in any case where the aggravating circumstances were absent. A later statute (42 Geo III, c 107 (1801)) provided that the stealing or killing of any deer on enclosed land would be punishable by up to seven years' transportation. But there is no evidence that this Act was widely used. Along with the 1775 Act and the Black Act 1723, it was repealed in 1827 (7 and 8 Geo IV, c 27) and not replaced. This decline in the use of capital statutes in relation to poaching and other activities on enclosed land may be seen as an example of the complexities underpinning the 'bread and circuses' balancing act between customary rights and land ownership. But their underlying aims had already been achieved. Enclosure's impact on the traditions and customs of rural life had been as devastating as its impact upon the economics of it and, in particular, upon 'those self-governing and customary elements in the structure of the pre-capitalist village economy' (Thompson, 1980, p 239). The capital provisions may have been removed, but the landowners' rights had been enshrined in law.

There is an important caveat here. On the few occasions when a legal challenge to an enclosing landowner was mounted, the courts did not always uphold the landowner's right to use his property as he wished, even though he appeared to have a *prima facie* legal right to do so. In a number of cases, the existence of a customary right of access for purposes which were deemed to be for the public benefit was actually regarded as grounds for rejecting the landowner's claims. In *Fitch v Rawling* (1795), the defendant's right to play cricket on land which the plaintiff had enclosed was upheld. Buller J spoke approvingly of 'the liberty and privilege of exercising and playing of all kinds of lawful games, sport and pastimes'. He rejected the plaintiff's contention that customary rights should only be upheld as being for the public good if it could be shown that 'the activities were for the recreation and health of the inhabitants'. Lawful games and pastimes were *a priori* for the public good and such customs should be upheld, said the learned judge. In *Hall v Nottingham* (1875), a parishioner's customary right to enter recently enclosed land, erect a maypole and dance around it, 'and to otherwise enjoy on the land any lawful and innocent recreation at any time of the year', was upheld. In reaching this decision, the court was aware that its decision 'might absolutely deprive the freeholder of the use of his land'.

But, despite the existence of such enlightened attitudes to leisure, there were still limits to the extent to which the courts would give priority to these customary rights, even if those seeking access to the land had been able to establish custom or long user. For instance, claims would not be upheld if they conferred a financial benefit upon those who sought to invoke them. In *Wickham v Hawker* (1840), a custom of engaging in hawking and gaming was deemed to be a profit rather than a mere leisure pursuit and, accordingly, was not enforceable as a customary right, and the same conclusion was reached on similar facts in *Bland v Lipscombe* (1855). In *Lancashire v Hunt* (1894), an injunction to prevent the training of racehorses on enclosed land owned by another was similarly upheld. So, the courts' willingness to uphold leisure interests only took effect in cases where the customary right at issue was solely a right to engage in leisure for leisure's sake. If continuation of the right would provide a financial benefit to those who wished to uphold it, while at the same time depriving the landowner of *his* financial benefit, it would not attract judicial sympathy.

Before one could argue the existence of a customary interest before the courts, one had to have sufficient social and economic capital to have access to the privileged portals of the legal system. Historians accept that the extent to which individuals sought recourse to the law to challenge the effects of enclosure on their lives was limited, although they give different explanations for this absence of legal protest. Neeson believed that 'resistance occurred only in exceptional circumstances, where unusually large commons had been lost, where small absentee owners let their lands or where enclosure was forced through without due process' (Neeson, 1984, p 114). The Hammonds (1911) believed that this limited legal resistance to enclosure reflected the realism of those who had been most adversely affected – the rural poor – who knew that legal opposition would be futile and prohibitively expensive. But, whatever the reasons, it was undoubtedly the case that recourse to the law was rare indeed. It was also the case that *illegal* opposition in the form of threatening letters or disturbances had little effect, too. They made no impression at all upon parliament, and the full force of the Enclosure Acts and other legislation could be used to quell them.

There were undoubtedly isolated, sporadic outbreaks against individual enclosures, but nothing approaching a coherent, articulate protest against the lack of protection that was being accorded to leisure pursuits and other rural traditions. Neeson's work on opposition to enclosure in Northamptonshire suggests that the best chance of successfully opposing an enclosure was through the efforts of 'early local opposition, voiced when proponents of enclosure first mooted their plans' (Neeson, 1984, p 117). But, once an Enclosing Act had been passed, very little could be done to prevent its implementation, although there were occasions when popular protests against such an Act were decidedly threatening. The passing of one particular Act prompted its opponents to advertise a two day football match on the site, inviting 'all gentleman gamesters and well-wishers to the cause now in hand ... to appear at any of the publick houses in Haddon, where they will be joyfully received and kindly entertained'. The 'gentlemen gamesters' pulled up and burned £1,500 worth of posts and rails in the two day orgy of destruction that followed. Other forms of protest included parliamentary counter-petitions which detailed the detrimental effects that enclosure would have. But Neeson considers these to be 'more useful as guides to what kinds of grievance were felt rather than measures of how much [opposition] there was' (Neeson, 1984, p 125). And, of course, those who had the financial and cultural capital to articulate their protests in this way were the only ones who could even contemplate access to the courts if all else failed.

Even though most customary pursuits of the rural poor were closely linked with harvests, fairs and agrarian feasts, and may accordingly have attracted a degree of judicial sympathy, the reality is that laws on enclosure sanctified the rights of landowners to the great detriment of the rural poor in particular. The judgments on the legality of leisure interests that the enclosure movement engendered may be properly regarded as one of the earliest cogent bodies of 'sports law'. And the veracity of Hay's condemnation of enclosure as 'the private manipulation of the law by the wealthy and powerful – a ruling class conspiracy in the most exact sense of the word' (Hay, 1974, p 52) may be ascertained by considering the history behind it.

Enclosure's detrimental impact on leisure pursuits was not limited to those interests of the rural populace. When the population of urban areas exploded during the Industrial Revolution, attempts were made to import some of these rural pursuits into the ever expanding towns and cities. But, by this time, they had become synonymous with public disorder, drunkenness and licentious behaviour on the part of those who ought not to have had the time for such conspicuous consumption of the frivolities of leisure:

> Genteel attitudes towards many aspects of popular culture had become increasingly unsympathetic. Customs which had once been tolerated came to be questioned and sometimes heartily condemned. This hostile outlook could hardly fail to have a significant impact on the customary practices of plebeian society, especially when the strictures stemmed from legislators and magistrates, employers and zealous clergymen [Hay, 1974, p 53].

This hostility helped to dispel 'animal sports' (namely, dog fighting, cock fighting, bull baiting and badger baiting), prize fighting, rough music and skimmity-riding in the towns (Thompson, 1993). And the rapid growth of urban areas led to a decline in the toleration of football and other games that had managed to gain some semblance of an urban foothold. As early as 1757, one London magistrate had spoken sympathetically of rural pursuits as 'laudable trials of manhood, to the improvement of English courage ... But, in [London], diversions calculated to slacken the industry of the useful hands are innumerable' (Malcolmson, 1973, p 161). The judiciary's limited tolerance of rural leisure pursuits was not extended to those that took place in the burgeoning urban powerhouses of the Industrial Revolution, as the judicial pronouncements on prize fighting illustrate.

CONCLUSION

Social and religious probity, economic pressures, urbanisation and the enclosure movement all contributed to the demise of animal sports and other leisure pursuits enjoyed by the rural poor in the 17th and 18th centuries. Following industrialisation, the enjoyment of leisure by the working classes in the towns and cities engendered widespread distrust and hostility. This contributed to the demise of the prize fight and mass participatory football, at least until the social reformers and the Muscular Christians got involved and turned the latter into something far more acceptable; something which epitomised the role of sport in Elias' civilising processes. Boxing was similarly acceptable because of its associations with the Corinthian ideal and the public school ethos. It was thus distinguishable, both socially and legally, from prize fighting, which always had the potential to incite civil disorder and disobedience; its putative legality had little or nothing to do with the fact that it was 'less violent'. Thompson stated that 'The passing of Gin Lane, Tyburn Fair, orgiastic drunkenness, animal sexuality and mortal combat for prize money in iron-studded clogs calls for no lament' (Thompson, 1980, p 451), but:

> ... riot and questions of control of the 'crowd' have been central features of modernity since the beginnings of the Industrial Revolution ... The regulation of leisure increasingly meant the 'disciplining' and 'policing' – in a Foucauldian sense – of working class culture in such a way that 'respectable' and 'rough' became dividing, and divisive, categories for control of the working class population [Redhead, 1995, pp 42, 43].

It must be remembered, however, that what the court had in mind when boxing was legalised in *R v Coney* (1882) was three three-minute rounds, where the emphasis was on skill and technique, rather than the contemporary professional fight game: 'The questionable legality of boxing as we now know it came about by default rather than design [Gunn and Ormerod, 1995, p 183].'

The prize fight epitomised the pre-industrial pursuits and sinful recreations which were synonymous with drinking, gambling and licentiousness and which late Victorian informed opinion was so keen to marginalise. But these civilised sports (in the Elisian sense) were 'the fulcrum of this newly civilised "masculinity", promoting the cohesiveness of the team effort and the sanctity of "fair play" in creative tension with the ideology of competition' (Williams and Taylor, 1994, p 216). Charitable and religious bodies' attempts to promote the public school ethos of Muscular Christianity led to their encouragement of team games in general – and football in particular. Ironically, it would fall to the clubs, pubs and factory associations of working class men to bring football to these individuals, and the significance of the relationship between them will be explored throughout this book. For the moment, it suffices to say that the impetus for these bodies' success lay in the fact that '"the [football] match", for those who remembered older, rural forms of sport, helped to fill the passing of ... violent and disorderly festivals and traditions' (Williams and Taylor, 1994, p 217).

CHAPTER 2

ONE HUNDRED YEARS OF SERVITUDE: CONTRACTUAL CONFLICT IN ENGLISH PROFESSIONAL FOOTBALL BEFORE *BOSMAN*

INTRODUCTION

English professional football's relationship with the courts predates the European Court of Justice's (ECJ's) decision in *Belgian FA v Bosman* (1996) by 100 years. *Bosman*, notoriously, prevents clubs from demanding 'transfer fees' for out-of-contract players who move from one club to another and prevents the imposition of restrictions on the number of 'foreigners' who can play for a particular club. The *Bosman* ruling itself, and its consequences, are outside the scope of this paper (see Morris *et al*, 1996, for discussion). The author's fear is that many smaller professional clubs will no longer exist in 20 years' time, partly as a consequence of *Bosman*, although it should be said that many others eschew this Doomsday scenario and assert that such fears are 'almost certainly unfounded' (Morris *et al*, 1996, p 902). Whatever the long term ramifications, it is undoubtedly the case that never again will small clubs' main source of revenue – the transfer fees paid by bigger clubs for the smaller ones' best players – be available in respect of players whose contract with the smaller club has expired. Those players are now free to move to whichever club offers them the best personal deal (in terms of salary and duration of contract), and their previous club receives not a penny from the transaction.

Even the legality of transfer fees demanded in respect of players who are still under contract at one club when they move to another is open to question. They remain lawful for the time being, if only because the legality of such deals was not considered by the ECJ in *Bosman*. However, whether the European or domestic courts would enforce a contract for personal services in respect of a player under contract who sought to move from one club to another without his first club's permission and without the payment of a fee is a matter of much dispute. For contrasting views, see McCormick (1999) and O'Leary and Caiger (2000). On balance, the author shares McCutcheon's opinion that, 'if a contract satisfies the basic requirements of fairness which the law of equity mandates, legal policy should tend towards its enforcement by negative injunction' (McCutcheon, 1997, p 100).

The European Commission recently suggested that *Bosman*'s detrimental effects on smaller clubs could be ameliorated if the football industry compelled larger clubs to give the minnows more financial support (Chaudhary and Thomas, 1999). This is an attractive proposition, which has far more validity than the suggestion that football is 'special' and should be granted an exemption from the European Community's (EC's) competition laws – a suggestion which is a non-starter so far as the Commission is concerned (Pons, 1999). Similarly, the introduction of mandatory salary caps would be open to legal challenge on the basis of restraint of trade (Boyes, 2000); and, in any event, salary caps would do nothing to safeguard the future of the minnows. Anyway, if governing bodies sought to compel, or even merely cajole, the Manchester Uniteds of this world into redistributing some of their wealth to the likes of Hartlepool and Chesterfield, the only consequence would be to hasten the introduction of a European 'superleague'. The Commission's suggestion overlooks the inescapable fact that, throughout the history of professional football, successful outfits have been more concerned with their own financial best interests than with safeguarding the future of the sport. That is not going to change. It is football's curse and is not the European Commission's problem.

However, the main purpose of this chapter is to show that, at least as far as English football is concerned, the most damaging effects of *Bosman* could have been avoided, notwithstanding the myopia and self-interest of those who run the game. The lawfulness of the transfer system had been argued before the English courts in three cases – *Radford v Campbell* (1890), *Kingaby v Aston Villa FC* (1912) and *Eastham v Newcastle United FC* (1963). *Radford* was heard shortly after the Football Association's reluctant sanctioning of professionalism but before the payment of transfer fees became the norm. This case was actually decided in the player's favour, Nottingham Forest being refused an injunction to prevent the player from signing for Blackburn Rovers on the ground that its application had been motivated by malice. However, *Kingaby* and *Eastham* both show how successful clubs were able to use the transfer system for their own ends, to the detriment of the players and clubs with less financial muscle. Kingaby lost because his counsel eschewed an obvious legal ploy in favour of a far more risky policy that must have made sense in the wake of *Radford*, while *Eastham* resulted in only limited reforms to the domestic transfer system.

This chapter will also show that a challenge to the transfer system on the basis of the European Union laws on competition and freedom of movement had been on the cards for more than 20 years before *Bosman*. Shortly after the UK joined the European Economic Community in 1973, the ECJ's rulings in *Walrave and Koch v UCI* (1975) and *Dona v Mantero* (1976) confirmed that 'professional football [was] on a collision course with the Treaty of Rome' (now called the EC Treaty) (Weatherill, 1989). Despite these warnings, the game's governing bodies in England and Wales (along with most of their counterparts throughout Europe) refused to countenance changes to their employment practices beyond the limited changes that had been forced upon them by *Eastham*. This chapter will show that professional clubs in Scotland, immune as they were to the ramifications of *Eastham*, continued to use draconian employment practices well into the 1990s.

14

ON THE PAROCHIALISM OF
PROFESSIONAL FOOTBALL

> Professional football was deformed at birth. The game was never honourable,
> never decent, never rational or just. Class was the root of all professional
> football's evils; those who played the game for money, the heroes who drew
> the crowds, were working class; those who administered the game, the
> directors and football club shareholders, were, as the greatest player of the age,
> Billy Meredith, contemptuously described them, 'little shopkeepers who
> governed our destiny' [Dunphy, 1991, p 7].

The various folk games of 'football' that were being played in England and the
rest of Europe by the 14th century are generally accepted as the forerunners of
the modern version, although whether the origins of contemporary football
can be traced even further back remains a matter of debate. The existence of a
direct link with the Roman games of *harpastum, paganica* and *follis* is regarded
as 'intrinsically improbable' (Russell, 1997, p 6), although it is perfectly
possible that the roots of the game predate the signing of the Magna Carta in
1215. Village feasts, religious festivals and holidays provided suitably
important occasions on which these game could be played. Teams of up to
1,000 men and women were commonplace. But physical violence was the
norm and, although these folk games were not merely ill disciplined carnivals
or simply an excuse for a punch-up, by the 19th century they were extinct or
under threat from the social and economic forces that influenced the
development of leisure during the Industrial Revolution (Birley, 1993). With a
few isolated exceptions, the great mass participation games of football did not
survive beyond the 1840s.

Notwithstanding the decline of these large scale events, there remained
some level of participation in small sided, spontaneous and informal games of
street football among working class men who lived and worked in the
burgeoning industrial towns and cities. While it is impossible to ascertain just
how many of these street games were played and the number of people
involved in them, a survey of popular recreations in the industrialised English
Midlands in the middle of the 19th century noted the continuing and
widespread existence of 'foot ball' (Russell, 1997, p 8). In any event,
participation was sufficiently widespread to excite the disapproval of
Parliament, for the Highways Act 1835 provided for a fine of 40 shillings for
those convicted of playing the game on the highways. It was also sufficiently
widespread to provide a base upon which to build during the 1870s and
1880s, when public school educated men tried to encourage working class
men to participate in their more 'civilised' version of the game – sides of equal
numbers, playing to agreed rules within a defined space and with some
regulation of the degree of violence or force that could be used (Elias and
Dunning, 1996).

The role of public schools in the expansion and regulation of football was of fundamental importance. Versions of the game had been played in these schools since the 1740s and, by the middle of the 19th century, all of the prestigious schools had their own set of rules and their own approach to playing the game. This multiplicity of rules meant that the Old Boys of these establishments encountered problems in deciding whose rules would hold sway in matches against other Old Boys' sides, but, in 1863, 17 London-based clubs established a uniform set of rules. Those rules made provision for catching the ball on the bounce, allowed 'hacking' on the front of the opponent's leg only and provided for the limited use of tripping. The clubs that subscribed to these rules adopted the title of 'the Football Association' (FA) and, although others took umbrage at the restrictions placed on handling and hacking and set up the rival Rugby Union, a ruling body for the 'Association game' (subsequently corrupted to 'soccer') had finally emerged. In the years immediately after the founding of the FA, the game remained largely the preserve of public schools and their Old Boys and, even at the end of the 1860s, the number of FA-affiliated clubs was no more than 50. In the 1870s, however, football's popularity among the lower social classes exploded, and local newspapers carried reports of over 800 games in Birmingham alone during 1879–80 (Russell, 1997, p 13).

The law may have been used on occasion to clamp down on 'folk football', but other legal developments were of no small significance in the 'modern' game's expansion into the lives of working class men. Saturday half-holidays became the norm in most industries; in 1874, engineers and builders secured a maximum nine hour day; the Factory Act 1875 provided for a 56 hour working week for those working in the cotton industry. The shorter working week heralded unprecedented opportunities to play the game, and the improved rail system, rising literacy levels, the mass media and the penny post have all been cited as factors that contributed to the astonishing development of football among the working classes (Walvin, 1994). However, perhaps the single most significant factor in the expansion of the game was the passing of the Education Act 1870. This resulted in an expansion of the number of working class pupils who were admitted to elementary schools and a concomitant expansion in the number of teacher training colleges, which were necessary to ensure the requisite number of qualified individuals to teach in them. Most teacher training colleges had Association football teams, and 'their diplomates were often the mainstay of early clubs, especially in industrial areas' (Birley, 1995, p 268).

This expansion of the game into working class communities heralded a shift in the balance of power on the pitch. The dominant clubs ceased to be Old Boys' sides from the South of England and, from the early 1880s, factory or industry-based teams in the north of the country became far more successful. However, those in charge of the FA continued to be men whose social standing was far higher than that of the best players. Their perceptions of football, how it should be played and who should be allowed to play it were still based on the public school model. Only in 1885 did the FA consent to working class men being paid for playing; even then, its acceptance of professionalism was contingent upon it being able to determine whom professionals could play and how much they could earn. Their player registration scheme, although legal in itself, was the model for subsequent, unlawful restrictions on players' employment rights that remained in place until the *Bosman* ruling.

THE FA'S PLAYER REGISTRATION SCHEME AND THE *RADFORD* CASE

By 1885, the Northern clubs which attracted the biggest crowds and had the best playing records (Aston Villa, Notts County and Blackburn Rovers) were making secret payments to the players who represented them. 'Professional football' was a stark reality, but the FA refused to acknowledge its existence, let alone sanction the practice. Consequently, clubs continued to make payments routine – underhand payments to their players in the form of 'boot money', where wads of cash would be placed in their boots before a game. Alternatively, players would be found employment with a sympathetic local employer – ideally, the club chairman or a club director – who would not be perturbed if he failed to perform on the factory floor, so long as he performed on a Saturday afternoon (Russell, 1997).

The FA's eventual reluctant decision to allow professionalism merely represented their acceptance of the inevitable, but its recognition of professional players was accompanied by the introduction of terms and conditions which allowed it to closely regulate those players' activities. The FA allowed professionals to play on condition that they would not be allowed to captain a side or hold other positions of influence within the game. Furthermore, it introduced a regulatory system that allowed it to oversee the transfer of professional players from one club to another. Players would have to re-register with their club every year and could not play for any club other than the one they were registered with. They were free to join another club at the end of each season – even if their old club did not want to let them go – but players could not change clubs *during* a season unless they had the permission of the club that held their registration. They also needed the permission of the FA.

The limited degree of freedom of movement that this system allowed was enough to prevent it from being an unlawful restraint of trade, and it soon became a fundamental part of the game's structure. Indeed, so successful was it in regulating professionalism that, shortly after the foundation of the English Football League in 1888, the League authorities introduced a new player registration scheme, which was ostensibly designed to safeguard the interests of all League clubs. The difference was that this new scheme involved the use of more stringent – and quite probably unlawful – restrictions on player movement.

But football had its first brush with English law less than two years after the introduction of the League and before the introduction of this League's registration system. In *Radford v Campbell* (1890), Nottingham Forest sought an injunction to prevent Campbell from playing for Blackburn Rovers. In March 1890, Campbell signed a contract which committed him to playing for Nottingham Forest in the 1890/91 season. However, before that season started, he signed another contract with Blackburn Rovers. At that time, Rovers were the most successful and prestigious club in the country, being founder members of the English League in 1888 (which Forest only joined in 1892) and winners of the FA Cup on five occasions between 1884 and 1891. As mentioned above, Rovers had been paying their players long before the FA agreed to professionalism, and Campbell received the princely sum of £4 10 s per week from them.

The application for an injunction was refused at first instance and Forest appealed to the Court of Appeal, where the case was heard by no less a personage than the Master of the Rolls, Lord Esher. The short report of his judgment is worth quoting in full:

> The Master of the Rolls said that this jurisdiction of the court must depend upon the circumstances of every case. It was not in every case in which a man was about to break his contract that an injunction should be granted restraining him from doing so. What was there at stake in the present case? There was no question of character or of property except that it was said there would be a diminution in gate-money. But the real point was the pride of the club; they wanted to win their games, and in order to do so they had engaged these professionals. Ought the solemn machinery of the court in granting an injunction to be invoked in order to satisfy their pride in winning their matches? If the defendant broke his agreement an action would lie against him, and it might be even that an action would lie against the other club for enticing him to do so. But it was unnecessary to decide that now; all that needed to be said was that North J [at first instance] was right and that this was not a proper case for granting an injunction [*Radford v Campbell* (1890)].

Lord Esher's contempt for the sport, and particularly for professionalism and the clubs' obsession with 'winning their games', drips from the judgment; the court ought not to involve itself with something so trivial as football. And, although it is probably impossible to know for certain, it surely must have been the case that Herbert Kingaby's counsel was mindful of *Radford* when he embarked upon his disastrous courtroom tactics some 20 years later.

But Forest's ambitions were no different to those of many other clubs who aspired to the heights that the likes of Rovers had reached. They had turned professional in 1889, and Campbell must have been a quality player to attract such a huge salary from Blackburn. Aside from having their best players poached, Forest's main concern was the success of their near rivals, Notts County. By the late 1880s, both clubs were playing in the Trent Bridge area of the city (Forest shared the county cricket ground) and, in 1890/91, while Campbell was playing for Blackburn and Forest were playing in regional competitions, County had their best ever season and finished third in the League. However, Forest were admitted as founder members of the new Second Division at the start of the 1891/92 season, expansion of the League being a consequence of the professional clubs realising that their interests were best served by giving more clubs the opportunity to play at the top level. Similarly, they appreciated the financial benefits that lay in giving more fans the opportunity to pay for the privilege of watching the best clubs and the best players.

These clubs also appreciated the need to remove the imbalance of power that existed within the game, usually between clubs based in large cities and those located in the smaller towns. If the small teams simply could not match the crowds of the big ones (the clubs argued), the big teams would dominate the competition as a consequence of being able to pay the highest salaries and, like Blackburn Rovers, recruit all the best players. If this was not prevented, it would cause a decline in interest and support for the smaller clubs and, quite possibly, their extinction. Accordingly, the League's officials decided that restrictions had to be placed on richer clubs' ability to tempt players into joining them from other clubs. This was deemed necessary in order to ensure an equal spread of talent and to keep the League competitive, thereby maintaining spectators' interest in all clubs. In order to achieve this, the League's officials filched the registration scheme through which the FA had regulated professionalism since 1885, and adapted it to suit their own requirements. Accordingly, from the start of the 1893/94 season, a player had to be registered with the club he intended playing for and, once he had registered, he could play for no other club. One can only speculate whether the player registration provisions would have developed differently if *Radford* (1890) had been decided in Forest's favour.

THE FOOTBALL LEAGUE'S PLAYER REGISTRATION SCHEME AND THE *KINGABY* CASE

In many respects, the League's registration scheme was little different to that instigated by the FA. The one crucial difference was that, if a player wanted to move clubs at the *end* of the season, he would need his old club's permission before being able to take up a new offer of employment. This provision applied if the player had refused to sign a new contract with his old club, and even if that club had no intention of playing him – or of paying him a salary –

in the forthcoming season. Consequently, a club could, in principle, refuse to release a player's registration and thereby prevent him from being able to play for another English League side. A player in such a position would be obliged to seek employment with a club in the (English) Southern League or (from 1890) the Scottish League, where the standard of play and the wages were lower but the clubs were not bound by the English League's punitive registration provisions. For most players, the alternative option was to quit the game altogether and return from whence they came – to full time employment in the mines, the factories or the cotton industry.

The potential harshness of the player registration system was ameliorated by the fact that clubs, which were always seeking to raise money to supplement gate receipts, quickly realised that they could forfeit a player's registration in return for the payment of 'compensation' by the club who wanted to sign him. It was argued that this 'transfer fee' provided further protection for the smaller clubs, because they could keep their best players until financial constraints made it prudent to sell them to larger clubs. If a player's registration was transferred and the selling club compensated, it would hope to receive enough money to replace the player *and* pay any outstanding debts. The fact remained, though, that, under the League's rules, a vindictive club could bring a player's career to a premature end simply by adhering to the letter of the registration scheme. Not all clubs badly needed the cash that transferring the registration of an average player would bring, and, certainly, there were occasions when a club's refusal to release a player was motivated by nothing other than malice. Aston Villa's treatment of Herbert Kingaby was one such occasion.

But *Kingaby v Aston Villa FC* (1912) needs to be considered within the context of two other significant developments that occurred within professional football around the turn of the last century – namely, the move towards the imposition of a maximum wage for players and the establishment of a professional players' trade union. Shortly after the inauguration of the retain-and-transfer system, various clubs had started to lobby for the introduction of a £4 per week maximum wage that would operate alongside that scheme. Clubs needed to reduce their costs after undertaking expensive ground redevelopment during the early 1890s and said that placing limits on the amount that could be paid in players' wages would help to achieve this. Although a maximum wage had obvious benefits for the smaller clubs, the richer ones were happy to pay whatever was needed to secure the services of the best players. Bigger clubs would also disregard the provisions on players' signing-on fees. The League's maximum permitted signing-on fee of £10 was routinely, but covertly, ignored by the most successful sides, which would pay as much as £75 for the right man (Birley, 1995, p 37), and, in 1893, a proposal at the League's Annual General Meeting to introduce a maximum wage was defeated.

Those in favour of a maximum wage continued to lobby other clubs, and the campaign grew stronger as the League's domination by a handful of clubs continued (in the 13 seasons between the founding of the League in 1888 and the imposition of the maximum wage in 1901, three clubs won the League Championship 10 times between them). Most players gave little thought to the maximum wage – the mooted figure was comfortably in excess of what the majority could ever hope to earn – but they were far more concerned when, in 1897, the Scottish League banned its member clubs from 'poaching' disaffected English League players. Thus, faced with the removal of one of the few opportunities that players had to continue their careers outside the English League, attempts were made to form a players' union; but membership never rose above 50% of all players and it foundered in the face of general apathy. In 1901, there was another vote on the maximum wage issue, and, given the apathy among the workforce, clubs were able to push through its introduction at the rate of £4 per week.

It was not until 1907 that players were finally able to establish a credible union – the Professional Players' Football Union. That an impressively large number of players was willing to support unionisation on this occasion was due, not to a new found radicalism among the rank-and-file, but to those players' consternation at the authorities' treatment of one of their number, Billy Meredith of Manchester City and Wales. Meredith was the first player to 'blow the whistle' on corruption within the game, after he was banned for 18 months in 1905 for attempting to bribe opponents into throwing matches. His club, which had fully supported Meredith's corrupt endeavours, denied any involvement in these attempts and left the player to face punishment alone. In pique, the 'Welsh Wizard' revealed details of City's illegal signing-on payments to new players and club officials' role in bribing opponents and their persistent violations of the rules on the maximum wage and player bonuses. Meredith's revelations resulted in all the players from the club's 1903 FA Cup-winning side being suspended from the game. They were also banned from playing for Manchester City again and certain club directors were banned *sine die*. Meredith joined near neighbours (and arch rivals) Manchester United once his ban had been served, but his experiences had made him a bitter man and his was to be a pivotal role in the new Union. His fellow professionals, mindful that Meredith's only mistake was to allow himself to get caught, came to appreciate the virtue of safety in numbers and enthusiastically supported his initiative. However, the Union's inception heralded a period of conflict between players and management over the maximum wage and, more pertinently, over the retain-and-transfer provisions. This conflict culminated in *Kingaby v Aston Villa FC* (1912).

In the early part of his playing career, Herbert Kingaby had been the archetypal journeyman professional footballer. He had played for a London side, Clapton Orient, in the Southern League while holding down a full time job, which restricted his availability for matches played on Saturdays and on public holidays. In 1906, he was sold to Aston Villa for £300 and was paid the maximum wage of £4 a week. Two months after the purchase, Aston Villa had second thoughts about the player's ability and offered to sell him back to Clapton for a mere £150. However, cash strapped Clapton could not afford him; no other club was interested in signing him; and Aston Villa – one of the richest and, arguably, the most successful club in the country – was not willing to lose £300 by allowing him to move without receiving a fee.

Kingaby's main obstacle to freedom of movement was the fact that the vagaries of the retain-and-transfer system allowed Villa to keep him on their retained players list, even though they had no intention of giving him a new contract after his one year deal had expired. Kingaby could not join another League club once he had been placed on Villa's retained list, but, as he was no longer contracted to them, he was not receiving a salary. Faced with the abrupt termination of his English League career – no contract, no wages and unable to join another English League club – he joined Fulham, which was a Southern League side and, therefore, was not bound by the English League's retain-and-transfer regulations.

Until now, Kingaby's travails had been little different to those of other players who had joined Southern League clubs because their previous employers had neither offered them a new contract nor allowed them to join another English League team. But his case became more complex in the summer of 1910, when he joined nearby Leyton Orient,[1] which played in the Second Division of the English League. Shortly after Kingaby's transfer, the Southern and English Leagues finally reached an agreement over recognition of the latter's player registration and transfer systems. This agreement prevented disaffected Football League players from joining Southern League clubs, but, more significantly for Kingaby, under the complicated terms of that agreement, he was re-registered as an Aston Villa player and was unable to play for Leyton or any other team, unless Villa agreed to transfer him. Villa *did* agree to transfer him – subject now to the payment of a transfer fee of £350, which was way beyond Leyton's budget and far in excess of any objective valuation of this ageing player's worth.

Faced once again with the immanent termination of his professional career, Kingaby sought legal redress against Aston Villa, contending that the club's actions were an unlawful restraint of trade. He sought assistance from the Union when the legal bills began to mount and, given that the case appeared to be a strong one and Kingaby had hitherto conducted himself impeccably in his dealings with the League and his various clubs, they agreed to provide financial and other support. At the very least, there was a *prima facie* argument that the system was an unlawful restraint of trade, following the decisions in

---

1   Not to be confused with nearby Clapton Orient, which was Kingaby's first club. The name 'Orient' is taken from the Orient Shipping Line, for which many of these two teams' players worked.

Mitchel v Reynolds (1711) and *Leather Cloth Co v Larsont* (1869). The Union had obtained legal advice to the effect that Kingaby's case was a strong one. At trial, though, counsel for the player made a gross and inexplicable error of judgment by concentrating on Aston Villa's allegedly malicious use of the transfer system, making no reference to the law on restrictive practices as developed in those earlier cases. It seems (the pleadings in *Kingaby* (1912) were briefly referred to in *Eastham* (1963)) that counsel, almost certainly mindful of *Radford*, simply contended that the club had acted maliciously and had used retain-and-transfer to stymie Kingaby's career in an act of revenge. He sought damages for breach of contract, conspiracy and maliciously procuring breaches of contract, and an injunction.

The 'malice' argument proved to be a disastrous ploy. Because counsel had failed to challenge the fundamental legality of the retain-and-transfer system, the case proceeded on the presumption that the transfer system was lawful and the club had acted lawfully in seeking a transfer fee for the player. Under those circumstances, Aston Villa's motives were irrelevant, because even the most malicious or capricious of motives could not render a lawful act unlawful. The club had no case to answer, said Lawrence J, who withdrew the case from the jury and confirmed that there were no grounds for challenging either the 'malicious' transfer fee or the transfer system itself as being a breach of the player's contract of employment. In *Kingaby*, 'no tort against the plaintiff had been committed and there was no evidence of malice' (*Eastham v Newcastle United FC* (1963), p 156, *per* Wilberforce J). Costs were awarded against the Union, resulting in near bankruptcy and, more ruinously, adverse publicity.

The Union's fortunes did not improve after the War, for, although membership had swelled from 300 in 1915 to well over 1,000 by 1920, this did not herald a new era of radicalism among the rank-and-file. Widespread unemployment heralded declines in attendance at a time when many clubs had, once again, committed themselves to expensive ground improvement programmes in the expectation that the post-War spectator boom would continue indefinitely. Inevitably, this caused financial difficulties at many clubs (Russell, 1997, pp 76–107). But those clubs believed that their problems were due to players' excessive wages, rather than over-expansion. In the spring of 1922, they persuaded the League authorities to arbitrarily impose a £1 cut to the maximum wage (£9 a week at that time) and force clubs to reduce the wages of players who were on less than the maximum (Harding, 1991, p 158). Players were legally entitled to be paid at the rate agreed between them and their employers, but, in the wake of *Kingaby*, the game's authorities believed that they could disregard the law of the land and arbitrarily impose new terms into players' contracts.

On this occasion, though, the authorities were proved wrong and the Union achieved a significant victory. In an unreported case from May 1923, Henry Leddy of Chesterfield FC established a player's right to be paid at the contracted rate, notwithstanding the Football League's attempt to unilaterally alter the terms of contracts agreed between players and their clubs by lowering the maximum wage to £3 per week (*Leddy v Chesterfield FC* (1924) – see Harding, 1991, Chapter 18). However, the principle of the maximum wage was unaffected by this ruling and it remained in place for almost 40 years after Leddy's case. Retain-and-transfer remained, too: players' careers could still be stymied if clubs refused to release them when another club made an offer, and George Eastham's courtroom challenge to the legality of that system was even further away.

THE ABOLITION OF THE MAXIMUM WAGE AND THE *EASTHAM* CASE

In the years immediately preceding *Eastham* (1963), the dual system of the maximum wage and retain-and-transfer had become increasingly discredited. There were numerous instances of financial irregularity at high profile clubs where players had been paid 'boot money' and received other perks in contravention of the maximum wage provisions; and, periodically, the Union represented players who faced suspension over receipt of such payments. In 1957, it fought a bitter, protracted but much publicised action on behalf of players from Sunderland FC (Harding, 1991, pp 144–51), and each allegation of illegal payments further undermined the credibility of the maximum wage. The Union continued to lobby for its abolition and, in 1961, faced with the real possibility of a players' strike, the League finally agreed. As soon as the maximum wage was abolished, Johnny Hayes of Fulham FC and England was offered a new contract, on a salary of £100 per week. This was five times more than the previous maximum and seven times more than the then average manual wage (Russell, 1997, p 150). Retain-and-transfer was sacrosanct, though, and the League would contemplate no amendment to it.

It was at this stage that George Eastham entered the fray. In April 1960, this Newcastle United player had made the first of several unsuccessful requests to be released from his contract with that club. Disheartened, Eastham quit the game and took a job outside football, but, in October 1961, the Union approached him with a view to his being a test case on the legality of retain-and-transfer. He agreed and, even though Newcastle relented and granted him a transfer to Arsenal for a fee of £47,000 in November of that year, Eastham, like Kingaby, agreed to go ahead with the case.

The contractual straitjacket under which George Eastham had laboured had changed little since the era of Kingaby himself. It was still the case that most players were employed on yearly contracts, running from 1 July to 30 June. As the one year contract neared its end, one of four scenarios would come into play:

(a) The player could re-register for the same club at any time between 1 April and the first Saturday in May. In effect, the contract was simply renewed.

(b) The club could retain the player on less favourable terms by serving a notice between 1 May and 1 June, giving details of the terms it was offering. If the FA considered the offer to be too low, it could refuse the retention, but, if it felt the terms were reasonable, the player could not sign for any other club. Players were allowed to petition the FA with their reasons for wanting to move to another club, but, if the FA refused to intervene, clubs could retain a player indefinitely.

(c) The player could be placed on the transfer list at a fee fixed by the club.

(d) If the club did not want to keep the player and did not seek a fee for him, it could release him and he would be free to conduct negotiations with other clubs at any time from the end of June. (Osborn and Greenfield, 1998, p 35.)

At the end of each season, the details of all transfer-listed players and the fee required in respect of them would be sent to the League. The complete list of all the players who were available for transfer would then be circulated to all the clubs. A player's registration could be transferred once the fee had been paid (or a lesser one negotiated), but, so long as a player was on the transfer list, the club was under no obligation to pay him a wage. In these circumstances, a player was actually in a worse position than his 19th century predecessors had been. He was not entitled to payment but, equally, was not free to join a new club. Unlike Kingaby, he could not move to another League, because retain-and-transfer now operated in virtually every country where the game was played professionally, and most Leagues respected the others' rules on player movement. For instance, in 1950, Neil Franklin of Stoke City and England had been persuaded to break his contract and join Bogota of Colombia. Unable to settle, Franklin returned to England and was banned for a year for breach of contract. He never played for the national side again (Harding, 1991, p 250). The only alternative was to leave the professional game altogether, which was the course of action that Eastham had originally taken.

Eastham v Newcastle United FC was heard in the Chancery Division over the summer of 1963, and Wilberforce J found in favour of the player by ruling that the combined retain-and-transfer system was an unreasonable restraint of trade. His judgment amounted to a scathing indictment of the retention element of the transfer system, which the judge regarded as going far beyond what was necessary to ensure that clubs were able to protect their legitimate interests.

The League had relied on the arguments that had been used to justify retain-and-transfer when it was first introduced in the 1890s – and that would be relied on again, for the most part, in *Belgian FA v Bosman* (1996). The League argued that the retain-and-transfer system prevented the bigger clubs from taking all the best players and, consequently, helped to maintain the element of competition and spectator interest. Wilberforce J concluded that, if the League was genuinely concerned with giving clubs the power to extend players' contracts, it would not have used a mechanism which did not come into play until after a player's employment had been terminated in order to do so. Simply giving a player a retention notice did not mean that he was still an employee. The player had to take further action – namely, he had to sign whatever new contract the club offered him – before the club would start paying his wages again: 'The retention provisions differ from an option to extend the contract which, once exercised, causes the employee to continue to be an employee [*Eastham v Newcastle United FC* (1963), p 147, *per* Wilberforce J].' A further criticism was that the system prevented players from obtaining employment with a different club at a time when they were no longer employees of their old club and were not being paid by it.

> If a League player is merely on the transfer list, he may escape, either by persuading the management committee to give him a free transfer, or by going to a club outside the League. He cannot so escape if he is on the retain list. In fact, by placing a player on the retain list – possibly at a reduced wage – the club with which he is registered can prevent him from signing on with any other club ... Any system that interfered with the player's freedom to seek other employment at a time when he was not actually being employed by another club would seem to me to operate substantially in restraint of trade [*Eastham v Newcastle United FC* (1963), p 147, *per* Wilberforce J].

A player who was on both the retain list and the transfer list could apply to have his transfer fee reduced, in the hope that this would persuade another club to buy him. But this did not ameliorate the excesses of the system, even though, between 1956 and 1963, 75% of the players who had used the appeals mechanism either had their transfer fees reduced or were awarded a free transfer.

> What makes the transfer fee so objectionable ... is its combination with the retain system. When it is so combined – that is, when a man is retained and it is made known that his club is open to offer, or when a man is put on both the transfer list and the retain list – he cannot escape outside the League. All he can do is (in the latter case) to apply to have the transfer fee reduced. But, even if it is reduced, no club in the League may pay it, and yet he cannot go outside [*Eastham v Newcastle United FC* (1963), p 150, *per* Wilberforce J].

Wilberforce J concluded that the League's legitimate interests did not justify its use of the retention system, and that the transfer system as a whole was unjustifiable, insofar as it operated in conjunction with the retain element. He also refuted the League's contention that, as the retain-and-transfer system operated in all of the world's professional leagues, it should be taken as evidence that those who knew best considered the system to be in the general interests of the game.

> I do not accept this line of argument. The system is an employers' system, set up in an industry where the employers have succeeded in establishing a united monolithic front all over the world, and where it is clear that for the purpose of negotiation the employers are vastly more strongly organised than the employees. No doubt the employers all over the world consider this system to be a good system, but this does not prevent the court from considering whether it goes further than is reasonably necessary to protect their legitimate interest [*Eastham v Newcastle United FC* (1963), p 150, *per* Wilberforce J].

THE POST-*EASTHAM* REFORMS

The *Eastham* judgment amounted to only a partial victory for the players, though. It was unnecessary for the League to dismantle the transfer system itself and, indeed, the transfer part of retain-and-transfer remained largely unchanged until the *Bosman* ruling. Wilberforce J's critical comments were levelled solely at the retain part of retain-and-transfer and, if that aspect was abandoned, the rest of the system could be left largely intact. Accordingly, in 1963, a new transfer system was agreed which took into account the judge's criticisms of the 'retain' element. Every player's contract was now a matter of free negotiation between him and the club, without the binds of the maximum wage. Once a contract had expired, the club could only renew it on terms that were no less advantageous to the player than the old ones had been, and the new contract had to last for at least the same period (unless both parties agreed otherwise). If the club was unwilling to do that, the player was entitled to a free transfer; if the club decided to get rid of the player, the original contract would continue to run until he was transferred. Disputes would be referred to the League Management Committee and thence to an independent tribunal incorporating League and Union representatives.

Eastham precipitated the introduction of a new transfer system – one which did away with the retain element, but which gave players in the English game a far greater degree of freedom than they had hitherto enjoyed. First, the new system made it easier for a player to obtain a 'free transfer' at the end of his contract, for, at the end of each season, clubs had to state which players would be placed on the transfer list but were only allowed to move them on payment of a 'transfer fee'. Unwanted players who were not on the 'transfer list' list would thus be entitled to seek a free transfer.

More importantly, *Eastham* changed the position of players who were in dispute with their club, even though the club wanted to re-sign them. In the event of a club wanting to re-sign a player who refused to put pen to paper, the new system made provision for the dispute to be referred to a new, independent transfer tribunal for arbitration. Invariably, this would mean the club either giving the player a new contract on terms that were acceptable to him or granting him a transfer to a different club. The days of clubs being able to bring players' careers to an end if they refused to accept whatever terms the club offered were over. Another important change to the system occurred in the mid-1970s, when the League and the Players' Union agreed that clubs who wanted to re-sign a player had to offer him a contract whose terms were no less favourable than those of the previous one (Osborn and Greenfield, 1998, p 40). Faced with this further erosion of its power of hire and fire, clubs began to offer players longer contracts. The one year deal soon became obsolete, except in the case of young and inexperienced players and those nearing the end of their careers, whose bodies may not have been able to withstand the rigours of more than another year in the game. Contracts of three years' duration became standard. Now, post-*Bosman*, seven and nine year deals are not unheard of.

A BLAST FROM THE PAST: SCOTLAND'S PLAYER REGISTRATION SYSTEM

Thus was established the mechanism that would govern players' contracts in England until the ECJ intervened. It had taken almost a century to achieve this limited degree of contractual freedom, but, as the EC's laws on competition and freedom of movement became ever more complex and sophisticated, it became increasingly obvious that English football's transfer system breached the provisions of the EC Treaty. Despite the reforms that followed *Eastham*, some of the most Dickensian aspects of the system remained in place and players were still the chattels of the clubs they played for.

Even worse was the plight of professional footballers north of the border, for Scottish law was unaffected by *Eastham* and some clubs' practices had changed little since the founding of the Scottish League in the 1890s. The most notorious (and, one trusts, the last) example of Scottish football's draconian employment practices concerned Chris Honor and Wesley Reed, both of whom played for Airdrie in the early 1990s. In the summer of 1993, they both reached the end of two year contracts with the club and were offered new deals. In accordance with the usual practice, when the two had first signed for the club, they had been given a basic wage plus a 'signing-on fee', payment of which was spread throughout the duration of the two years of their contract, rather than all being paid when they first signed. Like their English League post-*Eastham*, the Scottish League's rules (specifically, Scottish League r 60) provided that, if a club wanted to offer a player a new contract, the terms offered to him had to be no less generous than those of the previous contract. But that provision did not take the 'signing-on fee' into account, so, when new contracts were discussed, each player was offered only the equivalent of his basic salary under the previous contract. This was perfectly legitimate under a strict interpretation of r 60, but it amounted to a huge reduction in the players' salaries. Honor had effectively been earning £33,000 per year, but all bar £12,000 of this was a signing-on fee: his basic wage was only £250 a week and this was the sum that he was offered under the new contract. Reed would similarly see his income drop to approximately £13,000 per year, having previously been earning £20,000.

Both players refused to sign the new contracts, and at this stage they came to realise that Scottish players' situations had hardly improved since the days of Herbert Kingaby, and certainly not since the era of George Eastham. Because the club had offered them new contracts on terms that were, technically, no worse than the terms of the previous one, it was able to demand a transfer fee before allowing them to leave. In the interim, it could retain the pair on monthly contracts at a salary of £250 per week. Airdrie sought £100,000 for Reed (who had signed from the English club, Bradford City, for £95,000), although that figure was reduced to £65,000 once Reed had been out of the game for a year. Honor had signed from Bristol City for £20,000 and, when Cardiff City expressed an interest in signing him, Airdrie's chairman, George Peat, said that the player was available – for £70,000 (Mullin, 1996, p 5). Chris Honor now plays as an amateur for Bath City (Spink, 1997) and makes a living selling garden ornaments; attempts to trace Wesley Reed have proved fruitless.

CONCLUSION

Scotland's was the kind of transfer system that the game's governing bodies, and the clubs, were so keen to defend in *Bosman*. Ostensibly designed to protect small clubs and ensure the wellbeing of their players, it was, as Wilberforce J had so presciently noted, an employers' system, initiated in the Victorian era and designed to protect the vested interests of officials and club owners. That system was defended to the last by successive generations of 'little shopkeepers', even though, in *Walrave and Koch v UCI* (1975), the ECJ confirmed that sport was subject to EC law if it constituted an economic activity under Art 2 of the EC Treaty. In *Dona v Mantero* (1976), the Court held that professional footballers enjoyed the benefits of the Treaty provisions on freedom of movement of persons and of provision of services.

However, *Dona* also affirmed that, in some circumstances, the application of nationality restrictions to those who played in national teams would be a 'non-economic' issue and, therefore, would be exempt from the EC Treaty's provisions. The Advocate General expressed the opinion that:

> There is nothing to prevent considerations of purely sporting interests justifying ... some restriction on the signing of foreign players ... so as to ensure that the winning team will be representative of the State of which it is the champion team ... Even sporting activities run on a business basis may nevertheless fall outside the ... fundamental rules of the Treaty in cases where the restrictions on the ground of the player's nationality are based on purely sporting considerations. Provided that such restrictions are appropriate and proportionate to the end pursued [*Dona v Mantero* (1976), p 582].

This decision reinforced the football authorities' belief that 'purely sporting considerations' meant that the imposition of quotas and the transfer system were 'appropriate and proportionate' and justified the provisions of the EC Treaty being disregarded, despite the Commission's protestations to the contrary. Despite the fact that EC law had applied to the Swiss-based UCI, football's authorities still protested that EC law did not extend to clubs, national associations and international governing bodies, such as UEFA, that were based in countries which were not EC members. Indeed, in 1988, the then UEFA President, Jacques George, opined that '[UEFA] can make up whatever rules we want, as long as they are within Swiss laws, as we have nothing to do with the [EC]' (Miller, 1993, p 14).

Monsieur George was in for a rude awakening, courtesy of another journeyman professional.

CHAPTER 3

'THEY'RE PLAYING R SONG': *BOSMAN* AND BEYOND

INTRODUCTION

The previous chapter illustrated how domestic football bodies spent much of the first hundred years of their existence trying to avoid compliance with the law of the land, as it applied to the retain-and-transfer system. Notwithstanding the changes precipitated by *Eastham* (1963) in England, the transfer system was unlawful under European law, but UEFA attempted to turn back the tide rather than deal with the harsh reality. The cataclysmic effects of the European Court of Justice's (ECJ's) ruling in *Belgian FA v Bosman* (1996) could have been avoided but for UEFA's intransigence. That the fundamental principles of European Community (EC) (now European Union (EU)) law were incompatible with both the transfer system and the provisions on foreign players was evident long before *Bosman*. The 'Superstate' nature of the EC meant that the rules of UEFA were not immune to EU law, even though UEFA is based in Switzerland, which is not a member of the EC.

For those who are not *au fait* with the laws and politics of the EU, a very brief overview might be useful.

A HISTORY OF THE EC AND ITS INSTITUTIONS

The EC had its roots in two institutions – the Organisation for European Economic Co-Operation (OEEC) and the European Coal and Steel Community (ECSC). The OEEC was an intergovernmental organisation, set up in the late 1940s to help to co-ordinate the reconstruction of post-War Europe and funded by the US under the Marshall Plan. The ECSC was instigated under the Schuman Plan of 1950, which proposed far greater co-operation between Europe's political, economic and military organisations than had previously been the case (Davies, 1996). Accordingly, the ECSC had far greater influence than the OEEC, in that it took power away from national governments and gave it to new, independent institutions which were instigated under the Treaty of Paris 1951. These new institutions had responsibility for the development of the coal and steel industries in all of the six Nation States that had signed that Treaty. The development of those industries was no longer the responsibility of the States themselves. This ensured that none of those States had the capacity to independently gear their coal and steel production towards military purposes.

The original members were France, West Germany, Belgium, Holland, Luxembourg and Italy. Britain believed that its interests were better served by close relationships within the Empire, rather than with its European neighbours. It joined the European Free Trade Association, but this was a far less ambitious scheme which relied on intergovernmental co-operation, rather than on taking power away from the Member States and giving it to newly created institutions.

The ECSC paved the way for closer economic co-operation in spheres other than the coal and steel industries and, in 1957, the six Member States signed the Treaty of Rome, which created both the European Economic Community (EEC) and the European Atomic Energy Community (Euratom). Like the ECSC and the OEEC, both of the new Communities possessed autonomous institutions that operated separately from the Member States. In 1967, a Merger Treaty streamlined the administration of the ECSC, Euratom and the EEC, so that, for all practical purposes, they became one institution.

Under the Treaty of Rome 1957, the scope of the EEC was to be significantly broader than that of the other institutions. The elimination of customs duties and other trade restrictions, and the free movement of goods, services, persons and capital between Member States and common commercial policies towards countries outside the Community, were the fundamental aims. The integration of coal and steel had merely been the starting point. The long term aims, according to the Preamble to the 1957 Treaty, were 'a determination "to lay the foundations of an ever closer union among the peoples of Europe" and a resolve to pool resources "to preserve and strengthen peace and liberty"' (Weatherill and Beaumont, 1995, p 5). The UK became a Member in 1973 (two previous attempts to join having been repulsed by French opposition), along with the Irish Republic and Denmark.

The number of Member States has continued to rise and the scope of the Treaty of Rome was significantly extended, notably by the Single European Act (SEA) 1986 and the Treaty on European Union 1992 (otherwise known as the Maastricht Treaty). The SEA inserted a new Art 8(a) into the Treaty of Rome (now Art 7(a)), which committed Member States to 'adopt measures with the aim of progressively establishing the internal market over a period expiring 31 December 1992'. It also extended the EC's sphere of competence to such fields as economic and social cohesion, research and technological development and the environment.

The Maastricht Treaty substantially amended the Treaty of Rome and altered its name from the Treaty Establishing the European Economic Communities to the European Community Treaty (EC Treaty). It is primarily 'a statement of political intent, containing relatively few legally specific commitments' (Weatherill and Beaumont, 1995, p 9), but the name change reflects the fact that the Community's ambit is not restricted to economic matters alone. Its fields of activity now include culture, public health, industry and consumer protection. As discussed below, sport is not (yet) a formal Community competence, so there is no Community-wide sports policy. But a great many Community powers and decisions have already had a strong impact on sports issues, and this can only increase as the Community's ambit reaches into these new areas. Culture and consumer protection will be of particular significance in this respect. In addition to amending the Treaty of Rome, the Maastricht Treaty created a new institution – the EU – which is empowered to develop a common foreign and security policy and to extend its influence into matters of justice and home affairs.

Articles 7 and 8 of the EC Treaty entrust the tasks to be carried out by the Community to the Council, the Commission, the Parliament and the ECJ. The Council and Commission are assisted by an Economic and Social Committee and a Committee of the Regions, both of which have an advisory role. The nature and functions of these bodies may be briefly summarised as follows.

The *Council of Ministers* is the forum through which Member States express their opinions on issues within the Community's competence. Its composition changes according to the subject under discussion. Its functions are outlined in Arts 202–10 of the EC Treaty. Meetings are dominated by attempts to reconcile national interests with Community policies and balancing competing national agendas. The Council is the main legislative organ of the Community. It has the final say on the adoption of most legislative proposals made by the Commission (the European Parliament has limited powers of veto on some matters), so its decisions are of fundamental importance to the Community as a whole. Its legislative powers are not absolute, for it has to consult (and, in some cases, co-decide) with the Parliament and the Economic and Social Committee on certain issues. The Council reaches its decisions by vote, but there are three different voting systems in existence, and which one is applicable depends upon which Treaty Article the proposed legislation emanates from.

The *Commission*, based in Brussels, is concerned with the interests of the Community itself, rather than its Member States, and is responsible for the day to day administration of Community matters. Great Britain, France, Germany, Italy and Spain each appoint two Commissioners, while the other Members each appoint one. Commissioners are appointed by the Member States for a period of five years and are often, but not always, former politicians of high standing (Chris Patten and Neil Kinnock are the current British appointees). Once appointed, their duties are to the Commission, rather than to the national governments or their former political allies.

The Commission's main duties are to prosecute breaches of the Treaty by Member States, individuals or other institutions; to formulate recommendations and deliver opinions on matters arising under the EC Treaty; and to exercise any other powers conferred on it by the Council of Ministers. Its day to day work is undertaken by a number of Directorates

General (see below), which are staffed by civil servants from the Member States.

The *European Parliament* is the only Community institution whose members are directly elected by the citizens of the Member States. It comprises over 620 directly elected members and elections take place every five years. Its problem has traditionally been one of credibility. Initially called the Assembly under the original Treaty of Rome, its powers were severely limited, although it exerted a rather tenuous, informal influence over the Commission and the Council. The change of name was provided for by the SEA 1986 and reflects a belief that 'Parliament' carries a greater prestige than 'Assembly' and will thus command more respect from the public. Its powers were enhanced by the SEA 1986 and the Maastricht Treaty 1992: its consent is required in respect of the accession of new Member States and it now carries out a proper scrutiny of the work of the Council and the Commission. It also has the power to bring cases against other Community institutions before the ECJ.

The composition and functions of the *ECJ* are outlined in Art 220 of the EC Treaty. The Court consists of one judge from each of the Member States and eight Advocates General, with the judgment of the court being by way of a single ruling, rather than the majority decision prevailing. The Advocates General give their opinion on the issues in the case and their opinions are heard before the court's decision is given, 'thereby providing the judges with learned, though not binding, assistance' (Weatherill and Beaumont, 1995, p 30). The Advocate General's advice is usually followed, however, and is in many cases far more illuminating than the ruling of the Court itself. The decision in *Bosman* (1996) is a classic example of this, where the opinion of Lenz AG has been of great significance.

The domestic courts of the Member States can refer cases to the ECJ for a preliminary ruling under Art 234 of the EC Treaty, while individual citizens can invoke a similar procedure under Art 241. The overall function of the ECJ is to give effect to the aims and objectives of treaties. When considering the legality of States' or individuals' activities in relation to the Treaty or the provisions of the various directives, it considers what decision would best serve the 'spirit of the Community', as laid down in the Preamble to the Treaty. In other words, the judges of the ECJ give particular consideration to whether their decisions assist in the drive towards an 'ever closer union'.

Since 1989, the ECJ has been assisted by a Court of First Instance (CFI). Under the SEA 1986, the CFI can be given the authority to hear actions brought under any aspect of the EC Treaty, other than Art 234 references. Appeals against its decisions may be made to the ECJ, but on points of law only (for example, on the basis of a lack of competence on the part of the court, a breach of procedure or an error of legal interpretation). There is no right of appeal on the basis of the CFI's findings of fact.

SPORTS CASES IN THE ECJ BEFORE *BOSMAN*

In *Walrave and Koch v UCI* (1975), the ECJ affirmed that sport was subject to the provisions of Community law if it constituted an economic activity within the meaning of Art 2 of the EC Treaty (as amended). This provides that:

> The Community shall [promote] a harmonious and balanced development of economic activities, sustainable and non-inflationary growth respecting the environment, a high degree of convergence of economic performance, a high level of employment and of social protection, the raising of the standard of living and quality of life, and economic and social cohesion and solidarity among Member States.

Accordingly, any sports practice is an 'economic activity' within the meaning of Art 2 if it contributes to or impacts upon, *inter alia*, growth, economic performance and employment levels within the Community or the standard of living or quality of life of the people who live within it.

Walrave and Koch concerned the activities of two Dutch nationals who were employed as pacemakers on motorcycles in medium distance bicycle races. The bicycle racers would ride in the lee of the motorcycle and could reach speeds of up to 100 kmph, which would be impossible without the assistance of the pacemakers. In 1973, the sport's governing body – the Union Cyclisme Internationale (UCI) – introduced a new rule which stated that the pacemakers had to be of the same nationality as the riders they were assisting. The plaintiffs (who were generally recognised as two of the best pacemakers in the world) brought an action before the Dutch court, seeking a declaration that the rule breached Art 48 (now Art 39) of the EC Treaty. The plaintiffs won their case at first instance and were granted both a declaration that the new rule was void and an injunction prohibiting the UCI from preventing the plaintiffs from working for racers who were not Dutch nationals but who were nationals of other EC Member States.

The UCI successfully appealed against the ruling and, on further appeal, certain issues were referred by the domestic court to the ECJ under Art 177 (now Art 234) of the EC Treaty. Those issues concerned, *inter alia*, whether the rules governing sports events were exempt from the provisions of the Treaty. The Court was also asked whether the fact that the UCI was based in Switzerland and most of its member countries (there being over 100) were not members of the EC meant that the provisions of the Treaty were not applicable to the UCI in any event.

The second question was dealt with quickly. The Advocate General made the point that:

> ... any sovereign State is entitled to enact that a particular type of provision in the rules of an international association of private persons shall be deemed unlawful in its territory and shall not be applied there. One is familiar with

enactments of that sort in the field of competition law. In my opinion, what is true for a sovereign State is true also for the Community [*Walrave and Koch v UCI* (1975), p 328].

The Community is a 'Superstate' with laws, powers and obligations that apply to those who deal with it, even if they are not Community members.

On the question of whether an exception from the provisions of the Treaty should be made for the rules of sport organisations that are designed to ensure that 'national teams' should consist only of nationals of the country, Warner AG said that such an exception should be made:

> Suppose that an officious bystander, at the time of the signing of the EEC Treaty ... had asked those round the table whether they intended that (the relevant Treaty Articles) should preclude a requirement that ... a national team should consist only of nationals of the country it represented. Common sense dictates that the signatories, with their pens poised, would all have answered impatiently, 'of course not' – and perhaps have added that, in their view, the point was so obvious that it did not need to be stated [*Walrave and Koch v UCI* (1975), p 329].

And, in giving its judgment, the ECJ agreed, saying that the question of national team composition was 'a question of purely sporting interest and as such has nothing to do with economic activity' (p 332).

Walrave was applied in *Dona v Mantero* (1976), where the ECJ held that professional and semi-professional football enjoyed the benefits of the Treaty provisions on freedom of movement of persons and provision of services. However, the case also affirmed that, in some circumstances, the application of nationality restrictions to those who played in national teams would be a 'non-economic' issue and, therefore, would be exempt from the EC Treaty provisions.

The case arose after the plaintiff had been asked to 'scout' for players who were willing to play for Rovigo, an Italian club, of which the defendant was chairman at the material time. One of the plaintiff's ruses in this regard involved placing an advertisement in a Belgian sporting newspaper, asking players who were interested in playing in Italy's sunnier climes to get in touch with him. The defendant refused to consider employing Belgians and refused to reimburse the plaintiff for costs incurred in placing the advertisement. The rules of the Italian Football Federation banned players who were not Italian nationals from playing in the Italian leagues, and the plaintiff had not thought to clarify this before placing the advert. The defendant argued that he ought not to be obliged to reimburse the plaintiff if there was no way that the players who responded to it could play in Italy, unless and until the rules were changed. The plaintiff argued that the Italian Football Federation's provisions were invalid because they contravened the provisions of Arts 7, 48 (now Art 39) and 59 (now Art 48) of the EC Treaty.

The Advocate General opined that the Italian Federation's rules were, indeed, a *prima facie* breach of Community law. However:

> There is nothing to prevent considerations of purely sporting interests justifying ... some restriction on the signing of foreign players ... so as to ensure that the winning team will be representative of the State of which it is the Champion team ... Even sporting activities run on a business basis may nevertheless fall outside the ... fundamental rules of the Treaty in cases where the restrictions on the ground of the player's nationality are based on purely sporting considerations, provided that such restrictions are appropriate and proportionate to the end pursued [*Dona v Mantero* (1976), p 582].

This decision reinforced the football authorities' belief that 'purely sporting considerations' meant that the imposition of quotas and the transfer system were 'appropriate and proportionate' and justified the provisions of the EC Treaty being disregarded, despite the Commission's protestations to the contrary. Indeed, there was a number of skirmishes between the two sides on this issue before the *Bosman* case.

THE TRANSFER AND QUOTA SYSTEMS PRE-*BOSMAN*

UEFA had traditionally regarded itself as immune from external legal regulation and entitled to run its fiefdom in whatever way it saw fit. At various times, UEFA has been accused of acting in restraint of trade, placing unlawful restrictions on individuals' freedom of movement, engaging in racial discrimination and encouraging concerted practices. But the two practices that caused most concern within the Community were the use of 'quotas' to control the number of foreign players at each club and the transfer fee system.

Quota systems

Back in 1978, a meeting between UEFA and the Commission led to minor changes to certain discriminatory practices and UEFA affirming its commitment to complying with EU law in full by abolishing the quota system and amending its transfer provisions. But, by 1984, it had taken no steps in this respect and the Commission stated that it would instigate legal proceedings against UEFA if free movement was not introduced by the start of the 1987/88 season. In 1986, an internal Commission report revealed that the 1978 agreement had not been implemented as UEFA had promised. UEFA was called to another meeting with the Commission in 1987, at which it agreed to make more minor changes, modify some of its quota practices from the start of the 1990/91 season and undertake a further review of quotas and transfers in 1991.

However, in 1989, the Van Raay Report on restrictive practices in the European football industry proved to be a damming indictment of UEFA's ongoing discriminatory practices and questioned whether UEFA's commitment to change was genuine. The European Parliament recommended a programme for reform and the Commission threatened to resort to legal action to free the industry of restrictions altogether if UEFA continued not to toe the line. In April 1991, UEFA introduced a 'gentlemen's agreement' which provided that, from July 1992, there would no longer be limits on the number of foreign players that any club could play in domestic matches. From that date, the domestic leagues would be responsible for setting their own upper limits. However, those leagues would have to comply with a UEFA-imposed *minimum* of three non-nationals (that is, those who were not eligible to play for the national side) plus two 'assimilated players' per team. An assimilated player was one who had played in that country continuously for at least five years, three of those years being at youth level.

In practice, the national leagues used the UEFA minimum quota as their maximum. For its part, the Football League in England set no limits on other Britons appearing in domestic competitions but allowed a maximum of three 'real' foreigners. So, while there were no limits on the number of Scottish, Welsh or Northern Irish players who could play for English clubs, there were stringent limits on the number of players from other EU Member States or States outside the EU who could play for any club.

So far as the competitions run by UEFA were concerned, the gentlemen's agreement initially allowed for a maximum of four foreigners per *squad* from the 1990/91 season, although only three of them could be on the pitch at any one time. The provisions caused a degree of confusion. Eintracht Frankfurt fielded four foreign players (one more than the domestic regulations allowed) in a Bundesliga match against Bayer Uerdingen. There was a celebrated occasion in 1992 when Leeds United's match against VfB Stuttgart in the European Champions Cup had to be replayed because VfB, having started the game with two players who were not German nationals, added two more as substitutes. Therefore, they had all four of their foreign squad members playing at once – one more foreigner than the rules allowed. UEFA may have made some minor concessions, but its quota system still breached EU laws. It fell to the ECJ to clarify matters.

The *Bosman* case

> The organisation of football appears to be on a collision course with more than one area of the [EC Treaty]. This should not occasion surprise. European attitudes are beneficial to football, in that the sphere of attractive and lucrative competition is widened. But they also constitute a threat to the game [Weatherill, 1989, p 87].

In 1986, Jean-Marc Bosman signed professional forms with a Belgian club, Standard Liege. Two years later, he joined another, smaller Belgian club (SA Royal Club Liegois) on a two year contract with a monthly salary of approximately 120,000 Belgian francs. Shortly before this contract expired, in the spring of 1990, he was offered a new deal: a one year contract with his wages slashed to 30,000 francs – the lowest wage that the club could offer under the rules of the Belgian FA. Unsurprisingly, Bosman refused to sign the new contract and he was placed on the club's transfer list.

Under the rules of the Belgian FA, for one month at the end of the domestic season, a player on the transfer list was allowed to move to another club, even if his old club objected to the move. The old club could not block the transfer by asking for an unreasonable and prohibitive transfer fee, because, in such cases, the Belgian FA determined the fee to be paid. They used a complex mathematical formula that involved multiplying the player's annual wage by a figure of between two and 14 (depending upon the player's age). When this formula was applied to Bosman, the figure reached was almost 12 million francs.

This was far more than other Belgian clubs were willing to pay, but, in May 1990, Bosman negotiated a one year transfer to a French Second Division club (US Dunkerque) for one-10th of that figure. Dunkerque also had an option to sign him permanently if they paid another 4,800,000 Belgian francs by the beginning of August. However, RC Liegois doubted that Dunkerque would be able to raise the cash, so did not apply to the Belgian FA for the necessary clearance certificates to allow Bosman to move to France. The deal collapsed. RC Liegois suspended Bosman in accordance with the rules of the Belgian FA (under which he would have been re-classed as an amateur player if the club had not done so).

In late 1990, Bosman started proceedings in the domestic court. He sought an order that RC Liegois pay him a salary while he found a new club, and asked the court to prohibit the club from seeking a transfer fee for him. He also requested that the case be transferred to the ECJ for determination of the ultimate issue – the legality or otherwise of the Belgian transfer system. All three requests were granted at first instance but, on appeal, the referral to the ECJ was overturned.

Over the next three years, Bosman plied his trade at three lower division clubs in France and Belgium on a succession of one year contracts while his legal proceedings dragged on. In August 1991, UEFA was joined as a defendant in his action (which was now an action for damages) against RC Liegois. He also started a separate case in the Belgian courts against UEFA itself, contending that its rules were a breach of Art 48 (freedom of movement between Member States – now Art 39) and Arts 85 and 86 (imposition of restrictive practices and abuse of a dominant position – now Arts 81 and 82) of the EC Treaty. In April 1992, he amended his claim so as to seek an order that neither its transfer rules nor the rules concerning overseas player quotas were applicable to him.

In June 1992, the Belgian Court of Appeal restored the first instance court's decision to make a reference to the ECJ under Art 177 (now Art 234) of the EC Treaty. The reference sought a preliminary ruling on the compatibility of both the Belgian transfer system and UEFA's rules with the provisions of Arts 48, 85 and 86. The questions that the ECJ was asked to consider were as follows: first, when a player whose contract with a particular club had expired joins another club, does the EC Treaty prohibit the first club from requiring payment from the club that sign him? Secondly, do the provisions of the Treaty prohibit a national or international sporting association from restricting the right of foreign players from other countries in the EC to play in the competitions that that Association has organised?

The first point to be addressed concerned the extent of the ECJ's jurisdiction over UEFA's rules and regulations. UEFA is a confederation of FIFA, the game's international governing body, and UEFA's regulations require FIFA's approval. Both UEFA and FIFA are based in Switzerland and are governed by Swiss law. However, 'its members are the national associations of some 50 countries, including in particular those of the [EC] Member States which, under UEFA statutes, have undertaken to comply with those statutes and with the regulations and decisions of UEFA' (*Belgian FA v Bosman* (1996)). To illustrate the extent of UEFA's influence, in the qualifying stages for the 1998 World Cup, there were nine European groups, accommodating an unprecedented 51 countries and playing across a geographical area that extended from Iceland to Azerbaijan. Israel is also a member of the UEFA confederation, for obvious political reasons.

So far as the Advocate General was concerned, the fact that UEFA was based in a non-Member State, that the majority of countries playing under its auspices were non-Members and that the practices complained of had been *formed* in a non-Member country (that is, Switzerland) were all immaterial so far as Community law was concerned. If a company or other body based in a non-Member State engages in practices that affect competition or freedom of movement within the Community, then the provisions of the Treaty will be applicable so long those practices have been *implemented* within the Community. See, for example, *Ahlstrom Osakyhtio v Commission* (1988), where a concerted practice (namely, a cartel among wood pulp producers), 'though formed outside the Community, was implemented within it and accordingly fell within the Community's jurisdiction under the territoriality principle uncontroversial in international law' (Weatherill and Beaumont, 1993, p 614). The issue was irrelevant, despite UEFA's ejaculations about the benefits of being based in Switzerland. 'The present proceedings concern application of [UEFA's] rules within the Community and not the relations between the national associations of the Member States and those of non-playing countries,' opined the Advocate General in *Bosman* (p 159). There are obvious tax advantages for governing bodies which choose to base themselves in Switzerland, but they are still subject to EU law if their decisions impact upon the Community's citizens.

Once the jurisdictional issue had been resolved, the next plank of UEFA's and the Belgian FA's defence was the predictable one that recourse to law was not appropriate for dealing with sports issues. However, as explained above, *Walrave* (1975) and *Dona* (1976) had already established that Community law was applicable to sport if it constituted an economic activity. In summarising the effect of those two cases, Lenz AG opined that:

> ... (a) the rules of private sports associations are also subject to Community law; (b) the field of sport is subject to Community law *insofar as it constitutes an economic activity*; (c) the activities of professional football players are in the nature of gainful employment and are therefore subject to Community law; (d) either Art 48 or Art 59 [now Arts 39 and 49] applies to those activities, with no differences arising therefrom; (e) the Court allows certain exceptions to the prohibitions contained in those provisions [emphasis added].

UEFA argued that it was only the 'superclubs' of Europe whose activities could possibly be said to 'constitute an economic activity'. The provisions under Arts 48, 85 and 86 (now Arts 39, 81 and 82) of the EC Treaty ought not to be extended to the activities of humble little clubs such as RC Liegois in any event, for the restrictions were certainly proportionate and appropriate when applied to them. However, the Advocate General's opinion was that, once professional football had been deemed to be an economic activity, 'the size of that activity is immaterial, as is the question of to what extent it leads to a profit'. He had sympathy with UEFA's argument that transfers existed in order to subsidise the smaller clubs, and that applying the provisions of Art 48 of the EC Treaty would have consequences for the entire organisation of football, not just the professional game. But 'that argument relates to the *consequences* of the Court's decision, not the question of the *applicability* of Community law, and thus cannot be an obstacle to that applicability' (emphasis added).

The Advocate General's most trenchant criticism was reserved for the Belgian FA's argument that, as most professional clubs in Belgium did not make a profit, Art 48 ought not to be applicable:

> If I understand that argument correctly, the [Belgian FA] is submitting that the rules on transfers relate merely to the mutual relationships of clubs, while Art 48 is relevant only to the employment relationship between the club and the player. That argument cannot be accepted. The distinction suggested ... is of an artificial character and does not correspond to reality. The rules on transfers are of direct and central importance for a player who wishes to change club. *That is shown precisely by the present case: if it had not been for the transfer rules,*

nothing would have hindered Mr Bosman's transfer to US Dunkerque. It thus cannot seriously be maintained that those rules concern merely the legal relations between clubs [emphasis in original].

Lenz AG was equally dismissive of two other arguments put forward by UEFA. First, it suggested that, even if Community law was applicable to sport, Art 48 in particular was not appropriate for solving football's specific problems. The Advocate General reiterated that 'professional football is an economic activity and is therefore subject to Community law'. He also dismissed the arguments that the case concerned a dispute between a Belgian player and the Belgian FA and that it was a purely internal situation, to which Art 48 was inapplicable. The obvious response to such a suggestion was that 'the main action originates in a failed transfer from a *Belgian* to a *French* club ... There is thus evidently a situation which extends beyond the frontiers of one Member State' (emphasis in original).

Having reached the conclusion that Art 48 was applicable, the Advocate General went on to consider whether UEFA's quota rules breached its provisions. 'No deep cogitation is required to reach the conclusion that the rules on foreign players are of a discriminatory nature,' he decided, continuing:

> They represent an absolutely classic case of discrimination on the ground of nationality. Those rules limit the number of players from other Member States whom a club in a particular Member State can play in a match. Those players are thereby placed at a disadvantage with respect to access to employment, compared with players who are nationals of that Member State.

The rules may have only limited the number of foreigners who could *play* in any match, rather than the number of foreigners that a club could actually have on its books, but that still amounted to a restriction on freedom of movement: 'Every club which plans and acts in a reasonable manner will take the rules on foreign players into account in its personnel policy. No such club will therefore engage more – or significantly more – foreign players than it may play in a match.' By way of example, the Advocate General cited the two financially strongest clubs in his native Germany – Bayern Munich and Borussia Dortmund – who had just five and six foreign players respectively on their staff in the 1995/96 season, out of squads of 21 and 25 players.

In *Dona*, (1976), the ECJ had allowed the imposition of restrictions on the number of foreign players who could play in national leagues. But the justification for those restrictions lay in 'reasons which are not of an economic nature, which relate to the particular nature and context of such matches and are thus of *sporting interest only*, such as, for example, matches between national teams of different countries' (p 582; emphasis in original). The Advocate General in *Bosman* was troubled by the ramifications of this decision. He stated that, 'In view in particular of the fact that matches between national teams – as in the football World Cup – nowadays indeed have considerable financial significance, it is hardly still possible to assume that this is not (or not also) an economic activity' (*Bosman v Belgian FA* (1996), p 108). He was able to avoid the matter, 'since the question is not relevant to the present case'. Of more immediate concern were three other arguments put forward in an attempt to justify the discriminatory provisions:

> First, it is emphasised that the national aspect plays an important part in football; the identification of the spectators with the various teams is guaranteed only if those teams consist, at least as regards the majority of players, of nationals of the relevant Member State. Moreover, the teams that are successful in the national leagues represent their country in international competitions. Secondly, it is argued that the rules are necessary to ensure that enough players are available for the relevant national team; without the rules on foreigners, the development of young players would be affected. Thirdly, and finally, it is asserted that the rules on foreigners serve the purpose of ensuring a certain balance between the clubs, since otherwise the big clubs would be able to attract the best players.

All of these arguments have traditionally been trotted out by clubs and the various governing bodies when the need to defend quotas or the transfer fee system has arisen, and, on this occasion, the 'spectator identification' argument struck the Advocate General as particularly fallacious.

> As to the identification of spectators with the teams, there is ... no need for extensive discussion to show the weakness of that argument ... The great majority of a club's supporters are much more interested in the success of their club that in the composition of the team.

Even if the 'national aspect' arguments did have any merit, it:

> ... could not justify the rules on foreigners. The right to freedom of movement and the prohibition of discrimination ... are among the fundamental principles of the Community order. The rules on foreign players breach those principles in such a blatant and serious manner that any reference to national interests which cannot be based on Art 48(3) must be regarded as inadmissible as against those principles.

The Advocate General was also aware that the way in which young players were developed gave the lie to the argument that youngsters' development, citing Ajax Amsterdam as a rare example of a top club that had invested heavily and consistently in its youth policy. This applies as much to English clubs as it does to Dutch ones, for, with one or two notable exceptions, most clubs have relied on established stars from other Premiership sides or (post-*Bosman*) from other countries in an attempt to buy success. A quick trawl through the *Rothman's Guide* shows that transfer turnover has doubled since the inception of the Premier League, but that the amount of money being paid to smaller clubs by way of transfer fees is decreasing. Young players benefit enormously from playing with and against top quality players of whatever nationality, but 'it is admittedly correct that the number of jobs available to native players decreases the more foreign players are engaged by and play for the clubs ... That is a consequence that the right to freedom of movement necessarily entails'.

Professional football had consistently chosen to ignore the fundamental basics of Community law and hoped that it would be left alone. Those who ran the game were too proud and too short sighted to work out how it could best comply with its obligations under the EC Treaty. *Bosman* (1996) highlighted the need for clubs to develop lawful player development systems rather than rely on quotas and buying and selling established players amongst themselves.

The argument that restrictions on foreign players preserved a balance between clubs because they prevented the biggest sides from swallowing up all the talent and, thereby, widening the gulf between those clubs and the smaller ones, attracted a degree of sympathy from the Advocate General. But the onus fell on football's authorities to show that their significance was so great that they ought to be regarded as an exception to the provisions of Art 48 of the EC Treaty under the 'appropriate and proportionate' test. They had failed to discharge that burden. The Advocate General also pointed out that, while the rules on foreign players had been worked out with, or approved by, the Commission, this did not give them any particular legal significance or place them in a privileged position: 'The Commission is neither entitled nor in a position to amend the scope or meaning of the provisions of the Treaty by its actions. It is for the Court of Justice alone to give binding interpretations of those provisions.'

Lenz AG went on to say that young players and smaller clubs could be protected by means other than an unlawful restriction on freedom of movement. He suggested that a policy of collective wage capping or the distribution of funds on a more equitable basis might have the desired result, whilst preventing further breaches of the EC Treaty. The issue has come full circle, for the perceived need to protect smaller clubs had, of course, been one of the reasons why a maximum wage and retain-and-transfer had been introduced in England a century before. The *Bosman* ruling might oblige football's authorities to go down the 'redistribution of funds' route in preference to trying to carve out a path through the legal minefield of wage restraint and transfer systems. *Walrave* (1975) and *Dona* (1976) prevented UEFA and the Belgian FA from arguing that the restrictions were of a non-economic nature and that Art 48 did not apply. Having reviewed all of the authorities' other points at length, the Advocate General was moved to conclude that 'the transfer rules hitherto in force are not justified by reasons in the general interest'. The problem was that, although the end results of the transfer system might be in the sport's best interests, the means of achieving those ends had to be lawful. Failing that, there had to be sufficiently compelling reasons for maintaining a transfer system that was manifestly incompatible with Art 48. The authorities had failed to satisfy the court on either point.

The Court shared the Advocate General's view that the transfer system was unlawful under Art 48 and held that, because this was the case, 'it is not necessary to rule on the interpretation of Arts 85 and 86 of the Treaty'. However, the decision not to rule on Arts 85 and 86 meant that the legality of transfers that take place between two clubs based in the same State remained unclear. Article 39 (formerly Art 48) only applies to restrictions that prevent free movement between one State and another, but, as Weatherill points out:

> The juxtaposition of a domestic system requiring the payment of transfer fees and an absence of fees payable on cross-border deals affects inter-State trade patterns. The distortive effect on the wider market of a horizontal agreement between clubs relating to player acquisition brings it within Art [81(1)] [Weatherill, 1996, p 1021].

In other words, while the football authorities knew that, post-*Bosman*, the payment of a fee for an out-of-contract player moving from, say, Bröndby to Arsenal was unlawful, it was unclear whether the position was the same in respect of an out-of-contract English qualified player moving from Portsmouth to Southampton.

THE IMMEDIATE IMPACT OF *BOSMAN* AT GOVERNING BODY LEVEL

Within the game, it was generally believed that:

*   Art 48 (now Art 39) of the EC Treaty prohibited regulations that prevented a footballer who was a national of one Member State from moving to a club in another Member State once the player's contract with his former club has expired, unless a transfer fee had been paid;

*   it also prohibited 'quota rules', which restricted the number of players from other Member States who may play for any particular club;

*   the extent to which the provisions of Arts 85 and 86 (now Arts 81 and 82) of the EC Treaty applied to professional football remained unclear, since the Court felt that its decision in respect of Art 48 had made consideration of those provisions unnecessary;

*   Art 48 (now Art 39) of the Treaty had no application 'to situations which are wholly internal to a Member State, in other words, where there is no factor connecting them to any of the situations envisaged by Community law' (*Bosman v Belgian FA* (1996), p 156).

This last point is the one that has since caused most difficulty. Many commentators felt that it meant that transfer fees payable in respect of an out-of-contract player between two clubs in the same Member State were still lawful. However, Weatherill (1996) and others argued that the payment of *any* fee for a player has an impact on cross-border trade in the professional football industry and that the question of which States the two clubs were based in was irrelevant. In January 1996, representatives of the Premiership's top clubs lobbied UEFA for clarification of who was right: did *Bosman* prevent fees from being received in respect of transfers of out-of-contract players moving within the same country, rather than to another Member State? To this end, a meeting was arranged with representatives of the European Commission. Karel van Miert, the Community's Competitions Commissioner, stressed that 'national transfer fees were indirectly affected by the *Bosman* ruling. Any new system devised by UEFA would have to cover transfers within Europe and within European countries' ((1996) *The Guardian*, 6 February, p 24). However, after taking legal advice from two QCs, the Premier League remained convinced that *Bosman* only outlawed transfer fees in respect of cross-border transfers of out-of-contract players. The reason for this uncertainty was that the provisions of what is now Art 39 are concerned with access *to* a market, rather than behaviour *within* that market once access to it has been obtained; hence the governing bodies' belief that the decision only impacted on cross-border transfers. The argument of Weatherill and others was that:

> ... initial access may well have been obtained, but if further access is then immediately restricted, especially in comparison to fellow citizens coming in from abroad, then surely Art [39] comes into play. The necessary 'foreign element' of a foreign national, a citizen of another Member State, would be present, and the situation would rise above the 'wholly internal' as envisaged by the ECJ [Miller, 1996, p 49].

The quota system

Early in 1996, the Commission threatened UEFA with a seven figure fine if it failed to change its quota rules to take account of *Bosman*. UEFA's stance had been supported by FIFA (with General Secretary Sepp Blatter opining that the *Bosman* ruling 'went against the principles of football') and Tom Pendry (the then Shadow Sports Minister) called for European law to be amended so that football's transfer system and quota rules would be protected. But the Commission would not be denied. An exasperated spokeswoman for the Commissioner, Padraig Flynn, was adamant that the Commission would not stand idly by while UEFA flouted the Treaty and the 'clear ruling' of the ECJ in *Bosman*:

> Nobody is above European law. Individual States are not above European law, so you can't have a private organisation like UEFA saying that they are [(1996) *The Guardian*, 17 January, p 20].

Rick Parry, the then Premier League Chief Executive, also took the Commission's side. He said, 'I feel very sceptical that the Community will exempt football from its Art [39] on freedom of movement of workers because it is the bedrock of Community law ... The idea of a blanket exemption for sport is absurd' ((1996) *The Guardian*, 13 February, p 24).

UEFA countered by reminding the Commission that the existing quota rules had been the result of a gentlemen's agreement reached between the two in 1991, but, of course, the Advocate General in *Bosman* had expressly stated that this agreement had no validity at all. It was not for the Commission to rule on how Community law was to be interpreted. But UEFA continued to be characteristically bullish. In January 1996, it told national associations (by fax) to abide by the quota restrictions for UEFA competitions for the rest of 1995/96 'in the interests of continuity and fairness'. But its subsequent climb down was as humiliating as it was predictable. Shortly after this missive, Commissioner Flynn instigated proceedings under Art 171 (as amended by the Maastricht Treaty and now Art 228) and gave UEFA six weeks to comply with *Bosman* or risk the case being returned to the court and fines being levied. On February 19, two weeks before the deadline expired, UEFA announced that the so called 'three plus two' rule (three foreigners plus two assimilated players) would be scrapped forthwith. However, it called upon all those clubs who were still involved in UEFA competitions to observe a gentlemen's agreement until the end of the 1995/96 season. The Commission said that it was 'partly satisfied' with this, but stressed that UEFA would have no way of enforcing such an agreement if any club unilaterally decided to flout it ((1996) *The Guardian*, 21 February, p 24). In October 1996, UEFA announced that all references to player nationality would be removed from its regulations governing club competitions and that it was also working on a new international transfer system.

The transfer system

Further amendments to the transfer system followed soon after. In March 1997, FIFA announced that 'a compensation fee will no longer be paid between clubs in Community countries if the relevant player's contract has expired, irrespective of the player's nationality' ((1997) *The Guardian*, 27 March, p 26). Jean Marc Dupont, Bosman's lawyer, said that the decision was 'logical': 'It would not be moral for a club to have some players from Community countries having rights and the rest from elsewhere in the world being wage slaves [(1997) *The Guardian (Sport)*, 22 March, p 12].'

This announcement prevented another law suit over the precise effect of the *Bosman* ruling, for it coincided with the then Wimbledon player Vinnie Jones' purported intention to take the FA to court over the issue of transfer fees for out-of-contract players who moved from one English club to another. It was also rumoured that Sheffield Wednesday's Des Walker had considered commencing similar proceedings, while Newcastle United threatened to challenge the whole domestic transfer system in order to avoid paying £2 million for Shay Given, who joined them from Blackburn when his contract expired. The broad interpretation of *Bosman*, prohibiting transfer fees in respect of *all* out-of-contract players, neatly sidestepped this issue. However, the Premiership and the Professional Footballers' Association (PFA) are apparently in favour of this prohibition on fees being applicable only in respect of out-of-contract players who are over the age of 24. In their opinion, a transfer fee should still be payable in respect of younger players as 'compensation' for clubs' expenditure in 'training and development'. The Football League has yet to agree to the implementation of the scheme, but, in any case, it would appear to be fundamentally at odds with the provisions of Art 39 of the EC Treaty. There is certainly nothing in the *Bosman* judgment that could be cited as a justification for an age-based restriction.

THE IMMEDIATE IMPACT OF *BOSMAN* AT DOMESTIC CLUB LEVEL

On players' contracts

The contractual provisions applicable to players at British clubs are straightforward enough, at least until they are out of contract or seek to move elsewhere.

Players' contracts always terminate on 30 June of the relevant year. If the club wishes to retain the player, it must offer him a new contract by the third Saturday in May, with terms no less beneficial to the player than those of his previous contract. The player must be given a minimum of one month to consider the offer, and the club is obliged to continue paying his wages during that time. If the club does not want to retain the player on an improved contract, it may offer the same terms or make him an offer on lesser terms. If the player turns either of these down, he is entitled to a free transfer. Alternatively, the club may allow him to leave on a free transfer in any event, or make the player no offer and release him. If the player and the club cannot negotiate a new agreement by 30 June, they may agree a 'conditional contract', which will run until the player can find a new club or they reach agreement on new terms.

Once a player finds a new club, he will sign the standard form contract drawn up by the Professional Football Negotiating and Consultation Committee. The contract contains some 28 clauses and an additional schedule containing remuneration details, to be filled in by the clubs (Osborn and Greenfield, 1998, p 51). The player is obliged to play 'to the best of his ability' (breach of which obligation, incidentally, allowed Leyton Orient to sack Roger Stanislaus for using cocaine on the day of a match). They are allowed to contribute to the media in a 'responsible manner' and participate in other sports, so long as it is not one 'which might endanger his fitness ... or infringe any insurance policy taken out by the club'. Clubs can also prohibit players from living 'at any place which the club deems unsuitable for the performance of his duties under this agreement' (cl 11). This is as likely to be used against players who live an unreasonable distance from the training ground as those who find lodgings conveniently situated above McDonalds or the local bookmakers. Disputes over transfer fees and negotiations about contractual terms are supposed to be private and confidential under both the Premier League's and Football League's regulations.

On quotas

So far as quotas are concerned, the Premier League amended its rules in the wake of UEFA's climb down, so that a team could field no more than three players 'who were not citizens of the EU or the European Economic Area' (EEA) (*Premier League Handbook 1996/97*, s B, para 10). This is a little confusing, since the EEA is usually taken to comprise those countries that are Member States of the EU *and* those that are Member States of the European Free Trade Association (EFTA) but have ratified the EEA agreement. The effect of this provision was to prohibit restrictions on the participation of players who were citizens of the 15 EU Member States, citizens of Iceland, Norway, Liechtenstein (members of EFTA that ratified the EEA Agreement) and, probably, Switzerland (an EFTA member that has not ratified the EEA agreement). Were this provision still in force, the waters would have been muddied still further by virtue of the Associate Member agreements reached with countries that will join the EU in the near future.

The FA's rules were different. The rules of the FA Cup for 1996/97 prohibited the playing of more than three players 'who are not citizens of the EU or EFTA'. In theory, this gave Swiss citizens playing for a Premiership club – Stephane Henchoz when Blackburn were in the Premiership, and Ramon Vega of Spurs – an unfettered right to play in the FA Cup, even though their right to play in the Premier League was, arguably, subject to restrictions. Similarly, the Football League's foreign player rules prohibited restrictions on players who were 'citizens of countries within the EEA or colonies of the UK' that each club can play. A literal interpretation of this provision could have resulted in clubs packing their squads with players from the UK's 'colonies' – Bermuda and Gibraltar.

Three weeks after the *Bosman* judgment, the German FA and the Bundesliga came to a gentlemen's agreement not to use extra foreign players until the end of the 1995/96 season. In April 1996, transfer fees for out-of-contract players were abolished and an unlimited number of 'non-German' players were allowed, so long as each club had at least 12 German players on their squads. This was soon amended to allow an unlimited number of 'UEFA players' and restricted to three the number of players that a club could sign from non-UEFA countries (thereby lawfully discriminating against 'foreigners' from outside the EC).

The Spanish Association's regulations already allowed for free transfers for out-of-contract players and, in spring 1996, the existing restrictions on foreign players were amended so that clubs were no longer restricted to playing a maximum of four 'foreigners' (a term which included nationals from other Member States). The number of nationals from other Member States who can play for each club is now unlimited. Since the 1998/99 season, clubs are allowed to register a maximum of six players who hail from outside the EC (in squads that may contain no more than 25 players) and may field four of those in any one match. Some Spanish players were not enamoured of these changes, however. In January 1997, they announced that they would consider taking strike action if clubs did not agree to a maximum of three non-EC players each for the 1997/98 season, with subsequent annual reductions to a maximum of one 'foreigner' per club by 1999/2000. Gerardo Movilla, the Spanish Players' Union President, pointed out that there were over 200 non-EC players in the Spanish First and Second Divisions (mostly from South America, of course), which was more than the total of all the EC Members combined.

In March 1996, Belgium scrapped its entire domestic transfer system and its limits on the number of all foreign players (not just EC nationals). Portugal and Austria both lifted all restrictions on all non-nationals from the start of the 1996/97 season. At the same time, Serie A players in Italy came out on strike in an attempt to secure the limits that the players themselves wanted to be imposed on the number of non-EC nationals.

THE EU BODIES' IMPACT ON SPORT

The impact of the various institutions of the EC upon football and other sports is vast, and most sports organisations are only just beginning to comprehend the all-pervasiveness of EU law; at least in this respect, football is ahead of the game. Parrish (1998) states that 18 of the 24 European Commission's Directorates General have an impact on the operation of sport. The activities of Directorate General (DG) IV has the greatest impact, being responsible for general areas such as broadcasting rights, ticketing, product endorsement, government funding of sport and – crucially for football – restrictive practices such as transfers and restrictions on foreign players. However, formal responsibility for sport rests with DG X, which has responsibility for cultural issues. Its work on sport and EU law exposes the lie behind the suggestion that the *Bosman* ruling came as a shock to those wielding power and influence in the football industry.

Sport and the European Commission

In 1993, the European Commission's DG X commissioned a report from accountants Coopers and Lybrand on EU law's impact on sports. A cross-section of sport's governing bodies (including UEFA), government departments and individuals were consulted and the conclusion was that sport certainly affected by a vast range of EU laws and policies, both directly and indirectly. However, the report found there was very little co-ordination within the EU on sports issues. In particular, the report said that DG X should ensure that sports' interests were taken into account when EU policies were being drawn up. In response, a dedicated Sports Unit was created within DG X to carry out this task and to attempt to ensure that a coherent approach to sports issues was adopted by the 18 Directorates General whose decisions impact on sports matters. This Sports Unit also manages the EU's sports funding programme.

So far as football was concerned, the Coopers and Lybrand report drew attention to UEFA's power under Art 14 of its own regulations to prohibit matches that were played in one country from being broadcast in another country. Coopers and Lybrand took the view that this regulation was potentially an abuse of a dominant position and, therefore, an infringement of Art 86 (now Art 82) of the EC Treaty. It took on board UEFA's submission that limits on televising matches were necessary to ensure match attendance, although this is a view that few other sports seem to share and is not substantiated by any empirical evidence. However, it stressed that UEFA ought to take steps to 'eradicate abuse of Article 14' (Coopers and Lybrand, 1993, p 192).

The report also stressed that making the purchase of tickets dependent on the purchase of other services (such as travel and accommodation) and prohibiting nationals of one Member State from buying tickets from an agent in another State were manifest abuses of EU law. It should be possible to eliminate such abuses, the report said. Yet it was precisely these practices that caused such a furore in the run-up to France 98, five years after this report emphasised their illegality. The Commission's investigations into that ticketing fiasco concluded that the Organising Committee could not be expected to know that their policy broke the law – but Coopers and Lybrand had worked that one out many years previously and the Organising Committee had plenty of time to take its findings on board. The report was also wary of sports bodies granting 'official' labels to certain products in return for payment, and said that the bodies concerned had to make it clear that this was sponsorship, rather than endorsement of a particular brand. Significantly, though, the report concluded that, 'so long as the economic importance of [sport sponsorship] remains relatively limited, the EC should not intervene' (Coopers and Lybrand, 1993, p 8). Neither 'relatively limited' nor 'economic importance' was defined.

The report contained some cogent criticisms of various sports bodies' policies in respect of transfer systems and foreign quotas. Needless to say, football came out badly under both categories. Indeed, by the time that the report was published, a number of footballers had made complaints in respect of the transfer fee system, which (the report said) possibly amounted to an abuse of a dominant position under what is now Art 82. The football authorities had always said that these fees amounted to compensation for player development and were, therefore, vital to small 'feeder' clubs. As the *Bosman* case was already in the pipeline, the report refrained from making long term recommendations, although it did say that football authorities should implement certain temporary measures, such as ensuring that contractual terms were clear and that domestic governing bodies' rules complied with national labour law. In the event, no domestic bodies took such steps pending the resolution of *Bosman*, even though their officials were invited to make observations on the discrepancies between the EC Treaty's provisions on freedom to work in another Member State and the quota rules.

Football, basketball and (to a lesser extent) athletics and cycling were identified as 'problem sports'. In seeking to justify its restrictions, UEFA adopted the 19th century perspective and argued that lifting the restrictions would lead to top teams hoarding talent, causing a decline of youth policies and a loss of support for small local sides. The report accepted there may have been some merit to these arguments, but stressed that sports bodies had to move towards bringing their rules into line with EU law on free movement.

Sport and the European Parliament

The European Parliament now has considerably greater powers than those originally assigned to it under the Treaty of Rome 1957. The Maastricht Treaty 1992 and the Amsterdam Treaty 1997 have provided the Parliament with new legislative and budgetary powers and powers of scrutiny over the Commission. This has enhanced its impact on sport, as on all other matters. Its various committees have produced a number of sports related reports, including the 1989 Van Raay Report on the free movement of professional footballers (see below). It has also had some influence on football through debates, questions and communications with relevant parties. In January 1998, after asking the Commission to investigate a possible breach of Art 86 (now Art 82) of the Treaty (abuse of a dominant position), Parliament called for UEFA to reverse its decision banning the winners of the Coca-Cola Cup (as it then was) from competing in the UEFA Cup. Two weeks later, UEFA acceded to that request. Chelsea were the immediate beneficiaries of this policy change. They won the Coca-Cola Cup in 1997/98, went on to win the UEFA Cup in 1998/99 and thus qualified for the Champions League in 1999/2000.

Sport and the Council of Ministers

At its meeting in Amsterdam in 1998, the European Council inserted a non-legally binding declaration into the Amsterdam Treaty 1997, which called upon EU institutions to take note of the views of sports organisations when making decisions that have an impact on sport. The sports bodies themselves (and especially the European Olympic Committees and European non-governmental sports organisations) had hoped for a legally binding declaration along those lines, because the Council of Ministers makes many decisions that have a great impact upon sport.

RECENT AND POSSIBLE FUTURE DEVELOPMENTS

In July 1998, a Belgian court held in *Balog v Royal Charleroi Sporting Club* (1998) that FIFA's international transfer fee system was as much an unlawful violation of EU law as UEFA's Europe-wide one was. The court ruled that the agreement reached by FIFA and UEFA, allowing clubs to claim compensation for releasing non-EU players even though they have reached the end of their contracts, was unlawful. The case concerned the Hungarian, Tibor Balog, who successfully brought an action against his former club, Charleroi FC, for claiming a transfer fee when his contract with them ended, on the ground that to claim a fee would, once again, breach the EU's competition laws. The court granted interim measures, allowing Balog to join another Belgian club, Westerlo.

The previous year, during a dispute over Brazilian striker Ronaldo's move to Inter Milan, the European Commission had warned FIFA and UEFA that the international system of transfers for non-EU players was equally restrictive. Commission sources said that *Balog* only reinforced its position that competition policy applied to the commercial aspects of sport. Similarly, the International Board of Rugby Union amended its rules in January 1996, so that players leaving a club in one country to join a club in another had to wait for six months before they could play for the new club. The Commission immediately made it known that EU law was being breached and that reducing the length of the residency qualification would make no difference. The Board backed down, thus allowing French international Philippe Sella to play for the English club Saracens as soon as he joined them in February 1996 ((1996) *The Guardian*, 3 February, p 20).

The recent decision in *Malaja v French Basketball Federation* (2000) ensures that reciprocal agreements which have been made with States outside the EC and the EEA mean that players from those countries will be classed as 'non-foreigners'. An association agreement with Turkey, reached in accordance with the terms of Art 39 of the the EC Treaty, contains provisions regarding the free movement of workers. There are also association agreements with a number of Central and Eastern European countries that hope to become members of the EU in the near future, and with Morocco, Tunisia and Algeria, which provide for equal treatment at work and freedom from discrimination on the grounds of nationality.

At the risk of stating the obvious, it should be stressed that the ramifications of *Bosman* are not limited to football but extend to any sports that can be said to constitute an 'economic activity'. As Coopers and Lybrand predicted, the fallout has been particularly acute in basketball. In Spain, a 'two foreigners' rule had to be changed after European club champions Costa Naranja pointed out that the Briton, Andrea Congreave, could no longer be considered to be a 'foreigner'. Early in 2000, Polish basketball player Lilia Malaja won a case before the French courts that effectively recognised the right of nationals from Associate Members of the EU to be treated in the same way as EU nationals. She was denied a transfer from a Polish club to a French one because the French Basketball Association placed restrictions on 'foreigners', but she successfully challenged their rules on the ground that the Art 39 association agreement between Poland and the EU prevented the application of those restrictions to her. The initial effect of this decision will be to extend the right to work to the nationals of the 23 countries who already ply their trade in the EU; however, it will not allow workers to come to EU countries to begin employment. Recently, the Advocates General have given preliminary rulings on discriminatory provisions governing transfer deadlines in professional basketball (*Lehtonen v FRSB* (1999)) and whether amateur judo constitutes an 'economic activity' for the purposes of EU law (*Deliege v ALFJ* (1999)). Both of these cases remain destined for the ECJ: see www.curia.eu.int.

So far as football is concerned, the decision in *Malaja* means that 'those [foreign nationals] who are already here will enjoy exactly the same post-*Bosman* freedom to cross borders once their existing contracts come to an end' (Gardiner, 2000, p 1). In 1993, Hungary's Astvan Kozma was forced to leave Liverpool because he had not played enough games for the club in the previous season and his work permit was thus withdrawn. The effect of *Malaja* is that any other player from an Associate Member State who is already playing for a club in a 'full' EU Member State will not suffer the same indignity.

The status of players from outside the EU, the EEA or the Associate Member States has also undergone recent change. Players from Africa (such as Liberia's George Weah and Rigobert Song from Cameroon) and the Americas (including Costa Rica's Paulo Wanchope and the US's Kasey Keller) in particular are still required to obtain a work permit before they may play in the UK. The Department for Education and Employment has responsibility for issuing permits, and the rules governing them were amended in July 1999. Before that date, a foreign player would not usually be eligible for a work permit unless he had played in approximately 75% of his national side's matches in the previous two seasons. He was also required to be one of the six most highly paid players at the club wishing to sign him. The work permit was only for one year's duration; thereafter (as Kozma discovered), an extension would only be granted if the player was turning out regularly for the club and was making 'a significant contribution to the British game'. In *R v Secretary of State for Employment ex p Portsmouth FC* (1988), it was held that the 75% test was not to be applied too rigidly: if a player had missed international games through injury, that should be taken into account.

Under the new rules, the wage requirement has been removed and work permits apply to the entire duration of a player's contract. However, the requirement that one must be an international player is retained and the FIFA ranking of the player's national side is added to the list of factors to be taken into account when determining whether a permit will be granted (Welch, 2000). Gordon Taylor of the PFA said the changes would 'open the way for cheap foreign imports' ((1999) *The Guardian*, 3 July, p 24). Tony Banks, the then Minister for Sport, felt that they would 'allow clubs to recruit the best available international talent [whilst providing] opportunities for home grown young players' (Welch, 2000). Only time will tell whether Taylor's fears are well founded.

On the whole issue of quotas and transfers, football's authorities are not giving in quietly. In March 2000, EU officials met FIFA's Sepp Blatter (not a man for whom many within the Commission have much respect) and UEFA's Gerhard Aigner and, once again, they made a case for football being exempt from the EU's employment laws. FIFA suggested that a club side should always have six players eligible for the national team on the field of play – a proposal which would obviously conflict with the *Bosman* ruling on quotas and, it seems, not one which the Commission is willing to contemplate in the foreseeable future.

The governing bodies' main problem, it seems, is that they and the European Commission are miles apart on the important issues. Since the Commission so obviously has the law on its side, the governing bodies have to do all the running if they are to persuade the Commission to treat football nicely. Given UEFA's and FIFA's obstinacy in the years before *Bosman*, it seems that there are few within the Commission who believe that they owe football, or (more accurately) the men who run it, any favours – one gets the distinct impression that much of this is personal.

This gulf continues to manifest itself in these organisations' approaches to quotas and the transfer system. The Commission is of the opinion that FIFA's current stance on transfer fees remains at odds with EU law. It appears that, so far as the Commission is concerned, forcing clubs to pay transfer fees for players whose contracts have not yet expired breaches EU law. At least, that appears to be the position of Jean-François Pons, the Deputy Director General of DG IV and the man with responsibility for sport and EU competition policy. During the Nicholas Anelka saga, it was argued (rightly, it is submitted) that, even though the player was still under contract, he could terminate that contract upon payment of damages and move to whichever club offered him the best personal deal. Arsenal's decision not to pursue the case through the courts (they transferred him to Real Madrid for £22 million) probably preserved the last vestiges of the transfer system, in the same way that Derbyshire's releasing Chris Adams from his contract ensured the continuance of professional cricket's equally dubious player registration scheme.

FIFA, of course, shares the domestic governing bodies' view that the payment of a transfer fee for players under contract does not conflict with *Bosman*. In contrast, Pons says the following:

> The Commission takes the view that both the prohibition on all transfers following unilateral termination (assuming compensation for breach of contract has been paid) and the obligation on a new club to pay a transfer fee to the old club in cases of termination by mutual consent infringe Art 81(1) without being able to benefit from exemption under Art 81(3).

> The Commission has taken the preliminary view that through the establishment of the above mentioned rules, clubs have agreed:

> - to reject their freedom to take on players who have unilaterally terminated their contracts;
> - not to recruit players without payment of a fee, and to decide who should be responsible for fixing and paying the fee.

> According to the preliminary position taken by the Commission, these arrangements have as their object and their effect the restriction, to an appreciable extent, of clubs' freedom of action, which represents a violation of Art 1(1) [europa.eu.int/comm/competition/speeches/index_1999.html].

If Pons' comments do reflect the Commission's position, and there is no reason to believe that they do not, it is difficult to see progress being made on either the quota or the transfer fee issue. There may be some light at the end of the tunnel in the guise of Mario Monti, the head of DG X, who, on 17 April

2000, suggested that there could be some scope for derogation from the Treaty if it was required for 'genuinely' sporting reasons. This would not allow breach of fundamentally important aspects of the Treaty such as the provisions relating to freedom of movement or competition law. However, Monti inferred that there may be scope for the payment of 'compensation', so long as that was limited to the cost of a player's training and development. Furthermore, commenting on the need 'to apply the competition rules in a manner which does not question the regulatory authority of sporting organisations vis à vis genuine "sporting rules"', Monti stated:

> Rules which are inherent to a sport or which are necessary for its organisation or for the organisation of competitions so called 'sporting rules' should not, in principle, be subject to the application of competition rules. Sporting rules applied in an objective, transparent and non-discriminatory manner do not constitute restrictions of competition. This approach is in line with the recent judgement in the *Deliège* case ... Selection rules applied by a Federation to authorise the participation of professional or semi-professional athletes in an international sports competition have inevitably the effect of limiting the number of participants in a tournament. Such limitation does not in itself constitute a restriction of the freedom to provide services as long as it derives from a need inherent in the organisation of the international sports event in question [europa.eu.int/comm/competition/speeches/index_2000.html].

Two other recent developments at EU level should be mentioned – namely, the fallout from the ticketing fiasco of France 98 and the holding of a major EU conference on sport. In the summer of 1999, the Commission imposed a symbolic fine of 1,000 Euros on the organisers of France 98 for their use of discriminatory ticketing arrangements. Non-French citizens were initially advised that tickets could only be purchased from national football federations and tour operators and, as a consequence, almost 570,000 of tickets sold for matches found their way to applicants who were able to provide addresses in France. These arrangements amounted to an abuse of a dominant position and, as such, were contrary to EU law, specifically Art 82 of the EC Treaty. While the Commission said that a hefty fine would normally be visited on those who abused their dominant position, it noted that the ticketing arrangements for France 98 were no different to those adopted for previous World Cup finals (even though the Coopers and Lybrand report of 1993 had stressed those earlier arrangements' illegality). It also noted that the Organising Committee had been most constructive in its dealings with the Commission. However, 'the Commission expects tournament organisers in the future to ensure that any ticketing arrangements comply fully with EU competition rules and will not hesitate to take action against them where they fail to do so' (Gardiner, 1999, p 13).

The first European Union Conference on Sport was held in Olympia in the summer of 1999. Organised by the Sports Information Unit of DG IV, the conference made recommendations on a European model for sport, future relationships between sport and television and the 'fight against doping' (*sic*). Most of the recommendations (available at europa.eu.int/comm/competition/speeches/index_2000.html) need not concern us here, for many glib, groundless and factually inaccurate assertions were made which take the EU no closer towards a coherent and worthwhile European policy for sport. Its conclusions speak of the need to 'keep sport safe from political and economic manipulation' (both of which have always been features of organised sport) and the fear that 'over-commercialisation' would 'eventually distort sport's values' (whatever those may be). Apparently, drug use 'violates the basic principles of sporting ethics and endangers the public's health', and the conference came out firmly against 'the drug culture' and 'permissiveness' generally. While the conclusions reached include some thoroughly worthwhile recommendations about, *inter alia*, protecting young people involved in sport, paying more than lip service to equal opportunities and the need to improve disabled people's access to sports facilities, these initiatives will be lost among the dross that accompanies them.

CONCLUSION

The *Bosman* (1996) ruling has had more effect on the contractual status of professional footballers in the few short years since the decision was handed down than the previous cases achieved in their entirety. Retain-and-transfer suddenly seems a quaint historical anachronism, quota systems a relic from a bygone age and player loyalty a contradiction in terms. The ECJ's decision has serious implications for the smaller clubs, particularly if the big teams persist in buying established players on long term contracts and for huge salaries, rather than taking a chance on players from the lower divisions. None of this is the fault of Jean-Marc Bosman, the European Commission or the ECJ, for the game's authorities had been given plenty of notice that their practices were a fundamental violation of EU law and that something had to change. FIFA's and UEFA's arrogance – their belief that the football industry was 'special' and that being based in Switzerland amounted to some form of sanctuary – was never tenable. Perhaps the only surprise is that football was allowed to get away with so many illegalities for so long; the governing bodies certainly cannot say that they never had the opportunity to put their own house in order.

At present, it seems that the European Commission is not minded to grant football an exemption from the rigours of EU law. Unless the Commission has a dramatic change of heart, a choice will have to be made between introducing a system that effectively regulates player movement while complying with the law and maintaining the status quo and letting the smaller clubs die for want of income. Manchester United's 'memorandum of co-operation' with Royal Antwerp – non-EU residents benefit from Belgium's less stringent immigration laws (a salary of £15,000 a year and you're in), obtain an EU work permit after 18 months at Antwerp and then join United – is an imaginative attempt to cash in on *Bosman*. It also reveals, not that there was ever much doubt, that the big boys are not at all concerned about the small clubs and they have no intention of nurturing the grassroots voluntarily.

On 31 August 2000, FIFA announced that it will abolish the transfer system in respect of players aged 24 and over. The announcement represented a long overdue attempt to satiate the European Commission, which believes that the very existence of a transfer system represents a fundamental breach of EU law, notwithstanding the changes to football's employment practices precipitated by the *Bosman* ruling. Bowing to the European Commission's insistence that professional footballers should have the right to change clubs, provided that they serve a period of notice, FIFA proposes that players be allowed to change clubs once a year during a specific period lasting a few weeks, and that contracts be no longer than one year's duration. If these proposals are implemented, clubs will no longer receive transfer fees for players, but they will be able to terminate players' contracts by giving a period of notice. This means that the top players will be able to negotiate even greater salaries, while those playing for smaller clubs will be in a far weaker position than their brethren at Old Trafford or Highbury. They will have no job security and no real bargaining power, and their services can more easily be dispensed with should they suffer a run of poor form or a career threatening injury. It seems that FIFA President Sepp Blatter and his colleagues, after 25 years of posturing, have finally been forced to concede that the transfer system has no future. Blatter asked the European Commission for time to work out a system of compensation for players aged 24 and over, possibly based on length of contract, remaining sum of salary or football experience. But, of course, all this presupposes that the Commission will be satisfied with a system that retains the payment of transfer fees for those players aged under 24: in law, there is no reason why it should be.

A European superleague is no more than 10 years away and, in 30 years' time, there may well be no more than 30 full time professional clubs in England and Wales. One hundred years from now, historians will be writing about football as an incredible social and cultural phenomenon of the 20th century which changed out of all recognition because those in positions of authority failed to look after it properly. It will not be possible to lay the blame at the door of the European Commission.

CHAPTER 4

MISSING THE TARGET: LEGAL RESPONSES TO 'FOOTBALL HOOLIGANISM'

It might be wondered, in passing, whether some recent developments in sporting practices – such as doping, or the increased violence both on the pitch and on the terraces – are not in part an effect of the revolution which I have too rapidly sketched. One only has to think, for example, of all that is implied in the fact that [sport] has become, through television, a mass spectacle, transmitted far beyond the circle of past or present 'practitioners', that is, to a public very imperfectly equipped to decipher it adequately. The 'connoisseur' has schemes of perception and appreciation which enable him to see what the layman cannot see, to perceive a necessity where the outsider sees only violence and confusion.[1]

Something has got to be done.[2]

INTRODUCTION

This chapter is concerned with the legal implications of 'what everyone knows' about football hooliganism. It looks at the misconceptions that 'informed' judicial responses to football related violence and disorder, particularly in the years before the Hillsborough disaster, and, since 1989, how those misconceptions have coloured the several Acts of Parliament that have been foisted upon football fans. It considers in particular how the perception of hooligans as 'not real football fans' has underpinned both the legislative and judicial responses to their activities and the policing tactics that have been deployed inside and outside football grounds. It draws upon theoretical analyses and participant observation of football hooligans throughout Europe (Armstrong, 1993; Giulianotti, 1995; Armstrong and Giulianotti, 1997) which illustrate the flaws in the widely held perception of 'hooligans'.

The phrase 'football hooliganism' has not been defined by Parliament and the courts have shied away from attempting to explain what it is and what it connotes. In this chapter, it will be suggested that the phrase is properly applicable only to a very particular form of behaviour. That the media, the courts and the legislature have deemed all criminal and tarred anti-social behaviour that occurs (spatially or temporally) at or near a football match with the broad brush of 'hooliganism' has had a profound impact on the civil

---

1   Bourdieu, 1978, p 829.
2   *R v Motley* (1978), *per* Pain J.

liberties of football fans. It has also led to the passing of a myriad of largely meaningless legislation. Hooligan activity is inextricably linked to the game of football and the stadia in which it is played. Hooligans tend to possess an impressive knowledge of the subtleties of the game and its history, and their behaviour can scarcely be said to be those of people who are 'not real fans'. The true nature of football hooligan gatherings is different to the popular assumptions about them, but these flawed assumptions have coloured legislative and judicial attitudes to football supporters for more than 30 years.

This chapter does not attempt to provide an exhaustive overview of the voluminous amount of sociological research that has been dedicated to exploring football's 'hooligan phenomenon' which has appeared over the past three decades. For those interested in joining these discussions *ab initio*, an appropriate starting point would be the analyses of those working from Marxist perspectives (for example, Clarke, 1978; Taylor, 1971). Their work portrays football hooliganism as a conscious attempt by working class fans to reclaim the game from an ever more passive middle class audience for whom football was merely a spectacle rather than a participatory experience. Of equal significance are the figurational perspectives (including, but by no means limited to, Elias and Dunning, 1986 and Murphy *et al*, 1990) which constitute some of the most respected scholarly contributions of the 1980s. The work of these writers remains fundamentally important. More recently, illuminating analyses have arisen in the work of Bale (1991; 1993; 1994) and in collections edited by Redhead (1993) and Giulianotti *et al* (1994) in particular. Others have made contributions that could most charitably be described as naïve and offensive, notably those that have alluded to the Hillsborough disaster as being a consequence of hooligan activity (Lewis and Scarisbrick-Hauser, 1994).

A GENDERED SENSE OF SPACE

Many of the most illuminating recent discussions of hooliganism have been predicated upon John Bale's exploration of the significance of space as a social and cultural concept. For Bale, space provides an outlet for the personal and collective expressions of social agency, and for the imposition and exercise of power. For a football club's supporters, the football ground is the space that provides this outlet, and this is the case for the most sedate supporters as much as it is for those with a propensity for hooligan activity. The ground is an emblem of local identity, an icon to the local community (Bale, 1991), from which clubs traditionally drew their followers – and from which clubs who lack the social cachet of the 'glamour sides' continue to do so. Insofar as the concepts of 'home', 'space' and 'place' remain important in an age of globalisation, the football ground offers a meeting place and an opportunity to congregate with others of like mind: it confers 'symbolic citizenship' (Holt, 1989) on those who enter. The presence of club scarves, banners, chants and the other paraphernalia of football represent the visible and audible expressions of a community identity. This identity has not altogether disappeared, despite the best endeavours of the game's image makers and successive governments that have tried to make the game more appealing to a 'new breed' of consumer.

The function of football as 'community identity' is as old as the modern game itself. After its codification and the explosion in its popularity among working class males from the late 1870s onwards, the football ground became the bastion of the working class male and a focus for his leisure activities (Clarke, 1992). In the last 20 years of the 19th century, football benefited from the emergence of an independent-minded element within working class masculinity that was immune to the attractions of rational recreation and preferred to watch sport on a Saturday afternoon, rather than play it. The millions of football supporters who emerged at this time did not hail from among the poorest of the working class, for they were excluded from games by the admission price, but came instead from the skilled working and lower middle classes. Wherever they came from, not all of their number were impeccably behaved all of the time.

Boys' organisations (for example, the Scouts and the Boys' Brigade) and, for older youths and men, active participation in the activities offered by boxing clubs, cricket and football teams had grown apace under the auspices of philanthropists, the Church and employers. But the terraces and the public houses were attractive alternatives for 'the "dangerous classes" who haunted the Victorian imagination' (Collier, 1995, p 221). The explosion in football attendances from two million in 1885 to six million less than a decade later led no less a personage than Robert Baden-Powell to lament the game's transformation. It was no longer a character building form of physical exercise but 'a vicious game ... Thousands of boys and young men, pale, narrow-chested, hunched up, miserable specimens smoking endless cigarettes ... hysterical as they groan and cheer in unison with their neighbours' (quoted in Birley, 1995, p 230). That is not to deny the presence of those from higher social groups within the football crowd, for it has always reflected social class structures. Some fans have always expressed their commitment in song, while others have expressed it through violence; and 'rough' and 'respectable' cultures have always mingled in the football ground. Indeed, 'it is perfectly possible that individuals criss-crossed between [these cultures] in the course of the 90 minutes' (Russell, 1997, p 58). Fights between football fans have been part of the attending experience since at least the 1890s (Mason, 1980). Dunning et al (1984) assert that 'spectator disorderliness was a problem of considerable proportions' before 1914 and suggest that over 4000 incidents of what one might term 'football hooliganism' occurred in the 20 years before the First World War. Russell discusses an incident in 1885 when 2,000 Aston Villa supporters attacked the players and officials of Preston North End. In 1909, goalposts were torn down and over 100 people were injured in a pitched battle between fans and police after the Scottish Cup Final. Fights were not always wholeheartedly condemned by onlookers (Hopcraft, 1968, pp 84–85).

Whether or not a particular incident amounted to 'football hooliganism' was as subjective a test at the end of the 19th century as it was at the end of the 20th, and misunderstanding and misinformation have always been the norm.

> Hooliganism was, and still is, a hugely subjective category: it is this very slipperiness that gives it its power in the hands of law and order lobbies. A few lads shouting in the street may well fit the term for a frightened resident near a football ground, but be of little moment for a policeman who has witnessed a full-scale riot and who is used to policing the city centre at night. Whether the press recorded such an incident as 'hooliganism' or 'horseplay', or simply ignored it altogether, depended very much on the inclinations of the journalist and the paper. At the time of a 'moral panic' over youth culture, it might receive attention; at other times it might be ignored. The issue is further complicated by the fact that late Victorian and Edwardians (or at least their police forces) ... probably had a higher tolerance of a certain degree of disorder in and around sporting events than has been the case in the last 30 years [Russell, 1997, p 62].

It has certainly never been true to say that 'everyone knows' what hooliganism is, or that 'hooliganism' (however one defines it) has ever been prevalent 'in many parts of the country during most Saturdays of the football season' (*R v Motley* (1978), *per* Lawton J).

A MANOR MAKETH MAN

Contemporary football hooliganism (as opposed to these earlier variants discussed in more detail in Mason, 1980, Russell, 1997 and elsewhere) first attracted the concerted attention of Parliament, the media and other 'moral entrepreneurs' (Cohen, 1972) in the period between England's winning the World Cup and the Beatles releasing *Sergeant Pepper*. The spatial arrangement of football grounds certainly contributed to the way in which hooligan activity developed. As Bromberger (1993) explains, at the 'typical' ground, the middle class supporters would congregate in the (one) seated area which ran the length of one side of the pitch. The aspirant, skilled working class would congregate on the terracing beneath and the manual workers – of whom the vast majority of the crowd was comprised – would mass in the cheaper, uncovered ends behind the goals. Most clubs placed a roof over some or all of the exposed terraces and the wealthiest ones added another seated area or two, but the basic layout at most grounds remained unchanged until after Hillsborough. The social and economic composition of the crowd within the various parts of these grounds was equally resistant to change. For financial and social class reasons, the covered main stand, which was the home of the relatively wealthy fans, was segregated from the other ends. In the rest of the ground, supporters enjoyed freedom of movement. This freedom allowed those fans offering the strongest support for a particular side (invariably the 'home' side) to 'follow' it inside the ground by standing behind whichever goal it was attacking. This spatial arrangement thus involved many fans mirroring the ritual on the pitch by 'changing ends' at half time so that they were standing behind the goal towards which their side was playing.

The home side would have a preferred 'end' for playing towards, and this would be reflected in the location of fans at the start of the match. 'Away' fans, usually being in the minority and in comparatively unfamiliar territory, were expected to gather at the 'away end'. Depending upon the number of away fans in attendance, less voluble groups of home fans might also congregate in the away end. The pre-match 'toss' between the teams, to decide who kicked off and which ends the teams would play into, rarely upset fans' expectations – reflecting the common perception that the fans behind the goal towards which a particular side was playing could give team members a psychological lift (Finn, 1994). The concept may be alien to those supporters who know only segregation, but, until the late 1960s, interaction with opposing fans had been an unremarkable part of the match day experience for decades, save for the very occasional skirmish. This spatial arrangement is prevalent at non-League grounds.

That there have always been outbreaks of violence associated with football matches is beyond dispute. On occasion, traditional rivalries could lead to violence between opposing groups of football fans, particularly at 'local derbies' and other 'big matches' as the fans changed ends, but violence precipitated by bad refereeing decisions or the last minute postponing of a game was probably no less frequent (Vamplew, 1978). However, while the ferocity and frequency of these skirmishes can be exaggerated, it is undoubtedly true that, from around 1967, these violent outbreaks became more frequent and more serious. They certainly became a cause for greater consternation, not least because the amount of media attention that the game now attracted meant that incidents that would previously have gone unnoticed now made the news. Many of these outbreaks can be attributed to the fact that some, although certainly not all, fans were no longer content to restrict their attempts to offer the most intensive support by chanting the names of players, denigrating the opposition or waving their scarves in unison. For some of these supporters, 'taking the ends' of rivals became the focus of their activities (Marsh et al, 1978).

These activities led to the development of a classic case of moral panic. In the immediate aftermath of England's World Cup success, Norman Chester was appointed to chair a wide ranging enquiry 'into the state of Association football at all levels' and to make suggestions as to how the game might develop in the future (Chester, 1967). So far as crowd behaviour was concerned, Chester rightly noted 'an increase in disorderly behaviour by spectators' and commented that 'both the governing bodies [that is, the Football Association (FA) and the Football League] have been very concerned at this development'. The year 1967 had witnessed some increase in hooligan activity at various grounds, particularly in London, and certain clubs (for instance, Chelsea and Manchester United) began to develop a reputation for having troublesome fans. Hooliganism's prevalence was certainly overstated, though, not least in the report into soccer hooliganism (Harrington), which spoke in excited tones of:

> Spectators carrying knives, hammers, sticks and spikes, choppers and other offensive weapons like powdered pepper which are not necessarily used for violent purposes but may be used in threatening displays. There is also the problem of singing or chanting bawdy or obscene songs and phrases, some of which are also threatening and provocative ... While riots must be regarded as almost unknown accompaniments of football in this country, their potential seriousness and danger were exemplified recently by football riots in Turkey, where many people were reported killed [Harrington, 1968, pp 8, 9].

The two year period after the publication of Harrington's report represented 'the Parliamentary and academic maturation of "football hooliganism", from irregular disturbance to definitive social policy arena' (Armstrong and Giulianotti, 1997, p 9). A gradual escalation in fan violence and a fear of social unrest manifested itself in media and parliamentary discourse. News reporting of football crowds moved from 'a traditional celebration of the amiable boisterousness of the English crowds to a rather panicky condemnation of terrace culture' (Russell, 1997, p 192). In 1968, the House's attention was drawn to 'the growing public concern about the increase in hooliganism in football generally' (*Hansard*, 29 February 1968). Fifteen months later, through reference to 'the continuing amount of damage caused by soccer hooligans' (*Hansard*, 1 May 1969), the issue was represented as a threat to private property for the first time.

Towards the end of that year, another Commons exchange revealed the possibility of Government intervention: the question of 'what further steps' could be taken was raised and one Honourable Member warned that, inevitably, 'there are serious riots on the way' (*Hansard*, 20 November 1969). Like all moral panics, 'hooliganism' became a self-fulfilling prophecy thereafter, as the game's negative image aroused the interest of those with a propensity to violence and, in the 1980s, of those involved in far-Right politics. Violence changed the face of football and, even though the implied threat was more of a concern than were actual outbreaks of it, 'going to the match' was too often accompanied by an aurora of violence, underpinned by a casual racism and sexism that few had the courage to challenge. While outbreaks of hooligan activity were non-existent at many clubs throughout the 1970s and 1980s and such hooligan 'firms' as existed there (the Chesterfield 'Boot Squad' and the Mansfield 'Kicking Crew') were nothing more than an occasional minor inconvenience and the subject of derision, attending football was often unpleasant and degrading. The quality of the experience was too dependent upon the activities of varying numbers of charmless young men who were not hooligans but possessed even less wit than the 'hoolies' did. In the face of their combined activities, many decent fans kicked the habit of attending, hardly ever to return.

And yet, even in the darkest days, 'hooligans, however broadly defined, made up only a tiny element of the several hundred thousand who regularly went to professional matches ... In the early 1980s, the arrest rate at football matches was at the very low level of slightly less than five per 10,000' (Russell, 1997, p 193). Incidents of what one might properly call 'hooliganism' – occasions when an 'end' was actually 'taken', when away fans invaded the pitch or when serious disorder resulted from an attempt by the supporters of one club to invade the space of another's – were rare. Certainly, these outbreaks were of such infrequency that the necessity for and value of the game's response to it – the introduction of crowd segregation and, after rampaging Scotland fans drunkenly attacked an innocent set of goalpost at Wembley in 1977, of perimeter fencing – is questionable. It is worth making the obvious point that these segregation mechanisms, introduced to 'make grounds safer', caused many people's deaths during the Bradford and Hillsborough tragedies.

THE RESISTIBLE RISE OF HARRY THE DOG

The opposition's reputation and the number of their supporters within the ground dictated the *modus operandi* of 'taking an end'. Segregation fences were introduced to prevent away supporters from simply entering through the turnstiles at the away end, walking around the ground to the home fans' end and confronting the home supporters with songs, gestures and taunts. Similarly, home fans could enter the away end, await their rivals' arrival and act according to the balance of numbers.

> During any confrontations or fights that ensued, non-participants caught in the midst of proceedings would back away. A 'hole' of empty space across the terracing would appear, around which stood members of the rival factions packed close together. Invariably, within half a minute one side would recommence hostilities, rushing across the space, and punching and kicking would ensue. Possible results ranged between complete victory for one side (signified by the disappearance of opponents into other spaces, including onto the pitch); a short moratorium on further hostilities broken following events on the pitch; or the 'postponement' of a genuine conclusion, usually due to police

interventions. The latter intensified as this most visible form of young rivalry attracted easy political and media attention [Armstrong and Giulianotti, 1997, p 12].

As a consequence of this 'media and political attention' to these incidents, fencing was introduced at most clubs in the mid-1970s (although some had introduced it earlier, Everton being the first in 1963) as they sought to prevent the movement of fans between one part of the ground and another. These physical impediments – metal barriers which ran the width of the terrace – certainly had the desired effect of preventing fans from taking ends, so much so that their use soon became the norm at every ground in the country. So successful was segregation that the practice was also extended outside the ground and outside match hours. Police forces across the country adopted a policy of intercepting visiting supporters who travelled by rail or coach at the train station or car park and escorting them directly into one section of the ground – usually the area behind the goal that was least favoured by home fans. In turn, this meant preventing those home fans who had traditionally stood behind that goal from doing so. After matches, visiting fans were routinely held inside grounds while the home fans dispersed.

Segregation had some unexpected consequences. It achieved the primary aim of keeping the ends free from invasion, save for isolated occasions when away fans managed to gain access to home areas in vast numbers, by breaking through police lines or breaking down the fences. But their introduction also enabled supporters who would have avoided a violent confrontation to deride and abuse one another in circumstances which prevented a physical response: the police and the fences ensured that actions could not speak louder than words. It also meant that 'real' hooligans were no longer charged with protecting their end from possible incursion and new ways of defending their sacred spaces had to be sought.

Thus, hooligans' activities changed in response to the changes that segregation had brought about, both inside and outside the grounds. Away supporters were still corralled into the ends that had traditionally been set aside for visiting fans (and which, accordingly, would be the last to be adorned by a roof, decent toilets and other embellishments). The home hooligans would still be there, but, instead of congregating behind 'their' goal and attempting to take the visitors' end, they had gravitated now to the terraces that ran the length of the ground and, in particular, to those parts that allowed them to get closest to the visitors. The new avenues of confrontation that emerged included the smashing of seats and gouging out lumps of concrete from decrepit terraces. These would be directed at the opposition fans or at the huge numbers of police that were now in attendance at most matches, sometimes resulting in severe injuries. In *Cunningham v Reading FC* (1992), a police officer successfully sued the club under the Occupiers' Liability Act 1957 for failing to maintain its ground properly. He had been injured by a lump of concrete which was gouged out of the decrepit terraces by a visiting hooligan and used as a missile. Vocal, young non-hooligans who wanted to be where 'the action' was but had no intention of joining any violent exchanges between rival fans or fans and the police, gravitated towards the fences, too. Their support manifested itself through shouting, singing, posturing and swearing, and they delighted in being identified as part of the 'hard core element'.

Now, the response of Parliament, the media and the courts to all of this was to define 'football hooliganism' as covering all those forms of boisterous, anti-social, malevolent or criminal behaviour that had always occurred at football grounds. Activities that had not previously attracted the attention of the criminal law – shouting, swearing, threatening and abusing opponents – were suddenly labelled 'football hooliganism' and met with ejection, arrest and a possible prosecution for breach of the peace. Furthermore (as will be seen below), a whole gamut of criminal behaviour, including assault, theft and criminal damage, that did not merit the 'hooligan' tag was thus similarly labelled, resulting in the imposition of draconian and exemplary punishments on the miscreants. The irony is that the real hooligans directed their gaze away from the grounds and started to conduct their activities elsewhere.

'LET'S GO FOR A WALK ROUND'

For the real football hooligans, the spatial significance of the ground had been transformed by segregation. Prior to the erection of the fences, the ground had been the only forum in which rivalries were played out. In the years after segregation, hooligan confrontations increasingly occurred in train stations and, to a lesser extent, in pubs and towns, city centres and the streets surrounding them. The composition of certain 'notorious' hooligan formations of the late 1970s and early 1980s – the Portsmouth '6.57 Crew', Hibernian's 'Capital City Service' and the West Ham 'Inter-City Firm' – encompassed those who travelled by scheduled train service rather than on the heavily policed 'soccer specials', which any self-respecting hooligan would eschew. Consequently, train stations became primary sites of hooligan activity, with honour to be gained in arriving by train at a 'reasonable' hour before kick-off, locating the home hooligans and 'running' them. These confrontations rarely descended into actual physical violence and injuries were not common, but they were the most spectacular and coveted victory available to either side. However, the high police presence that soon became a common feature at train stations on match days meant that the duration of any conflict was minimised. A heavy police presence also increased the likelihood of arrest and (worse) the shame of a police escort to and from the ground.

In order to avoid police attention at train stations, hooligans have started to deploy other travel arrangements, most notably using hired coaches, private cars or (increasingly) transit vans for journeys to away matches. If police escorts are eluded, the visitors are thus rewarded with a greater degree of autonomy in planning the day's entertainment – in particular, the freedom to choose which pubs to head for before the match. Ideally, these venues will be chosen beforehand, so that numbers may be swollen by those arriving in other coaches or by other means of transport. In consequence, public houses have become the primary space for contemporary hooligan rendezvous, and the favoured venues are those which give access to town or city centres but which are situated close to public transport arteries and are within striking distance of the ground. Pubs also require an accommodating (but still profit-oriented) management, willing to tolerate the occasional broken window or the stigma of their pub being viewed as a 'hooligan' home.

Thus ensconced, pubs allow the participants to play out various hooligan strategies, usually involving nothing more than 'a walk round' (in which the protagonists simply walk past the pub and intimidate the occupants). Other pub-oriented hooligan activities include 'sounding out', 'acting wide' and 'taking liberties' (Armstrong and Giulianotti, 1997a), and it is worth noting that such 'attacks' as actually occur are invariably limited to the surrounding of pub doors, the smashing of windows and the exchange of missiles. On these occasions, entry to pubs is hardly ever attempted, and those inside typically remain there unless their numerical superiority is unquestionably established (but, if that were the case, the initial 'attack' would never have occurred). The often exaggerated activity of 'pub wrecking' concerns the activities of those outside only; hooligan etiquette decrees that, where pub management and staff have extended a welcome, no serious or concerted damage will be done to the premises. Similarly, occasions of non-participants being caught up in the crossfire are extremely rare and provoke as much moral righteousness among hooligans privately as among the media and police publicly. According to Robins (1995, p 215), the vicissitudes of hooligan status ensure that honour is lost, rather than earned, when one group allows or promotes attacks or injuries on passers by.

The police have responded to the changing nature of hooligan activity by attempting to 'clear' pubs of their hooligan clientele or by forcing the management to close on the day of the game. However, the strategy of having hooligans out on the streets rather than in a pub can lead to greater policing problems, particularly when opposing hooligans have information regarding the others' potential or actual numbers, or where the time and location for hooligan exchanges can be agreed upon beforehand through personal communication. No longer are the core sites of football ground, train station and favoured pubs the venues for routine reproduction of numbers and competitive intent.

But endeavouring to arrange a hooligan confrontation does not necessarily mean that action will follow. The police, through tracking or discovering hooligan movements and occasionally being tipped off by paid 'insiders', can often emerge as the day's victors in preventing any contestation of public space, bar that which they are unable to eradicate (for example, banter and posturing between the rival factions). Additionally, their use of crime prevention technologies ensures that every act of fan 'violence' can be captured in detail (Giulianotti, 1994) by CCTV and plainclothes police officers who are stationed where perceivedly 'problem' supporters are gathered (Bale, 1993). The 'knowledge' generated on these fans, in the form of photographs and dossier reports, is filed with the ground's Football Intelligence Officer, who then relays the information to the National Criminal Intelligence Service's Football Unit in London. Many of the fans thus scrutinised possess no criminal record for football related or any other offences, but many Government ministers and high ranking police officers believe that the contents of these dossiers should be used to restrict fans' freedom to attend matches in England and elsewhere. 'Football hooligans' are now one of the major public demons referenced for the political legitimisation of CCTV in city centres (Armstrong and Giulianotti, 1997) – another example of how a broad definition of the phrase suits lots of moral entrepreneurs.

SENTENCING THE 'HOOLIGAN'

The courts have defined 'hooligan' particularly broadly and one finds many examples where sentences imposed on those who commit 'hooligan' acts are far in excess of those imposed for similar criminal behaviour which has not occurred at or near (temporally or spatially) a football match (Trivizas 1980; 1981; 1984). Salter (1985; 1986) carried out research into incidents of criminal conduct that were labelled 'football hooliganism' in the five years after the ruling in *Motley* (1978). He discovered that 'the following actions have been judged to constitute "football hooliganism" in the reported cases':

> Looking aggressive, jeering, shouting, jumping up and down, waving fists in the air, running in groups, issuing bloodcurdling and obscene threats involving baseball bats; invading the pitch; wrecking motorway service stations; taking a crutch away from its unfortunate owner and using it as a club; fighting with fists; kicking rival fans who are on the ground; smashing faces with hammers; robbing rival fans of their valuables and clothes; ripping up terracing; 'stampeding' around railway stations so as to scatter the public; denting car bonnets and roofs and obstructing the road; vandalising and overturning local people's cars after a match; assaulting local residents with iron bars and wooden clubs; shouting National Front and racist abuse; racially inspired and disabling attacks involving bottles and fists on British Rail employees, taxi

drivers and shopkeepers; and, lastly, throwing missiles at each other, local people, oncoming cars and the police [Salter, 1985, p 352].

In *R v Bruce* (1977), Park J spoke of the need to impose exemplary sentences on 'those who commit violence on the occasion of football matches' (p 150). In *R v Motley* (1978), the Court of Appeal upheld a sentence of Borstal training following conviction of two counts of assault occasioning actual bodily harm and two counts of damaging property. The appellant, a Derby County supporter, who was travelling home after a cup tie at Colchester, was involved in throwing missiles (including a 'piece of brick' and a beer can) out of the coach in which he and other supporters were travelling and in the direction of vehicles travelling in the opposite direction. The missiles struck at least two vehicles, shattering the windscreens and causing minor cuts to the drivers. He also admitted causing criminal damage inside the ground during the match.

In upholding the sentence, Pain J commented as follows:

All of us are now well aware of the problems which arise from the misconduct of football supporters, mostly during and after matches but sometimes before. The Government seems to be concerned about the matter and one step which has been taken recently in the Criminal Law Act 1977 is to increase the scale of fines which can be imposed for this kind of offence ... [D]uring the last two or three years, when this problem of order at and after football matches has had to be considered, many courts have decided the problem should be tackled by fines, community service orders, orders to go to attendance centres for a specified number of hours, probation orders and the like. It is manifest now that that kind of sentence has not deterred the hooligans who go to football matches intent on causing disorder. Something has got to be done in order to ensure as far as possible that this kind of conduct comes to an end [*R v Motley* (1978), p 277].

Taking advantage of the fact that 'this is the first opportunity which this court has had of expressing a view as to how this kind of conduct should be dealt with by the courts', Pain J opined that the 'something' to be done was the imposition of immediate custodial sentences. Those aged 17 and over 'should expect to lose their liberty', save in *very* exceptional mitigating circumstances, and these circumstances would not include a guilty plea or the absence of previous criminal convictions. The imposition of a sentence of detention should also be given serious consideration in respect of those aged between 14 and 16. His Honour was moved to assert, 'we are confident that, if the courts impose a policy of this kind for the rest of this football season, there may be an improvement next year'.

In *R v Dunphy* (1981), the defendant and three others, supporters of a side called 'Nottingham County' (*per* Milmo J) launched an unprovoked attack on a group of rival supporters. One of those supporters was kicked and punched and had several items of clothing and other belongings stolen. Upholding a sentence of six months' detention for robbery (the defendant had pleaded guilty and was of previous good character), Milmo J started his ruling with the statement that 'the case is one of football hooliganism'. He went on to use the h-word on three other occasions during his short judgment. He criticised the 'wholly inadequate' sentences sometimes passed by magistrates on hooligans: here, six months was 'not a day too long' and the defendant was 'wholly fortunate to escape a Borstal sentence' (*R v Dunphy* (1981), p 160).

In none of these cases could what happened be properly defined as 'football hooliganism'. Neither throwing missiles out of coach windows into the path of oncoming traffic nor vicious and unprovoked assault and robbery carried out by, and on, persons who had hoped to attend a football match are hooligan activities. But the courts' description of them as such and their comments on sentencing practice sets an agenda for other courts to follow.

And that agenda was followed, at least so far as the labelling process was concerned. In *R v Wood* (1984), Lawton LJ opined that the 'kind of conduct' of which the defendant had been convicted 'has become common on football grounds all over the British Isles. It is conduct which is causing disquiet ... We infer that those who have a propensity to use violence are not deterred by fines ... The time has come for the courts to impose [deterrent custodial] sentences' (pp 4, 5). The court upheld the imposition of Borstal training on the defendant, who was involved in a 'disorderly incident' at Oxford United's ground, during which a police officer's nose was broken and over 60 arrests were made. The jury concluded that the defendant had not inflicted that injury. In any event, he received a custodial sentence because, in resisting arrest, he had bitten the arresting officer on the forearm. Lawton LJ ruled that the appellant 'went too far in attempting to persuade the officer he had got the wrong man'. In fact, he was reacting violently because he feared that the arresting officer's actions were suffocating him. So violent were the appellant's throes 'that another officer had to hit him over the head with his truncheon in order to dissuade him from further struggling and disorderly behaviour' (p 4). It seems that Wood, before being half-choked by the arresting officer and rendered semi-conscious by the truncheon wielder, had initially been arrested for the grave offence of consensual outer clothing removal.

Lawton LJ continued:

> One of the forms of activity which the mindless youths of Oxford who attend these football matches indulge in is to rip off each others' shirts. That inevitably leads to further disorder. On his own admission, this appellant went to this football match dressed for the part, in that he was wearing an old shirt, anticipating that it might be torn off ... The appellant went there to take part in such disorder as there may have been [*R v Wood* (1984), p 3].

While the suggestion that the consensual removal of one another's clothing 'inevitably' leads to disorder is, at best, open to challenge, Lawton LJ's judgment allows one to add 'shirt ripping' to Salter's list of hooligan activities. In *Joyce v Hertfordshire Constabulary* (1984), chanting and singing the name

'Bjorn Borg' was used as an indication of a defendant's propensity for hooligan activity.

In contrast, in *R v Beasley* (1988), Tudor Evans J resisted the labelling process of his fellow judges and avoided describing as 'hooliganism' a 'deliberate, planned and organised' attack with bottles and stones on stationary vehicles and their occupants. He used the less laden phrase 'football violence', notably in relation to a defendant's previous convictions for abusing and threatening others at a railway station (p 507). Of course, the irony here is that, depending on the specific circumstances of those earlier convictions, the fact that they occurred at train stations may well have merited the use of the 'hooligan' tag.

In *Beasley*, custodial sentences of between three and five and a half years for affray were reduced to between two and a half and four and a half years for offences under the Public Order Act 1986. The Court of Appeal considered that the initial sentences were too harsh, particularly in light of *R v Keen* (1986). In *Keen*, sentences for Public Order Act offences during the disorder at Broadwater Farm ranged from 18 months on individuals whose involvement was no more than 'slight', to seven years for those convicted of throwing petrol bombs and injuring police officers and firemen. Beasley himself (who had three previous convictions, two of which were for threatening behaviour) was initially imprisoned for five years for kicking a car and throwing a stone at a transit van. One of his co-accused (who had no convictions) received four and a half years for throwing a brick at a transit van. An 18 year old (who had convictions for several football related offences) received four years' youth custody for the same offence. A third (who made a guilty plea and had no previous convictions) received three years for attempting to assault a car driver and throwing small stones. Another had received five and a half years (he made a not guilty plea and had many previous convictions) for his part in the affray. Each had their sentences reduced by one year by the Court of Appeal, Tudor Evans J accepting defence counsel's submission that the five and a half year sentence visited on the last defendant would be more appropriate for individuals who were convicted of actually organising such attacks.

Even though the Court of Appeal's 'broad brush' policy of what amounts to 'football hooliganism' was taken on board by the Crown Court and the magistrates, there is some evidence of a reluctance to impose the kinds of exemplary sentences that Pain J and others had advocated. Salter (1986) highlights the magistrates' approach in *Mail v McDowall* (1980) to the 'habitual chanting of Northampton supporters', which was accompanied by 'jumping up and down and fist waving' (*R v Motley* (1978), p 284). The local magistrates interpreted this behaviour as 'non-threatening' and, accordingly, acquitted the defendant of threatening behaviour. In the High Court, this interpretation rendered Donaldson LJ apoplectic. He 'could neither comprehend such crowd behaviour nor this interpretation of it, especially in the context of "what everyone knows" about violence at football matches' (Salter, 1986, p 284); neither could he understand why the magistrates were unmoved by the profanities that are commonplace in football chants:

> How the magistrates could think that a man who, in the company of others, is waving his fists in the air and is jumping up and down and saying ... 'We are going to kick your fucking heads in' (*sic*) was other than behaving in a threatening manner passes my comprehension.

But the magistrates had acquitted because of the very existence of the walls, wire and other segregation mechanisms that had been erected at all grounds by this time in an effort to 'stop hooliganism'. These barriers, they concluded, meant that it was not 'likely' that any breach of the peace would occur notwithstanding the defendant's utterances and actions. As Salter rightly suggests, the erection of what Donaldson LJ called a 'Berlin-type wall' 'possibly encourages threatening words and ritualised gestures by providing a perfect excuse for confined fans *not* having actually to carry out their threats' (Salter, 1986, p 285). The defendant's words, chants and gestures were meaningless hot air, but outsiders such as Lord Donaldson, as Bourdieu would have it, were ill-equipped to understand what was being played out. In *Parrish v Garfitt* (1985), a similarly ill-equipped court held that a defendant's voluntary presence among a football crowd whose behaviour was perceived as 'threatening' raised a *prima facie* case of threatening behaviour against him. One supposes that this presumption could be rebutted if the fan could show that he was where he was because the police had corralled him into that particular area of the ground, rather than because he had attached himself voluntarily to a 'hooligan element'.

Elsewhere, stringent sentences were being imposed on individuals for behaviour that would have passed unnoticed in any other walk of life. A Bristol City fan who shouted 'Wanker' at a group of rival segregated fans received a 24 hour attendance centre order, while a 'beckoning sign' directed by a Birmingham City fan towards heavily policed Arsenal supporters attracted a £400 fine (Salter 1986, p 290). However, there are also examples of magistrates imposing fines of less than £200 in cases where the Court of Appeal would have expected the imposition of custodial sentences. In *Hills v Ellis* (1982), magistrates granted an unconditional discharge to a defendant who was convicted of wilfully obstructing a police officer contrary to s 51(3) of the Police Act 1964. The defendant had simply attempted to tell an arresting officer that he had 'got the wrong man', following a *fracas* between two men after a game at the Tottenham Hotspur ground, and the prosecution accepted that his actions had evinced no hostility towards the officer. While the Divisional Court upheld the magistrates' finding that the defendant's motive in obstructing the officer was irrelevant for the purposes of s 51(3), it supported as 'very sensible' their decision to discharge him.

LEGISLATIVE RESPONSES TO 'FOOTBALL HOOLIGANISM'

Throughout the 1980s, then, forms of behaviour that would previously have passed without comment were likely to lead to arrest and attract the 'hooligan' label if they occurred within a football ground or close to it, and may or may not have attracted exemplary penalties. Loud shouting in the street, jostling and gesticulation could lead to eviction from the ground or arrest for the catch-all offence of breach of the peace, initially under the Public Order Act 1936 and later under the Public Order Act 1986. That is not to say that all earlier incidents had escaped the law's attention, though. Williams (1978) writes of the prosecution under s 5 of the 1936 Act of 'a supporter who threw an apple at a goalkeeper during a Fourth Division game between Chesterfield and Tranmere Rovers', way back in 1964. He also writes of 'three girls who "fought like wildcats" at a pre-season friendly between Ipswich Town and Dundee United in 1969' and who were similarly prosecuted. However, Armstrong and Hobbs (1994) believe that the first use of public order charges other than breach of the peace against football fans did not occur until 1973. This hardly gives the impression that rampaging hordes of fans were wreaking havoc every weekend or that the courts were unduly burdened by football cases. In 1985, a charge of riot was used, for the first time, against a Chelsea fan who tried, but failed, to kick a rival supporter outside the ground. For the grave offence of attempting to kick, this individual received a sentence of life imprisonment from Argyle J. Even the Court of Appeal thought that this was beyond the pale and reduced the sentence to three years' imprisonment.

However, from the mid-1980s, one sees the introduction of legislation aimed solely and specifically at the activities of football fans to complement the use of general public order laws.

The Sporting Events (Control of Alcohol, etc) Act 1985

The Sporting Events (Control of Alcohol, etc) Act 1985 is similar to the Criminal Justice (Scotland) Act 1981, which prohibits the consumption of alcohol at football grounds and on 'football specials' in Scotland. The McElhone Report had said that there was a strong link between football violence in Scotland and alcohol consumption, and that spectators became more aggressive and less inhibited when they had consumed drink. The Scottish Act was passed in response to the Report's recommendations. The Scottish FA said that the Act was a contributory factor in a decrease in crowd violence in the early 1980s, particularly at Celtic vs Rangers matches. However, the 1985 Act was implemented, even though a 1984 report by a

Working Group on football spectator violence in England said that legislation preventing the consumption of alcohol at grounds or on 'football specials' was not necessary. Indeed, in their evidence to the Working Group, the police authorities had specifically said that alcohol was not a major contributor to football related violence in England and Wales. That many football fans enjoy a drink before and after matches is beyond dispute, and, indeed, the significant role played by alcohol in the development of sport should not be understated (Vamplew, 1988). However, there is no evidence that, for the overwhelming majority of fans, a pre-match pint or four increases the likelihood of their being involved in hooliganism or other football related violence.

The failure to establish a causal link between alcohol and hooliganism was irrelevant so far as the Government of the day was concerned. The 1985 Act was introduced simply because 'something had to be done' after several distressing incidents of hooliganism and football related violence during the 1984/85 season. The riot at Millwall's game at Luton, the death of a young fan during violent scenes at Birmingham City vs Leeds United (which occurred on the same day as the Bradford fire) and, of course, the obscenity that was the Heysel Tragedy (Popplewell, 1995; 1996) marked English football's darkest hour. The Government was determined to have a new piece of legislation in force by the start of the 1985/86 season.

The provisions of the 1985 Act, then, were based on the dubious presumption that football related violence or 'hooliganism' (the two phrases being used interchangeably) could be prevented, or at least reduced, if the availability of alcohol to spectators before, during and after a football match was limited. Accordingly, s 1 prohibits the carrying of alcohol on 'football specials' and allows the police to stop the train and search the occupants if they believe that alcohol is on board. Section 2(2) makes it an offence to attempt to enter a football ground whilst 'drunk', a phrase which the Act fails to define.

Difficulties lie, however, in the practical enforcement of the provisions. Pearson (1999) found that alcohol was allowed on many independent or supporters' club coaches, with both organisers and consumers willing to risk the minimal chance of being stopped and searched by police. In addition, the Act does not cover private vehicles, be they cars or transit vans, which are the preferred modes of conveyance for the true hooligan – they certainly would not stoop to travelling on a 'soccer special'. Pearson also notes an understandable reluctance on the part of turnstile stewards to prevent the entry of those who may be 'drunk'. This may be due in part to a pragmatic and perfectly understandable unwillingness on the part of stewards to risk getting involved in an altercation with a drunken fan and his mates. Furthermore, the failure to define 'drunk' in the 1985 Act means that stewards and/or the police are required to make a 'spur of the moment' value judgment

– and for what purpose? Thousands of spectators pass through the turnstiles in various states of inebriation every week, but their presence has no effect on anyone else. The police have better things to worry about, club stewards simply are not paid enough to concern themselves with a harmless inebriate and, for other fans, the drunkard is just another character at the carnival. If drunkenness leads an individual to interfere with the enjoyment of those other fans, then a sharp rebuke from his peers or ejection from the ground in the company of a burly steward will surely follow. In extreme circumstances, it may lead to the miscreant's arrest and, possibly, his being charged with an offence under the Public Order Act 1986.

The Sporting Events Act also aims to prevent the consumption of alcohol within football stadia by making it an offence to attempt to take alcohol into a football ground (s 2(1)(b)) and prohibiting the consumption of alcohol within sight of the pitch (s 2(1)(a)). However, in the more 'civilised', consumer-driven environment of the 1990s, many clubs (including the notorious hooligan hotbed of Millwall) have been granted licences to serve alcohol and the 1985 Act does not prevent them from doing so, provided that the beverage is sold and consumed out of sight of the pitch. However, those who wish to combine going to the match with having a pint or two beforehand still tend to visit public houses near the ground, rather than avail themselves of the clubs' bars, where the fare on offer tends to be more expensive and of poor quality. At Premier League grounds in particular, the products are limited to those of the competition's sponsors, supplemented by burgers, pies and rolls of dubious provenance. These have little appeal to all but the most poorly educated palate and do not provide an incentive for fans to 'get there early'. The suggestion that fans who are late in leaving the pub cause disruption and delay others' access to the ground is a myth. Football fans are just as capable of planning their activities so that they are in their seats 10 minutes before the start as those who attend the opera or the ballet. When these delays do occur, they are invariably due to traffic problems, precipitated by roadworks, adverse weather conditions or delays on public transport. Very rarely, they occur because the police and the club simply underestimate the number of people who want to attend. They do not occur because a local hostelry has a particularly fine guest ale that thousands of fans want to sample before they go off to the football.

The Football Spectators Act 1989

Part I of the 1989 Act introduced the ill-fated 'membership card' scheme, which the then Prime Minister much favoured in her ceaseless crusade against the activities of 'the enemy within', be they football fans, striking miners or the unemployed. Fortunately, Taylor LJ's good sense prevailed:

> I have grave doubts about the feasibility of the national membership scheme and serious misgivings about its likely impact on safety. I also have grave

doubts about the chances of it achieving its purposes and its potential impact upon police commitments and control of spectators. For these reasons, I cannot support the implementation of Pt I of the Act [Taylor Report, 1989, para 424].

Part II of the 1989 Act has been implemented, however. Section 15 of the 1989 Act introduced restriction orders (now called 'international football banning orders'), which are used to prevent those convicted of football related offences from leaving the country whenever the national side is playing abroad. Section 15(5) provides that individuals who are subject to these orders must attend at a police station when the match is in progress.

'Restriction orders' have not been an unqualified success. Following the racist violence among England fans that occurred in Dublin in February 1995, only two of those subsequently charged were subject to these orders, although the National Criminal Intelligence Service claimed that at least 30 'known hooligans' had travelled to the match ((1995) *The Guardian*, 27 February). By the time of the disorder at the Italy vs England World Cup qualifier in October 1997, there were still only nine restriction orders in place, although 400 fans were subject to domestic exclusion orders under s 30 of the Public Order Act 1986. Consequently, in December 1997, the Home Secretary stated that all persons convicted of football related offences between that time and the World Cup in 1998 should be placed under restriction orders. By the start of the tournament, the number of restriction orders in force had risen to more than 70 (Pearson, 2000). On 1 June 1998, the Football Spectators (Corresponding Offences in France) Order 1998 (SI 1998/1266) was implemented. This provided that football related offences under French law and committed in France by British supporters would similarly become offences under Sched 1 to the 1989 Act, thereby allowing the British courts to impose restriction orders on England followers convicted of committing offences during France 98. Neither provision prevented English fans' involvement in outbreaks of violence during the tournament, particularly the riot in Marseilles, which was the most violent incident to occur during it.

The 1989 Act originally defined 'football related' offences as those which were committed no more than two hours before the kick-off of a designated football match, although offences committed before that time were deemed to be football related if they were committed on the journey to the game. Offences which were not classified as football related could not lead to the imposition of a restriction order and this undermined the effectiveness of the Act, insofar as it applied to 'genuine' hooligans, because hooligan activity quite often occurs before 1 pm on a Saturday. Soon after the Marseilles riot, it became clear that none of those arrested could have restriction orders imposed upon them. Consequently, the Football (Offences and Disorder) Act 1999 extended the definition of 'football related' for the purposes of the 1989 Act to include offences that occurred up to 24 hours before and after a game.

The Football (Offences) Act 1991

The Football (Offences) Act 1991 is the most notorious anti-hooligan measure. Alongside tougher sentencing policies in respect of 'football hooligans' and the development of the Football Intelligence Unit (FIU), the 1991 Act was supposed to 'solve the problem' of football hooliganism for good. The problem, of course, is that, although it creates three new offences, none of these offences can be regarded as dealing with the activities of 'hooligans', as properly defined. Furthermore, most of the football related activities it does deal with could just as easily have been dealt with under existing legislation, while those which could not be dealt with under the existing law (specifically via the 'racist chanting' provision) it deals with badly.

Section 2 of the 1991 Act makes it an offence to throw any object within a football stadium, while s 3 criminalises racist or indecent chanting within a designated football stadium and s 4 makes encroaching onto the pitch or the area surrounding it a criminal offence. Prior to this Act, convictions could be obtained for any of these actions under the 'threatening behaviour' provisions of the Public Order Act 1986, but convictions were infrequent and the creation of football-specific offences was deemed to be appropriate. The interesting aspects of the Act arise under ss 3 and 4.

Section 3 of the Act is the most problematic of the three provisions. It prohibits 'racialist [*sic*] or indecent chanting' within a football ground. The racism provision is dealt with below, for it is important to debunk the simplistic presumption that those engaged in hooliganism or 'indecent chanting' would lend their voices to racism, but both the 'indecent' and the 'chanting' aspects cause sufficient problems to merit detailed consideration here.

Although the term 'indecent' as used in the 1991 Act has never been defined, one could argue that most of the popular chants of recent years could be interpreted as 'indecent' by a sufficiently zealous police officer or magistrate. If that is the case, then their mere utterance would be an offence under s 3. The rationale behind this interpretation is that the 'racist chanting' offence of s 3 is fulfilled if any person is offended by it. The question of whether the chant is meant to be offensive is immaterial, as is whether the chant is aimed at the person who is insulted. To apply a hypothetical example to the letter of the law, if a player with a particularly limited understanding of the English language mistakenly misinterprets 'Who's the bastard in the black?' as 'Who's the black bastard?' and is offended, then, by virtue of the language of s 3, the offence has been committed. The intention of the person uttering it is of no relevance. Furthermore, the 'racist' part of the section can be committed even if the chant is not aimed at the person who is insulted by it. Of itself, this does not provoke concern, for it is desirable that the player in question does not have to be offended by 'monkey chants' directed at him before the s 3 offence can be made out. Plenty of fans or club officials would be able to stand before a magistrate and, in all good conscience, say, 'I was insulted by those chants', even if the player himself was not offended. The difficulty is that, if the same interpretation is placed on the 'indecent' provision as on the 'racist' one, any individual who is offended by hearing a particular word in a chant could appear for the prosecution and give evidence that, yes, they were similarly offended by that chant. This part of the prosecution's case would thus be discharged by the production of such evidence. This means that words which would pass unnoticed if uttered away from a football ground can become 'indecent' purely because of the physical location of the person who uses them and the sensibilities of an individual who happens to be within hearing distance. If clubs fear (rightly or wrongly) that the 'new' supporters they seek to attract – women, families, those from ethnic minorities and the middle class male, whom Richard Collier (1997) calls the 'family man of law' – will be perturbed by 'foul language', they could ask the police to make more use of s 3. Alternatively (and more likely, given that the police are well aware of the section's limitations), stewards could ask those individuals to tone down their language or risk being ejected for breach of the ground regulations.

The upshot is that 'What the fucking hell was that' or 'You're so shit, it's unbelievable' have become potentially 'indecent' when uttered by those attending a football match. Yet, the same chant uttered by fans watching the same game in a pub – where most 'real hooliganism' occurs, let us not forget – would provoke no response. The prosecution of fans making such chants away from the ground could only ensue if the words were deemed to be threatening or insulting under the Public Order Act 1986. Section 3 was enacted precisely because the 1986 Act was considered inadequate for dealing with the 'problem' of football fans, but that same public order legislation has remained the principal means of dealing with genuine hooligan activity, notwithstanding the passing of the later Act. Certainly, it would be naïve to argue that the intervention of the police or stewards could be justified on the basis that using such phrases within a football ground might provoke a violent response from the opposition's supporters.

The cultural capital (Bourdieu, 1992) accumulated by those who are familiar with the carnival that is football (Turner, 1984) means that their exposure to banter and their decision to return it or ignore it is an accepted and integral part of the game. 'Indecent chants' are not an indication of impending physical violence meriting fear for one's personal safety and, if numbers and disposition permit, a pre-emptive and violent response. Furthermore, chants which in themselves are not 'indecent' (for example, 'Come and have a go if you think you're hard enough'; 'You're supposed to be at home') can be far more threatening than most 'decent' ones. This is especially so if the chants are accompanied by aggressive body language or emanate from a large group of adult males sauntering through the streets en route to the ground or the pub, but the 1991 Act does not cover these either. Once again, the 1986 Act provides the law's only response. As an 'anti-hooligan' measure, s 3 was dead in the water from the day it came into force. Its 'indecent' element was merely an attempt to sanitise the match day experience for the edification of a new breed of consumer.

Section 4 of the 1991 Act provides that:

It is an offence for a person ... to go on to the playing area or any area adjacent to the playing area to which the spectators are not generally admitted ... without lawful excuse.

However, even by the time of the Act's passing, 'aggressive' pitch invasions, which had never been a particularly common feature in the English game, were even more a phenomenon of the past, by virtue of the perimeter fencing that had been introduced at all professional clubs' grounds. Most clubs which did not already have them introduced fences over the summer of 1977, following Scotland fans' invasion of the pitch at Wembley in the Home International of that year. The few pitch invasions with violent overtones that preceded the Act were dealt with under existing statutory provisions, notably the Public Order Act 1986. Section 4 was deemed to be a necessary response to the changes in perimeter fencing practices that came about in the wake of the Taylor report. Its effect was to tar with the brush of 'hooliganism' those pitch invasions which were not threatening but which have occasionally occurred at football matches for over 100 years. Before s 4, a successful prosecution for a 'non-threatening' pitch invasion depended upon whether the police were willing to construe, and the magistrates willing to accept, that an invasion borne out of excitement, protest or high spirits was threatening or disorderly behaviour. Under s 4, the mere act of invading the pitch will suffice. An invasion to protest about perceived managerial or directorial incompetence, or to celebrate promotion, is an offence under s 4, regardless of motive.

Fortunately, good sense on the part of the police has prevailed and it has to be stressed that the police's response to incidents at football matches is often far more considered and measured than that of the legislature, the courts and the media. Dealing with minor pitch invasions precipitated by excitement or despair from behind the goal usually becomes the responsibility of the match day stewards, for they have the same powers of arrest for pitch encroachment as the police. Although some safety officers expect their stewards to act as quasi-police officers and use these powers to the full, the usual policy is to accept that stewards are not paid enough to act as such; in any event, they lack the training to do so. Most clubs encourage their stewards to try to intercept fans who attempt to invade the playing area and to lead those who make it back to the stands. Stewards would be expected to eject those who make repeated attempts. But, as Pearson (2000) states, 'there are very few ejections and hardly any arrests for fans invading the pitch, and it was apparent [from his participant observation] that the vast majority of fans consider the chances of their being ejected or arrested for invading the pitch to be negligible'. Ejection is usually visited on those fans who actually access the playing area and disrupt the game, while arrest and prosecution are reserved for those who threaten, or actually assault, players, officials or stewards. None of these activities is the province of the hooligan properly defined, whose activities take place far away from the playing area and for whom engaging in something as juvenile as a pitch invasion would give rise to a grave loss of face.

Other legislative measures specifically aimed at the 'football hooligan' include the exclusion orders provisions under s 30 of the Public Order Act 1986. Various other sections of the 1986 Act (particularly the breach of the peace provisions) are routinely used, while the ticket touting provisions of s 166 of the Criminal Justice and Public Order Act 1994 represent one of the few occasions on which the Conservatives shied away from unbridled monetarism (Osborn and Greenfield, 1996). Section 60 of the 1994 Act has been used to stop and search fans travelling to matches. All of these provisions have been amended by the 1999 Act; as has s 3 of the 1991 Act, in order to remove a fundamental flaw which it contained – namely, its definition of 'chanting' in s 3. In the original Act, 'chanting' was notoriously defined in s 3(2)(a) as 'the repeated uttering of any words or sounds in concert with one or more others'. This meant that individuals' utterances were not covered by the legislation, although, in principle, they may have been deemed sufficiently threatening or insulting to warrant prosecution under the 1986 Act.

The Football (Offences and Disorder) Act 1999

It is worth noting that the 1999 Act was a Private Member's Bill but was drafted by the Home Office and, of course, had the necessary degree of all-Party support to pass through the House. It is regrettable that Simon Burns MP could not think of a worthy cause with which to share his good fortune at coming sixth in the members' ballot and was reduced instead to championing this piece of populist nonsense. Tony Banks, then Sports Minister, was quick to use the h-word. He celebrated the Bill as being 'the toughest anti-hooligan legislation of almost any country in the world' and said that its passing would 'greatly help [England's World Cup 2006] campaign after a 1998 World Cup scarred by rampaging fans in southern France'. Burns himself opined that 'the disgraceful behaviour by a small element of yobs and thugs at the World Cup ... shows that more needs to be done to tighten up the law to allow the police and the courts to take greater action' (www.ya.co.za/soccer/291298hooligans.htm). It was obviously far easier to 'tighten up' the flawed 1989 and 1991 Acts than it was to contemplate the possibility that those laws had missed the target.

The Act came into force on 1 October 1999, so, at the time of writing, there is no quantitative evidence of its effectiveness. It was spawned by a Government review of the football related legislation then in existence (www.homeoffice.gov.uk/pubs.htm), which had made suggestions for future reform, including the introduction of measures designed to prevent individuals from attending matches in the UK and abroad. It also proposed that the circumstances in which exclusion orders and restriction orders could be made under the Public Order Act 1986 and the Football Spectators Act 1989 respectively should be widened and that the laws on ticket touting and indecent or racist chanting should be strengthened.

Accordingly, s 1 of the Football (Offences and Disorder) Act 1999 replaces the phrase 'restriction orders' in s 15 of the 1989 Act with 'international football banning orders'. It empowers the court, when dealing with someone convicted of a football related offence, to make an international banning order, if it is satisfied that there are reasonable grounds to believe that making such an order would help to prevent violence or disorder at, or in connection with, designated overseas football matches. Furthermore, if the court chooses not to make such an order, it must state in open court why it is not satisfied that the reasonable grounds exist.

Section 2 amends, *inter alia*, Sched 1 to the Football Spectators Act 1989, in order to increase the range of offences in respect of which an 'international football banning order' may be made – a move which, at least, recognises that 'football hooliganism' does not occur at football grounds. Consequently, ticket touting and certain offences of violence or disorder that are committed within 24 hours of a designated football match and relate to that match may now result in the imposition of an 'international football banning order'. Offences do not have to be committed during the journey to the match in order to 'relate to it'. Committing the offences of conspiracy, incitement, aiding and abetting and counselling or procuring the commission of the substantive offence will also attract a ban. Under s 3, the court may order the miscreant to report to a named police station and may also order the individual to surrender their passport until the match is over.

Section 4 of the Football (Offences and Disorder) Act 1999 amends the duration of orders, so that a person who has received an immediate custodial sentence will be subject to a ban of between six and 10 years. In all other cases, the ban will be for between three and five years. However, the individual may apply for the ban to be rescinded after the expiry of no less than two-thirds of the time period. Section 5 amends s 22 of the 1989 Act, so that international banning orders can be imposed in respect of offences committed outside England and Wales. Section 6 replaces s 30 of the 1986 Act, re-names 'exclusion orders' and 'domestic football banning orders' and makes similar provision for s 1 in respect of bans for attending domestic matches.

Section 7 replaces s 31 of the Public Order Act 1986. Its effect is that offences in respect of which a domestic banning order can be made are the same as those in respect of which an international banning order can be made. Section 8 amends the 1986 Act so that a domestic banning order may be made for between one and three years. It also increases the penalties for breaching a domestic banning order. Section 10 amends the ticket touting provisions in s 166 of the 1994 Act so that the offence extends to the sale of tickets for designated football matches played overseas.

Finally, s 9 amends s 3 of the 1991 Act so that an individual who engages in a racist or indecent chant on his own is now guilty of the offence. Although it is too early to gauge the effect of this change, it is worth noting that, before the Football (Offences and Disorder) Act 1999 was passed, the police were reluctant to make arrests, even when a large crowd indulged in 'racialist or indecent' chant. The impossibility of arresting all those involved, the potential public order ramifications of making an example of one or two individuals (especially if they were in a crowded all-seating area) and losing the arresting officer to the tiresome chore of processing the arrest while the match was in progress militated against the use of s 3. Most importantly, the police were all too aware of magistrates' reluctance to rely on whatever identification evidence they would have been able to proffer. It seems most police forces took the view that satisfactory identification evidence could only be adduced by them tracking a particular individual over a number of matches and having a closed circuit camera trained on him throughout those games. Additionally, a plainclothes officer would have to be standing or sitting close to the offender and use a hidden microphone to pick up his utterances. Apparently, Lewisham police used precisely this tactic and successfully charged one racist from Millwall, with the assistance of the club and at a cost to the public purse of a little over £80,000.

The difficulties in providing satisfactory identification evidence, the expense of proving a case and the other flaws of the 1991 Act have resulted in the police preferring to leave the identification and punishment of those who commit any offences under the 1991 Act to the clubs. The more innovative policies devised by clubs include Fulham's issuing offenders with a 'yellow card', which explains that their language or behaviour is being monitored and any future lapses will attract a 'red card', resulting in ejection from the ground. Pearson (2000) mentions a highly publicised incident of bottle throwing during Manchester United's match at Everton in November 1998. Throwing an object inside a football ground was, of course, an offence under s 2 of the Act, but the club discovered the identity of the offender and banned him from Goodison Park for breach of ground regulations. The police took no action under s 2. Sheffield United have similarly banned for life a supporter who attacked a linesman at Portsmouth during the 1997/98 season.

As mentioned above, these restrictions have been combined with deterrent sentencing; the admission of dubious evidence in the trials of alleged football hooligans (Giulianotti, 1994); extensive extra-judicial mechanisms, such as the routine body searching of those about to enter grounds; and the work of the FIU. The FIU has the power to photograph and file the details of fans suspected of involvement in 'football related' crime (Armstrong and Hobbs, 1994) and these details have been used to prevent fans from leaving the country or to deport them back to the UK if they are suspected of involvement in football hooliganism but have never been convicted or even charged of a football related offence (Pearson, 1999).

CONCLUSION

During the Parliamentary debates on what became the Football (Offences and Disorder) Act 1999, Conservative MP David MacLean proposed that it should be amended to enable the courts to impose 'international banning football orders' upon those who were suspected of being football hooligans. That they had not actually been charged with a football related offence, let alone convicted of one, was a mere inconvenience that did not concern him unduly. This proposal was defeated, but it is worth noting that Kate Hoey MP (then Under-Secretary of State for the Home Department and now Minister for Sport) supported the idea. At the Bill's committee stage, she stated that:

> The power to make banning orders in respect of people without convictions is necessary ... From football intelligence, we know that some people commit offences or are involved in organising violence, but cleverly manage not to be where they may be arrested. We need to find a way of dealing with those people [Pearson, 2000].

It is worth considering precisely what the 'football intelligence', upon which this Minister and others have sought a solution to 'football hooliganism', actually amounts to. Armstrong and Hobbs, reviewing the Chair of the Association of Police Officers on Football Hooliganism 1987 lecture at the European Conference on Football Violence, noted that:

> [David Phillips' lecture] was the product of three sources: '... my own observations; our considerable football intelligence; and what I have read and heard from others.' The hooligan, [the] conference learned, had the following characteristics: a lack of interest in football [and] little knowledge of the game, his use of which was simply to pursue gang aims. Individuals in the gang were recognisable by being 'restless' and, at away games, 'hiding in nooks and crannies ... looking for opportunities to exploit' ... Psychological notions were introduced; 'the whole grounds are a volatile mix capable of ignition'. The level of sound in the ground can cause 'paralysis' and, because of this, the hooligans deliberately organise chanting and clapping ... Chanting in unison heightens

the hooligan's sense of power; 'the most violent are those that do this chanting'. Having generated such an atmosphere, the hooligan can perform his deeds [Armstrong and Hobbs, 1994, p 196].

Now, all of this is palpable nonsense. Reliance on 'my own observations; our considerable football intelligence; and what I have read and heard from others' relieves moral entrepreneurs of the need to trouble themselves with the reality. Far better to regurgitate once again that which 'everyone knows' about football hooligans. If this is the 'football intelligence' upon which successive governments, the media and the police have relied, it is little wonder that the laws which have been passed and the manner in which the police and the courts have implemented them have missed their target so completely. If governments seriously wanted to deal with 'football hooliganism', then a sensible first move would have been to take steps to actually understand the nature of the beast, rather than relying on self-opinionated psycho-babble. The 1999 Act merely regurgitates old myths in a desperate attempt to make England's fundamentally flawed bid to host the 2006 World Cup seem credible, by convincing FIFA and consumers, who, a decade ago, would have looked down their noses at football fans, that 'something is being done' about hooliganism.

Since the late 1960s, 'football hooliganism' has been constructed as a particularly widespread and dangerous phenomenon, characterised by police, judges, politicians and the media as 'the English sickness'. In *R v Kelton* (1989), Russell LJ remarked that an incident of violence involving football supporters on a cross-channel ferry was tantamount to piracy and commented that:

> I know of my own knowledge that the foreign press call this particular form of mindless violence 'the English sickness'. It is a sickness and a scourge that threatens to destroy civilised life in our country [Pearson, 2000].

When hooligan activity is thus construed, one understands why successive governments in 'our' 'civilised' country have been able to impose sanctions on all fans. The 'suits', 'canaries', 'crap hats', 'fashion victims', 'top boys' and all the other sub-groups whose presence contributes to the urban pageant that is football are lumped together for the purposes of the anti-hooligan agenda. The State is able to infringe upon the civil liberties of fans with impunity precisely because 'football hooliganism' has been defined so broadly and without criticism for so long. Many have questioned the reliability of such 'institutional truths' about football hooliganism, but the myths will not go away. The label 'football hooligan' has been applied to anyone whose drunken, criminal or anti-social behaviour can be linked, however tangentially, to 22 men kicking a bag of wind around; and for a very specific reason:

> The transition of British soccer stadia ... is bound inextricably with the spatial war waged on 'football hooliganism' by the judiciary, police and football authorities. Major spatial rearrangements of football grounds – segregation,

perimeter fencing and all-seated stands – have each been justified according to the need to eliminate the phenomenon of fan violence, so that the game's appeal to corporate or bourgeois finance may continue [Armstrong and Giulianotti, 1997, p 3].

CHAPTER 5

CROWD CONTROL OR CUSTOMER CARE?

INTRODUCTION

The public order concerns that football matches had occasionally given rise to since the 1880s first attracted the prolonged attention of the Government in 1923. The Home Secretary established a committee of inquiry to look into the disorder that accompanied the FA Cup Final of that year – the first to be staged at the new Empire Stadium, Wembley. The Committee's Report concerned itself with the division of responsibility for crowd control within football grounds. It recommended that 'the police should be responsible for all matters appertaining to the preservation of law and order and that, for arrangements for the convenience of the public, the ground authority should be responsible' (Shortt Report, 1924, para 22). It is worth noting that the Report also stated that, in order to discharge those duties relating to the convenience of the public, 'stewards should always be employed. It is in the highest degree important that any such stewards should be properly trained and ... organised as a disciplined body' (para 27). The intervention of the legislature was not deemed necessary, however:

> We are assured that the governing bodies are only too anxious to secure that their sport is carried out under conditions which will promote the public safety, and we feel that, at this stage, it is safe to leave the matter to them [para 47].

But the governing bodies did not 'promote public safety'; far from it. That no major crowd disaster occurred at a football ground until after the Second World War was more a matter of luck than a manifestation of the authorities' concern with the wellbeing of spectators. When barriers collapsed behind a goal at Burnden Park, Bolton in March 1946, 33 spectators died and over 500 were injured. Another Home Office inquiry, chaired by Moelwyn Hughes QC (Hughes Inquiry, 1946), noted that, instead of the projected 50,000 supporters, over 85,000 had turned up for an FA Cup tie against Stoke City. Supporters gained access after a man who wanted to leave the ground successfully picked the lock on an exit gate, and Burnden Park exceeded its nominal capacity over 30 minutes before kick-off. In fact, the capacity of the ground had never been properly assessed: along with other football grounds, its 'capacity' merely represented 'the greatest number that has been safely accommodated there on a previous occasion' (Scraton, 1999, p 18). Knowing no better, the turnstile operators allowed another 2,000 fans to gain entry to that section of overcrowded terracing before the game kicked off.

The game's authorities 'were roundly criticised for their lack of strategy, slow reactions and lack of organisation' (Scraton, 1999, p 18) and Hughes noted that one of the barriers which had given way was 'heavily rusted'. He formed a 'clear view' of the steps that had to be taken to avoid the recurrence of such a disaster and recommended that the capacities of grounds should be scientifically calculated, together with the introduction of a mechanical counting system to ensure that the capacity was not exceeded. However, Hughes also said that:

> The preceding safety measures cannot be secured without legislation. [The Shortt Report] anaemically recommended that adequate provision for safety be left to the pressure of the governing bodies in sport. The most important of these was, of course, the FA, which had not deigned to appear before the Committee ... The legislation should empower the Home Secretary to issue general regulations for different kinds of grounds and the broad conditions necessary for safety. No ground of any considerable size should be opened to the public until it has been licensed by ... the local authority. The issue of a licence would depend upon satisfying the authority as to the construction and equipment of the ground, its compliance with regulations and the proposed maximum figures of admission to the different parts [Hughes Inquiry, 1946, para 11].

Needless to say, these recommendations were ignored. In the years immediately after the Second World War, English football enjoyed another massive burst in popularity that saw attendances peak at an all time high of over 41 million in 1948/49. Even though attendances steadily declined to less than 28 million in 1961/62, post-War aggregates remained above the 28.1 million whom attended in 1938/39 in every season until the early 1970s. 'Football managed to sustain a far greater level of patronage than many of the other areas of mass entertainment that had boomed in the 1940s, most notably the cinema [Russell, 1997, p 133].' Not all was well, but a culture of complacency prevailed. Although a handful of big clubs (notably Manchester United and Tottenham) invested in lavish new grandstands in a conscious effort to attract the middle class punter, there was no general clamour for an improvement in facilities and, generally, crowds were well behaved. Against this backdrop, the legislature saw no cause to intervene and, where crowd safety was concerned, the game's authorities continued to do what they had always done. They did nothing.

SECRETS AND LIES

Few people will need reminding of what happened on that terrible day of 15 April 1989, or of how the failures of the game's authorities, the club and South Yorkshire Police contributed to the disaster. These have all been explored in Taylor LJ's Interim (1989) and Final (1990) Reports into Hillsborough. The 'required reading', though, is the work of Phil Scraton and others into the background of the disaster and lies, cover-ups and prevarication that followed (Scraton *et al,* 1995; Scraton, 1999). It would be pointless and offensive to try to summarise their research here, and anyone who cares about football should read it. Put simply, roadworks on the motorway between Liverpool and Sheffield meant that thousands of supporters arrived late at Sheffield Wednesday's Hillsborough ground – the neutral venue where Liverpool's FA Cup Semi-Final tie against Nottingham Forest was being played. So great were those delays that thousands of Liverpool fans were still outside the ground when the game commenced. Faced with a serious threat to public order and with too few turnstiles to cope with the number of fans, the police took the fateful decision to open a huge exit gate at the Leppings Lane end of the ground in order to let all of those fans in at once. Those supporters rushed into an area directly behind one of the goals that was already overcrowded. Supporters nearer the front were crushed against barriers or fences as the crowd surged in behind them, or were trampled underfoot in the panic that ensued.

Some police officers, who are trained to regard football fans as a threat to public order, mistook fans' desperate attempts to escape by scaling the fence for an attempted pitch invasion and used their truncheons to beat them back into the pen. Others simply froze as the enormity of what was happening hit home. Ninety five Liverpool fans were crushed to death. Another died later in hospital, following the House of Lords' acceptance (in *Airedale NHS Trust v Bland* (1993)) of parents' wishes that doctors should withhold medical treatment from a patient in a persistent vegetative state who had no hope of recovery.

The heartache of the grieving families was compounded by the mendacity of certain high ranking police officers, their underlings' temerity in seeking damages for nervous shock and – most of all – by certain newspapers' portrayal of the Liverpool fans in the days that followed. Those contemplating the purchase of a satellite dish 'to watch the footy' might still care to peruse the headlines from Murdoch's newspapers, especially *The Sun*, from the days following Hillsborough, before deciding to do so.

Worse, Taylor LJ's subsequent inquiry was merely the latest in a long line of investigations into soccer ground safety. The series of reports stretches back over 70 years and comprises several volumes, most of which have been left to gather dust. To summarise, the Shortt Report of 1924 had been written in response to the crowd disorder at the first Wembley Cup Final in 1923, while, in 1946, Moelwyn Hughes had inquired into the overcrowding at Burnden Park that resulted in 33 deaths (Hughes Inquiry, 1946). In 1966, Sir Norman Chester was asked to write a report into the state of the game and further reports followed in 1968 and 1969. In 1972, Sir Norman Wheatley wrote yet another report (Wheatley Report, 1972), this one following the Ibrox disaster, where 66 fans were killed after a stairway collapsed. The McElhone Report (1977) looked at crowd violence in Scotland. Another report into spectator violence was commissioned in 1984, a year before Popplewell J produced the first of his two reports into the Bradford fire (Popplewell Inquiry, 1985; 1986). Taylor LJ's Final Report into Hillsborough was published in January 1990.

Most of the recommendations of those reports had gone unheeded, save for occasional legislative tinkering and vague assurances from those in positions of authority that 'it will never happen again' or 'it couldn't have happened here' (Taylor Report, 1990, pp 4, 5). It was not until the 1970s that any of these reports precipitated worthwhile action. The first *Green Guide* (1973), the Safety at Sports Grounds Act 1975 and a second edition of the *Green Guide* (1976) were the tangible results of Sir Norman Wheatley's endeavour. Popplewell J's Report into Bradford led to a third edition of the *Green Guide*. The Fire Safety and Safety of Places of Sport Act 1987 and the Football Spectators Act 1989 were both on the statute books before Taylor LJ's Final Report was published. The fourth edition of the *Green Guide* and the Football Offences Act 1991 were responses to his recommendations. Furthermore, some fundamental elements of the 1989 Act were not implemented because Taylor LJ was so critical of them in his Final Report. The controversial football membership scheme was shelved for this reason.

In reading his Report, and despite the legislative intervention of the previous 15 years, one can sense the frustration that Taylor LJ must have felt as he realised 'that [Hillsborough] was allowed to happen, despite all the accumulated wisdom of so many previous reports and guidelines. [This] must indicate that the lessons ... had not been taken sufficiently to heart'. 'Insufficient concern' with spectator safety, allied to 'a preoccupation with measures to control hooliganism' and 'unforgivable complacency', were given as the reasons why central government and the game's authorities had failed to take fans' wellbeing sufficiently seriously. Old grounds, poor facilities, the legacy of alcohol-fuelled hooliganism and poor leadership from the game's hierarchy were singled out as the major reasons why the emphasis had consistently been on crowd control rather than spectator safety.

Consequently, Taylor LJ's Report precipitated wholesale, fundamental changes to stadium safety and the way that football crowds were controlled, which would not have been necessary if earlier lessons had been learned. The framework that was already in place to deal with stadium safety – specifically, the 1975 and 1987 Acts and the *Green Guide* – 'have not been strong enough to ensure that basic level of safety' (p 24) that was required in respect of football grounds. The facilities at football stadia would have to be urgently upgraded, with the abolition of high perimeter fencing and the removal of standing areas at grounds that attracted the biggest crowds being the main priorities.

In order to oversee the proper implementation of these new, technical aspects of ground safety, a reappraisal of the clubs' and governing bodies' relationship with the police and alterations to the work of the local authorities, an updated legislative framework would be necessary. The earlier Acts of Parliament and non-statutory guidelines were an inadequate starting point, and the finished article that Taylor LJ had envisaged would be radically different to what had gone before. The Football Licensing Authority (FLA) and the 'new breed' of football safety officers (prior to Hillsborough, only 10 clubs had one) had a fundamental role to play in shaping this changing landscape.

The local authorities were given day to day responsibility for ensuring that Taylor LJ's recommendations on stadium safety were properly enforced. They were already responsible for issuing safety certificates for sports grounds under the terms of the Safety at Sports Grounds Act 1975, under which they were the certifying authorities for any sport and leisure venues to which the general public had access. Taylor LJ recommended that local authorities be given new powers and obligations that would be applicable only in respect of venues where 'designated football matches' were played. Thus, the local authority would be obliged to formally licence designated football grounds once a year by issuing safety certificates to them. The local authority would have to carry out a rigorous inspection of the ground before issuing the safety certificate and make regular checks thereafter in order to ensure that clubs were carrying out their duties under the terms of their safety certificates.

The provisions of the safety certificate are of paramount importance to the clubs. Although they receive a lot of guidance on stadium safety from the FLA, their local authority, the Football Trust, the Football Safety Officers' Association (FSOA) and the Department for Culture, Media and Sport, the safety certificate is the only document that lays down clubs' legal obligations. Breach of its terms can lead to closure of the ground. Theoretically, the information received from the myriad other bodies is mere guidance, but, in reality, there is so much interplay between the various bodies that much of this guidance effectively has the force of law. Conflicts between them are rare. The Football Spectators Act 1989 requires the local authority to ensure implementation by the clubs of the relevant terms of the *Green Guide* (drawn up by central government) and the *Pink Book* (written by members of the FSOA). In turn, the local authority is answerable the FLA. As explained below, this body has statutory responsibility for making sure that the local authorities carry out their licensing functions properly. It also has ultimate responsibility for ensuring clubs' compliance with the terms of their safety certificate, and it can actually override a local authority and insist that certain provisions are incorporated into a club's safety certificate if it considers such a step to be appropriate.

A club's safety certificate will outline the technical specifications applicable to its ground, such as the maximum number of people allowed in a particular area or the minimum number of turnstiles in each area of the ground. But it also makes provision for the number of stewards that the club must employ, specifies the appropriate level of steward training and outlines the roles of the safety certificate holder and (if they are not the same person) the club's safety officer. Before discussing these issues, it might be helpful to give a little more detail about the organisations that have influenced the development of stewarding since the Taylor Report and the sources of information that clubs use to ensure that they comply with their safety certificate.

STADIUM SAFETY A DECADE AFTER HILLSBOROUGH

The FLA is an independent body, funded by the Department for Culture, Media and Sport. It was established under s 8 of the 1989 Act and was initially created to oversee the introduction of the football membership scheme, devise the framework under which that scheme would operate and ensure that clubs complied with its provisions. The Thatcher Government had introduced the scheme in the wake of the Heysel riot and several other high profile outbreaks of hooliganism in the mid to late 1980s. However, Taylor LJ's criticisms of the proposal led to a government climb-down and, although the relevant sections of the 1989 Act received royal assent, they have never come into force. He feared that the scheme could lead to additional congestion and disorder and was not convinced that the computerised mechanism, which worked well in tests, would stand up to the rigours of match day reality. He shared the police's concerns about the resource implications of the scheme and their fears about the ramifications for crowd behaviour when the system malfunctioned. He was not convinced that the scheme would eliminate hooligans from the grounds, but was certain that (at least in the short term) it would actually lead to an increase in trouble outside the grounds (Taylor, 1990).

The decision to scrap the membership scheme in the light of the Taylor report meant that the FLA would have to be scrapped as well, unless a new role could be found for it. Taylor LJ said that ensuring day to day compliance with his recommendations for new ground safety provisions should primarily be the local authorities' responsibility because of their experience in implementing the 1975 Act. However, he also felt that a new, independent body would be needed to ensure that the local authorities and the clubs carried out their respective duties under the new legislation properly. Accordingly, the sensible solution was to change the remit of the FLA so that it became responsible for ensuring compliance with all of the legislation that would soon be applicable to grounds where designated football matches were played.

After the 1992 election, the Department for Culture, Media and Sport was created and took over responsibility for stadium safety matters from the Home Office. Accordingly, the FLA is now subject to the overriding authority of the Department for Culture, Media and Sport. Under s 1(2) of the Football Spectators Act 1989, the Secretary of State has a discretionary power to make any game a designated football match.[1] Section 11 of the Act gives the Secretary of State an additional power to order the FLA to ensure that safety certificates issued by the local authorities contain any provisions that the Government wishes to impose. This provision could be used to ensure that any new statutory provisions regarding standing in all-seater stadia, for example, could be enforced, even if the FLA, the local authorities, the clubs and the governing bodies opposed them and were happy to let fans stand in those areas (McArdle, 1999c).

With that caveat in mind, the FLA has an ultimate power of sanction over the local authorities under s 10 of the 1989 Act, which allows it to review any decision of a local authority on whether to grant a licence to admit spectators to a designated football ground.

The local authority may refuse to grant a licence if, in its opinion, the club has made such inadequate provision for the safety of the spectators that it would be unable to comply with the terms of a safety certificate. If the local authority does grant a licence, the FLA's overriding statutory power allows it to force the local authority to incorporate any term into the club's safety certificate which it considers to be appropriate. In reality, the local authorities' discretionary power over the terms of safety certificates is of little relevance, so far as designated football grounds are concerned.

In order to ensure that the clubs and local authorities properly carry out their tasks in respect of safety certificates, the FLA employs nine regional ground inspectors, who have unrestricted access to the League and Premiership grounds for which they are responsible. Subject to a commitment in the FLA's Code of Practice that ground visits shall only be carried out at reasonable times (FLA, 1996), the inspectors may visit the grounds for which they have responsibility whenever they wish. Unannounced visits on match days are not unknown. If the inspector's investigation provokes concern, the FLA may vary the terms of the safety certificate, or suspend it altogether, by giving notice in writing to the club. The club will normally have 21 days to make representations before the suspension comes into force, but, if the FLA is satisfied that the case is sufficiently urgent, it may override that provision and suspend the licence immediately (s 12(5) of the Football Spectators Act 1989). The suspension can be lifted once the grievance has been addressed (for

---

1   See SI 1991/1565 and 1992/1554, both of which came into force when that power was still vested in the Home Secretary.

example, once necessary remedial work has been completed). Under s 10 of the Football Spectators Act 1989, it is an offence to breach any term or condition of the licence, although a 'reasonable precautions and due diligence' defence is available. Punishment is a fine not exceeding level 5 on the standard scale (s 10(15)).

To summarise, the FLA and the Government both have wide ranging powers that they can use to ensure that provisions are incorporated into the terms of the safety certificates that the local authorities impose on the clubs in their area. Although the FLA has the power to impose a 'model' safety certificate on the local authorities, it has preferred to use non-statutory guidelines in the form of the *Green Guide* and the FSOA's *Pink Book* to flesh out the contents of the safety certificate. This is where the distinction between law and guidelines becomes blurred. Although the safety certificate is the only document whose provisions are legally enforceable, all clubs use the non-statutory guidelines in order to give practical effect to the safety certificate's provisions. In fact, certain individuals from the FLA have suggested that it would be very difficult for a club which is not using those guidelines to persuade the FLA that it was able to properly implement the safety certificate's provisions.

As mentioned above, the *Green Guide* was originally produced in the 1970s and has been revised and updated on several occasions. The current edition was actually written by the FLA on behalf of the Department for Culture, Media and Sport in March 1997. The fact that this edition was the first update not to be written in response to a crowd tragedy explains why its emphasis is more on customer care than on crowd control. Earlier revisions had responded to specific events, so there was more emphasis on fire safety in the wake of Bradford and on crowd control in the review that took place in the aftermath of Hillsborough. The FLA believes that the provisions of the *Green Guide* have not become 'football-specific' simply because it has been written by a body which is, for the time being at least, solely concerned with the safety of designated football grounds. In its opinion, other sports can continue to make use of the *Green Guide*, so long as the crowd dynamics that characterise different sports events are taken into account.

Responsibility for ensuring that the terms of the safety certificate are implemented properly by the club usually rests with the safety officer. Some safety officers played an important consulting role when the FLA was updating the *Green Guide*, and the same individuals were responsible for writing the football-specific *Pink Book* on football stewards' training. The FLA is a member of the safety officers' professional body, the FSOA, and its members were similarly involved in the writing of the *Pink Book*.

FROM SEGREGATION TO SURVEILLANCE

Politically, the major justification for this new economy of control relates not only to the public disgust that spectacular displays of aggression generate among witnesses, but also to the everyday danger that 'law abiding citizens' may be caught up in the crossfire. These instances are extremely rare, but may precipitate as moral righteousness among hooligans privately as among the media and police publicly. *Pace* Robins (1995, p 215), the vicissitudes of hooligan status ensure that honour is lost rather than earned when one group allows or promotes attacks or injuries on passers-by.

THE ROLE OF THE SAFETY OFFICER

In addition to the technical specifications and a wealth of other information, the club's safety certificate will contain the name of the person within the club who is the holder of the certificate and who, therefore, has ultimate responsibility for ensuring the club's compliance with it. It is not unusual for the club itself to be named as the certificate holder, but, if that is the case, then, under s 1(9) of the Football Spectators Act 1989, the club is still required to appoint a 'responsible person' who will have day to day responsibility for safety. This 'responsible person' will be the safety officer, sometimes called the stadium manager (especially at clubs with bigger grounds). If the club is not the holder of the safety certificate, then the safety officer will be the named certificate holder.

The local authority is not required to specify the safety officer's duties within the terms of the safety certificate granted to the club, but the FLA's guidelines do include a model job description for the post. This job description has been accepted at most clubs, albeit with more variation in the light of local circumstances than is the case with the terms of the actual safety certificate. It outlines the safety officer's external relationship with, *inter alia*, the police commander for the ground, the fire and ambulance service personnel and the certifying authority's safety advisory group.

In the model job description, the safety officer has responsibility for ensuring that the CCTV, emergency telephones, fire fighting equipment and other safety systems are fully operational. He (readers will not be surprised to learn that they are all men) must carry out annual inspections of crush barriers, fences and gates and draw up plans with the police and other emergency services that will cover all contingencies, up to and including evacuation of the ground. Match day responsibilities commence 24 hours before the game, when the safety officer is required to ensure that any defects reported at the previous match have been rectified and that the fire warning and fire detection systems are in good working order. On the day of the match, he must undertake a physical inspection of the ground to ensure that no combustible or hazardous materials are stored in a way which could present a danger to supporters. He must also ensure that there are no materials that could be used as missiles, that all routes and exits from the ground are clear and that all gates open easily. He must liaise with the St John's Ambulance Service to ensure that a sufficient number of qualified first aiders will be in attendance and ensure that adequate first aid equipment (as laid down in the safety certificate) is available within the ground and is easily accessible.

Approximately two hours before kick-off, the safety officer will meet with the police's match day commander, satisfy himself that enough trained stewards are available and ensure that the (compulsory) computerised spectator counting system is fully operational. There must also be a manual counting system that can be immediately introduced if the computerised system malfunctions. Under s 1(8) of the Football Spectators Act 1989, the 'start' of a designated football match is deemed to be either the period beginning two hours before the actual or advertised start of the match or, if this is earlier, the time at which spectators are first admitted to the ground. This means that the stewards must be at the ground by 1 pm for a 3 pm kick-off. The FLA guidelines recommend a minimum of one ground safety steward for every 250 fans, although some local authorities have used their discretionary powers to stipulate a smaller ratio. One ground safety steward to 220 supporters is not uncommon among the bigger clubs. The safety officer must ensure that these stewards have been fully briefed and are carrying written instructions on what is expected of them. These instructions will usually take the form of a stewards' handbook, written by the safety officer and supplemented by a pre-match briefing.

The safety officers form the fulcrum of the whole stewarding operation. It is they who have responsibility for ensuring that the technical data included in the safety certificate, and the various guidelines that supplement it, are put into effect at their particular club. They are ultimately responsible for ensuring that their stewards are trained to the requisite standard and that any stewards hired from private agencies are capable of doing the job assigned to them. Their thoughts on the future development of stewarding, how they carry out the tasks assigned to them and what influence they feel they have over the decisions of central government and the FLA are the issues to be addressed in the rest of this chapter.

This research developed out of the postal survey of clubs' participation in the 'Kick-It' campaign (discussed below, Appendix 1). In that survey, clubs had been asked to identify the employee with overall responsibility for ensuring compliance with Kick-It. The overwhelming majority said that the safety officer was that person. This was quite a surprise, for one would have naïvely assumed that the Football in the Community officer, a club director or other person with executive authority would have been in charge. There is certainly nothing in the safety officer's model job description that suggests that this is the kind of role that should be assigned to them; nor did the Taylor Report make any recommendations along those lines.

On reflection, assigning this task to the safety officers rather than to the other usual suspects was a perfectly logical decision. Racist abuse or breaches of the Football Offences Act 1991 have ramifications for ground security and crowd safety that would properly fall within the safety officer's remit, especially as the stewards would be the ones in the front line when it came to dealing with such incidents. But the fact that so many safety officers had been given responsibility for Kick-It stimulated consideration of their precise role within the clubs and prompted the research that followed.

Approximately 30 of the clubs who had responded to the Kick-It survey said that they would be willing to have their 'responsible person' discuss the club's participation in Kick-It and related issues. Twenty three of these 30 clubs had identified the safety officer as the 'responsible person'. These safety officers were contacted and asked if they would participate in an interview that covered not only racism, but other aspects of their remit, including steward recruitment and training, their relationship with the police and the broad issue of stadium safety.

All of the safety officers contacted expressed a willingness to participate, and 16 semi-structured interviews were subsequently carried out with the safety officers of four clubs from each division.[2] In identifying the 16

---

2   The initials ascribed to each officer bear no relation to their real names. In view of the important role played by former police officers working for high status clubs, the following may be of interest to those who wish to know a little more about them and the clubs they work for. Fourteen safety officers' responses have been used in this chapter:

RL   Premiership, former police.
HC   Premiership, former police.
SH   Premiership, not former police.
KS   First Division, former police.
PW   First Division, former police.
LI   First Division, former police.
JH   Second Division, former police.
LE   Second Division, former police.
JS   Second Division, not former police.
CS   Second Division, not former police.
LW   Third Division, not former police.
AC   Third Division, former police.
DM   Third Division, former police.
NB   Third Division, not former police.

Thanks to all for their time, generosity and hospitality.

participants, care was taken to ensure that the sample was balanced in terms of geographical location of the clubs, average crowd sizes and (in the lower divisions) between all-seater stadia and 'traditional' grounds. Most of the interviews lasted between 45 minutes and one hour and usually took place on match days, four or five hours before kick-off.

Although there were clearly defined purposes to this research in determining steward recruitment and training strategies (these form the subject matter of Chapter 6, below), the more subjective issues of the safety officers' perceptions of their work and the future of stewarding were of just as much interest. Semi-structured interviews were identified as the best way of exploring these issues, but, like all research strategies, they have their advantages and disadvantages. The main criticism levelled at semi-structured interviews is that, essentially, they merely document how those interviewed account for themselves and their actions rather than being concerned with 'hard', quantifiable data. What an interviewee says about their role, the organisation that employs them and the people they work with is not always the truth, and this research was undertaken with the possibility of other people's agendas firmly in mind: 'Just as you are hoping to get something out of the interview, it is not unreasonable for the interviewee to get something from you [Robson, 1993, p 230].'

SAFETY OFFICERS' PERCEPTIONS
OF STADIUM SAFETY

That stadium safety pre-Hillsborough was an amateurish operation in which leadership and accountability was lacking is beyond dispute. Although the clubs were nominally in charge and (certainly so far as the Government of the day was concerned) bore responsibility for things that went wrong, the reality was that crowd control was strictly a matter for the police, albeit with varying degrees of assistance from club employees on occasion. The present incumbent at one of 10 clubs to have a safety officer before 1989 confirmed that the role of the stewards was limited to collecting gate money and basic customer care functions. Apart from that, 'we didn't have a proper safety officer as such. Just a guy who used to come in on match days and make a nuisance of himself' (JH):

> Everything in football was very amateurishly run – even here [one of the biggest clubs in the country]. It was a case of 'if they [the stewards] all turn up, all well and good. If not, someone else will sort it out. So there might not be anybody to open a gate in an emergency [SH].

> We needed stewards to get the games on and we would stick a yellow jacket on anybody who volunteered to do it. But the stewarding and safety operation was in the direct control of the police [LW].

The difficulties for the new safety officers were compounded by the desperately poor state of stewarding and stadium safety that many inherited. The fact that the recommendations from the plethora of previous inquiries dating back to the Shortt Report had mostly been ignored meant that clubs were suddenly being asked to carry out basic stadium safety work and remedial tasks that would have been done up to 50 years previously, had the earlier lessons on crowd control and ground safety been learned. As 'HC' noted, 'these recommendations were never implemented because the FA and the Government never expected another tragedy'.

Because of the preoccupation with hooliganism and the all-pervasive presence of the police, controlling the football crowd was a public order issue, rather than a customer care one. When most clubs started to recruit safety officers in the immediate aftermath of Hillsborough, it was inevitable that most of those who were recruited would have learned their trade in this environment, where public order was at the forefront and clubs' stewards played a very limited role – for the safety officers were invariably former high ranking police officers, well versed in the ways of high visibility, mass policing of football grounds, where customer care was of limited significance:

> Stewarding no longer entails just showing people to their seats and telling them where the ice cream kiosk is, but it did at that time. Anyone who came up here asking for a job was basically given a bib and told, 'Here, you're a steward'. The police did it all, really [RL].

> The police controlled the game far more than they were entitled to – and far more than they could be reasonably expected to. But they did it for the sake of the club and the sake of the fans. Without the support of the police actually taking on that role there wouldn't have been a football club here [KS].

So far as the clubs were concerned, the ideal candidate for safety officer was a high ranking officer who was contemplating early retirement; smaller clubs were particularly interested in those who might be tempted by a part time position. Eleven of the 16 safety officers interviewed for this research had police backgrounds and had ended their policing careers near the top of the ladder. It will come as no surprise to close observers of the football industry to learn that, of the 16 interviewees, only one had undergone anything remotely approaching a proper recruitment procedure. The others were already known to the club and had been informally approached by the club chairman and appointed 'on the nod':

> I'm a retired policeman, as most safety officers are. I spent 30 years with the local police force, finishing as superintendent. I was considering early retirement when Hillsborough happened and I was approached to see if I'd take this role on here [AC].

> I was in the police service for 30-odd years, finishing as Divisional Commander. When I left the force in 1990, the Chief Executive of the club asked me to look for a three day a week safety officer for them. I said I'd do it [LE].

Two of those who were not former police officers had public service backgrounds: one had worked in the fire service and had responsibility for training and safety across his region; the other worked in local government and had spent 15 years in charge of issuing and overseeing safety certificates for two big clubs. Two had worked elsewhere in the leisure sector. The fifth was actually a former professional footballer:

> I realised in my mid-20s that I wasn't going to earn enough from the game to retire altogether at 35, so I qualified as a surveyor by doing courses at night school. I finished my career at this club, and they realised they needed someone to be a part time safety officer. They knew I was qualified, so I fell into it [JS].

The fact that former police officers dominate the post of safety officer has been of great importance in the development of their professional body, the FSOA. Formed in 1992, the FSOA works very closely with the FLA to improve ground safety and enhance the role of club stewards, which is particularly important now that the game has turned away from mass policing. In 1995, the Association developed the *Pink Book*, acknowledged by the FLA as the definitive tome on stewards' training. Although one or two clubs have adopted other training packages that they believe are more stringent, or have controversially opted for a National Vocational Qualification (NVQ) stewarding package (see below), the *Pink Book* is what the vast majority of clubs currently use for training their stewards. The safety officers are responsible for ensuring that their stewards are trained to the levels laid down within it.

Although they have been at the forefront of creating stewards' training programmes, the future of the safety officers' role remit seems destined to be dictated by decisions taken elsewhere in respect of three controversial issues: the standardisation of steward training; a compulsory NVQ for stewards; and the use of agencies. Although the FSOA will undoubtedly be involved in the decision making process, given its close links with the FLA, there is a concern amongst some of its members that former high ranking policemen who work for high profile clubs have too much influence within the FSOA. There is a feeling that these individuals' views are not representative of the opinions of safety officers as a whole. It would be stretching the truth to say that this research revealed a schism between police and non-police or between big club and small club safety officers. But some officers were of the opinion that the Association's policies do not represent the views of the membership as a whole, and that it is merely a mouthpiece for retired police officers who now work at the biggest clubs. One criticised it as 'an unbalanced, biased body', dominated by 'policemen who see ... the safety officer's as being a policeman's role' (LW):

They think they are still police officers, running football matches like military campaigns. And that has to be a problem. Some police people were trying to work their tickets by taking early retirement as the need for safety officers arose and I'm not convinced that, long term, they are right for the game [CS].

Most of the time, [the FSOA] talks about trivia. It tends to be dominated by people who have held senior rank and who are with kudos clubs, whereas the real issues of finance and steward recruitment are down here, in Divisions Two and Three. I've been to places where the stewards are paid £6 because that's all their club can afford. There's a practical world and a theoretical world and the real issues are down here [DM].

The question of who speaks for the safety officers at the lowlier clubs is particularly pertinent, now that such issues as standardisation of training programmes and formal qualifications for stewards are firmly on the agenda. Since this research was undertaken, the Football Taskforce's anti-racism Report has recommended that stewards should undergo 'a mandatory NVQ or equivalent qualification' (Football Taskforce, 1998, p 5). Some of the safety officers (especially those working in Divisions Two and Three) believed that the introduction of formal qualifications would be economically ruinous for small clubs and would not precipitate any improvement in stewarding standards. There was a widely held belief that clubs would have to rely even more on agency stewards, because club stewards would simply be unwilling to take an NVQ, or would do so only if they received a decent wage once qualified.

NO VALUABLE QUALIFICATION

A little background to NVQs may be appropriate at this stage. In 1986, following a national review of work-based qualifications, the former Government set up a National Council for Vocational Qualifications (NVCQ) to devise and implement a new framework for vocational qualifications (the NVQs) and to oversee the establishment of bodies making accredited awards. The intention was to devise a training system that gave recognised qualifications on the basis of employees' proven ability to carry out their work successfully, with five levels of award being offered according to the complexity of the work undertaken.

Each NVQ amounts to a 'statement of competence', comprising 'units of competence', which are further sub-divided into 'elements of competence'. It is these elements that form the basis of the assessment. 'A unit of competence will be made up of a number of elements of competence which together make sense to, and are valued by, employers so that they warrant separate accreditation [Jessup, 1991, p 1].' The criteria for the NVQs state that these elements of competence must be capable of demonstration and assessment and must describe the *result* of what is done, rather than the procedures that were used for doing it (NCVQ, 1991, p 3). In other words, the qualification and its assessment must be performance-based: 'Assessment should be uncoupled from training in order to promote access, recognition of prior learning and candidate choice of learning mode [Eraut, 1994, p 192].' The conditions under which assessment takes place must be in the workplace or, if that is not possible, as close as is practicable to a workplace situation: 'The method of assessment should always enable eligible candidates to demonstrate competence, and place no unnecessary additional demands on them [NCVQ, 1991, p 6].'

As some of the safety officers inferred, it is difficult to see how the stewarding operation at designated football grounds could be better assessed under NVQ criteria than under the existing method. At the moment, club safety officers take responsibility for ensuring that their stewards are trained up to the appropriate level. This is overseen by the local authority and the FLA, which can step in if they feel that the club is falling short of what is required. A course that required stewards to attend college or engage in desk-bound learning would appear to be hideously wide of the mark. Certainly, it is difficult to think of how one could devise a role play situation of ejecting a drunken racist (for example) that would be sufficiently in tune with reality to correspond with the 'workplace situation' that the NCVQ demands.

The practical difficulty associated with the introduction of an NVQ or similar qualification was the one issue over which the safety officers were united, regardless of their career background and the size of the club they worked for. They stressed that standardisation of most elements of steward training is already in place, given the FLA's influence over the terms of the safety certificate and the degree of co-operation between it and the FSOA in drawing up the *Green Guide* and the *Pink Book*. Even the safety officers who had not been privy to this co-operative approach were supportive of the extent to which steward training had already been standardised. Their concern was that demanding a mandatory, formal qualification of all stewards would be unnecessarily expensive, without better equipping them to do their job.

However, only two safety officers could speak from experience. Their clubs had already put their stewards through NVQ training, but they were divided on the merits of the scheme. One club was sufficiently impressed to require its stewards and all other staff to go through some form of NVQ training up to level 3 (SH). However, the other (NB, who was working at a far smaller club) thought that an 'NVQ is an expensive way of doing [steward assessment]. Internal assessment is now seen as the way forward here'.

It seems that most safety officers are not opposed to standardisation *per se*, but favour the idea of the game having its own in-house qualification, rather than having a mandatory NVQ or other qualification imposed on them from without. The vexed question of who would bear the costs of any such qualification loomed large. Some of those interviewed felt that the clubs or the game's governing bodies would be more amenable to incurring this expense if it was devised and implemented by 'football people'. However, others believed that neither the clubs nor the game's authorities would be willing to commit themselves to the greater expenditure that any standardised formal assessment procedure would necessarily entail, regardless of who was behind it:

> The FSOA is working on a standard assessment package, going from initial interview and through to final certification for a fully trained steward. We hope to have that out by next summer [1999], but we're on a stumbling block about who pays. The football authorities want the clubs to pay for it, but the clubs say they haven't got the money [CS].

The safety officers offered various justifications for their support for an in-house certification rather than an NVQ. First, there was overwhelming cynicism about the motives of the various universities, further education colleges and other bodies that offer the existing NVQ courses in stewarding. Some felt that 'some people are going to make a lot of money out of these courses' (JH) and that the people behind them had little idea about what the stewarding operation actually involved. They certainly did not believe that NVQs would produce better stewards than clubs' own in-house training schemes were producing:

> I got a call from a guy at a local university recently. He said they'd just put together 'this wonderful new course on stewards' training', and would we be interested in it. I said, 'Sorry, but we do our own training, and so do most other clubs'. They didn't really understand how stewards are trained at the moment and thought that every club would want their poxy training package [RL].

> There are various universities and colleges trying to encourage us to send supervisors to them for a week or so. The club would have to pay for that and I don't think my chairman would be too keen. Of course, safety is paramount, but when you're at the bottom end of the scale any spare cash gets spent on players [AC].

One or two safety officers went so far as to question the need for even a standardised stewarding programme that the football industry itself would oversee, let alone a mandatory NVQ. They believed that the differences in ground capacity, stadium layout and other variables from one club to another meant that it would be impossible to produce a model training and assessment package that would be equally applicable to all clubs. This was one area where the small club/kudos club distinction was most apparent. Those safety officers who were not retired policemen working with kudos clubs had the strongest reservations about the whole issue of standardisation, if not actually going so far as to reject the idea altogether:

My other worry about the FSOA is that they are pushing for some form of certification before you can be a steward. I suppose they might be right, but surely it plays right into the hands of the organisations who will run the courses [LW].

Is [standardised assessment] really what the game needs? If you go down that road, the only people who will benefit are the ones who set up the stewards' training packages [DM].

Another major concern was the perceived difficulty in persuading clubs' stewards to undergo another form of mandatory assessment. All safety officers have experience of potential stewards putting themselves forward, then dropping out once they realise that there is a degree of training involved with some form of assessment at the end of it. Even those who had no reservations about NVQs in principle wondered how many of their stewards would themselves be willing to put up with the hassle. The risible sums that most clubs paid their stewards (and there are still places where they get £10 and a cup of tea) meant that they could not really expect them to do more than they were doing already. Assessment 'is a time consuming process and for most of them it would be more hassle than the job is worth' (JH):

I just wonder what will happen to the football industry when a lot of very good stewards are asked to sit formal examinations. They are part-timers who do it for a few quid. If I tried to force mine down that road, I'd lose most of them [JS].

I've always had good stewards who I can rely on and who know what they're doing, but the club can't afford to pay them to come to training sessions and they'd have to be very keen to do more [training] for nothing [JH].

The fear that a lot of good stewards would rather walk away from the job than undergo any type of assessment programme was widely held. Many safety officers were concerned that they would not be able to convince their stewards that an NVQ or any other 'work-based' programme would be no more onerous than the present club-based training programme that most of them were comfortable with:

The people I'm working with ... are here on a Saturday afternoon to do a job for four or five hours and to earn a few bob for a night out. So long as they have the intelligence to do what I need them to do, I'm happy [KS].

There's one exit gate man who's here week in and week out and he's been here for years. Now, I'm not being disrespectful to him, but [operating an exit gate] is about as much as he can cope with. He's not going to do an NVQ [LE].

These reservations seem to be borne out by the experiences of one of the two safety officers who had already put his stewards through NVQ training but who was turned off by the expense: 'One of the other drawbacks when we did NVQ was that quite a few people disappeared and didn't want to know about it. And they were good stewards [NB].'

THE FUTURE OF AGENCY STEWARDS

If standardisation (whether through an industry operated scheme or via the imposition of a mandatory NVQ) does occur, it could lead to a dramatic reduction in the number of stewards working at the smaller clubs. The main beneficiaries would be those private security agencies who provide stewards and who make up the numbers at those clubs that cannot recruit enough supporters willing to do the job. Agencies' attempts to secure a niche for themselves in the future of football stewarding have not been helped by fans' perceptions of them as inadequately trained and unnecessarily aggressive, as epitomised by the ongoing skirmishes between fans and Special Projects Security at Old Trafford. Fans' attempts to improve what they perceived as the embarrassingly sterile atmosphere at matches by standing up and singing at United home games during the 1995/96 season were met by the club warning that they could be ejected. Notwithstanding the club's difficult position, in that persistently standing in an all-seater stadium would infringe the provisions of the safety certificate, United did themselves no favours by entrusting agency rather than club stewards with enforcing this provision.

Although such incidents do have a negative impact on agencies' reputations with the fans, the safety officers' perceptions of them were based on their own experiences, rather than through media reports of admittedly isolated incidents of malpractice. But there was a widespread feeling that the implementation of the *Pink Book*'s provisions by even the most cash-strapped clubs is far more rigorous than the training programmes that most agency stewards are subjected to. Some safety officers said that agency stewards were often surprised at just how rigorous the clubs' training programmes were, and few were convinced that agency stewards had been trained up to at least *Pink Book* level.

But being trained to this level is what is required under the terms of clubs' safety certificates. The perceived inadequacy of agency stewards would appear to be a far more pressing problem for the game's authorities than demanding a formal qualification of clubs' employees. Some safety officers were willing to believe that some agency stewards may have received an adequate level of training, but the fact remained that the agencies themselves could not produce the training records that would provide satisfactory evidence of this. One officer spoke of having to get rid of one of the biggest agencies in the country because they simply could not prove the adequacy of their training:

> We like to know that everybody who comes into the ground has been trained to an acceptable level, but this lot's training records were non-existent. We said, 'If you can't produce the records we want, we're not having you'. That's why we have got rid of them [RL].

Others had been through similar experiences:

> Something we've fought long and hard for at FSOA meetings is that private agencies should have to prove themselves and show us their training records. They may be very well trained but I can't guarantee that, whereas I know that the ones who work for the club have been through a proper training course [HC].

At the larger clubs, the use of agency stewards was a less frequent occurrence than in the lower divisions, where it tended to be the norm. It seemed that safety officers at big clubs could afford to take a long term view of steward recruitment. They were able to devote sufficient resources to their recruitment and training, 'using agencies for a short period of time, to get over temporary shortage when we were recruiting and training our own' (SH). They had the luxury of a big enough fan base from which to recruit their stewards. In stark contrast, those at the other end of the scale did not have enough resources to treat recruitment and training as an investment and did not have enough fans coming forward to volunteer their services. These clubs were living a hand-to-mouth existence, so far as stadium safety was concerned:

> Being a small club with a small fan base is our biggest problem. We are not as successful as the rich clubs in terms of steward recruitment and when we run the training programmes it's hard to get people to come along ... Those we have are very loyal, but out of the 70 stewards we use on a match day, about 18 will come from a local security firm [DM].

Alongside fears about training levels and the inadequacy of their training records, the safety officers' other big complaint about agency stewards was that they never knew who the agency would be sending from one game to the next. It was not unusual for new stewards to turn up without any evidence that they had undergone adequate training, or, indeed, any training at all. It seems that, if the archetypal 'untrained bloke in a yellow jacket' does exist, he is working for a private agency rather than the club to which he is temporarily attached. One officer spoke of an agency sending over 240 different people in a four month period, to cover just 60 stewarding posts. And his experience was not exceptional:

> When we first took on an agency we said we had 70 positions for them to cover. We wanted the same people there every week if possible and we wanted to be sure of their training records. But, last season, those 70 positions took 273 people to cover. They were coming for one match and we'd never see them again. [RL].

> We use an agency that has been with us for a long time. We monitor their training and their records, and, quite frankly, of all the agencies we've looked at, we've not seen anyone with better training records. And they are efficient stewards, I suppose. Ideally, we'd like to have all our own stewards [JS].

The safety officers were particularly concerned that stewards' infrequent attendance at their ground prevented them from being sufficiently familiar with ground layout to carry out basic customer care functions. This did not just impact on the simple things, such as pointing people to the lavatories and showing them to their seats; they could not be relied upon to know where the exits or emergency telephones were, or to understand the code system that most clubs use to relay messages about potentially serious situations. This combination of circumstances led some safety officers to believe that stewards who had many years of experience but who were working one match per fortnight at 'their club' would quickly realise that they could earn much more by working at other grounds if they had a formal stewarding qualification. Certainly, nobody could blame the stewards if they chose to earn some decent money by doing agency work instead, perhaps working at three or four different grounds per week in the London area. There was a widely held belief that this would cause a stewarding crisis for smaller clubs, especially if they were located near other grounds where agency stewards could work without too onerous a journey:

> We can offer stewards 23 matches a season, plus Cup games. But there are so many clubs around here that an agency can give them three matches a week. If you're looking for money, you'll go and work for an agency and get £60 [HC].

Clubs who used agency stewards did so out of necessity. They used them because they could not recruit and retain enough club stewards to comply with the requirements of their safety certificate, not because they were happy with the level of training that agencies were giving the people they employed:

> A couple of years ago, we spent the whole summer training about 20 new stewards. It cost about £400, and this was in the days when the club had no money whatsoever. Within a couple of weeks of the season starting, they had all gone off and joined an agency [JS].

Most safety officers invite new applicants to work alongside an established steward for a few matches before deciding to invest in those people by putting them through the full training programme. In retrospect, using the summer months to train people who had no interest in the club and presuming that they would turn up and do the job once the season started – when the onerous aspects of stewarding become apparent – was distinctly unwise. It also highlights the dangers of recruiting stewards who are not fans of the club; for example, 'JS' had recruited the new stewards via the local job centre. There were many clubs (not all of which were in the lower divisions) which had avoided falling into this trap but still needed to supplement their club stewards by using agencies because of their inability to recruit of their own.

The difference in wages between club and agency stewards, and the latters' relative unfamiliarity with the grounds they work at, led some safety officers to believe that the stewards should be deployed in carrying out those tasks which could be characterised as 'public order' rather than 'customer care'. In the bad old days of the 1980s, these tasks would have fallen within the police's remit, but the move towards reducing or eliminating the number of police in attendance because of the costs involved means that stewards have had to take responsibility for dealing with some unpleasant situations. On occasion, this requires them to deal with, or at least contain, situations until the police arrive. At police-free games, it can be some minutes before enough police are available to deal with a situation. It should be remembered that the phrase 'police-free football match' is a misnomer. There are always enough officers within the ground or immediately outside to deal with unexpected public order problems. But one or two safety officers believed that, if such situations did arise, the sums they paid agency stewards justified asking them to deal with the matter:

> I just want [club stewards] to be able to talk to people – a bit of customer service, the ability to be polite. I don't particularly need them to be aggressive in the policing of [the fans] because we've got paid security stewards who get £60 a game. So they're the ones who are going to get punched in the face, if anyone is [JS].

It should be stressed that safety officers who believed that agency stewards should be called upon to handle the most difficult situations, with club stewards being guaranteed a relatively easy ride, were exceptional. The majority did not differentiate between stewards when public order tasks had to be carried out. They believed that agency stewards and club stewards should be treated equally in terms of what they dealt with, and that the limits of their 'public order' obligations should be the same. They pointed out that, under the Football Offences Act 1991, pitch invasion is an offence for which 'any person' has the power of arrest, not just a police officer:

> A number of our stewards have made arrests here for pitch incursions. If our training is working ... we would expect our stewards to be competent in carrying that out [PW].

That said, the limits that had been imposed on the roles of club and agency stewards alike tended to fall some way short of what the law actually empowered stewards to do. Safety officers were conscious that '[stewards] don't have the police's experience of dealing with violent people, and we wouldn't ask them to' (JH):

> The power of arrest under the Football Offences Act 1991 extends to stewards, but I would rather they assisted the police by providing evidence as a private person. They could arrest people who incur on the pitch and they have arrested people for racist abuse and for trying to get into the ground with drink [KS].

This reflects the safety officers' overwhelming belief that football grounds should never be police-free to the extent that stewards are expected to deal with all public order issues. The training and remuneration of stewards would never be enough to enable them to carry out the police's functions effectively, regardless of both whether they were obliged to take an NVQ or other form of qualification and whether the status quo remained. The game might be about to incur considerable expense by going down the NVQ route, but there is little evidence that it would either enable stewards to carry out new tasks or make them any better at doing what is already required of them:

> I'm critical of those people who are trying to make stewards into pseudo-policemen. They will never replace the police. Stewards are here for safety, not for public order, and if I was being paid £15 a game to enforce the criminal law I would certainly want some information from my employer about my insurance and my liabilities. Most clubs have not dealt with that at all [LW].

> We ask [the stewards] to be the first line. If they see someone misbehaving, we ask the stewards to politely calm them down. That's their job. We don't ask them to be heroes – we don't pay them enough to be heroes. We stress, 'Don't put yourselves at risk' [CS].

CONCLUSION

Clubs may not ask their stewards to 'put themselves at risk', but the reality is that risk is an inescapable, fundamental part of the steward's job. Every season, at least half a dozen occasions when stewards get injured or attacked in the course of their work will be reported in the national press, in addition to innumerable other incidents that never make the headlines. In October 1998, Coventry City steward Ron Reeves died after being crushed under the wheels of the Arsenal team coach. His death was a tragic accident; neither Coventry City FC nor the coach driver was to blame in any way (see (1998) *The Sunday Times (Sport)*, 1 November, p 1). But it served as a salutary reminder that, were it not for the likes of Ron Reeves being willing to carry out tasks that are essentially public order matters, fans would still be subject to the intimidatory, mass policing that was the norm for so many supporters in the 1980s. Stewards sometimes get paid no more than £15 per match for carrying out this service. But they will shortly be asked to carry out yet more training, undergo an NVQ or a similar assessment programme and then be held up for further scrutiny by the Football Taskforce and other worthies who think that stewards' main concern is with getting in to watch the match for free. This represents a fundamental misconception of what the stewards' function involves and is prompted by a small number of high profile incidents of misbehaviour by stewards, usually those employed by agencies and working at Manchester United or one of the other 'big clubs'.

Club stewards carry out vital tasks that most fans would have neither the inclination nor the courage to perform. They have level of basic medical training and firefighting skills that enable them to make important contributions to the wider community. One would hope that the FSOA will be willing to argue that any formal, standardised assessment that is introduced must be overseen by those who understand the stewarding process, rather than outside bodies looking to make a fast buck from the game. If they fail to do so, the smaller clubs in particular face a threat to their financial viability which is almost as grave as that posed by the *Bosman* (1996) ruling.

Changes to the stewards' role may not be immediate. At the time of writing, it seems that the FLA is to be replaced by a Sports Ground Safety Authority, possibly within the lifetime of the current Parliament. Rumours emanating from the Department for Culture, Media and Sport suggest that the 'designated football match' system of licensing will be abolished, but that the new body would keep local authorities' discharge of their licensing duties under close review. If this were to occur, it might allow time for a more considered appraisal of the future of stewarding, the role of private agencies and the logistics of introducing a formal assessment procedure. The alternative is that those responsible for policing the game will make some costly decisions that have no merit. At the very least, they need to remember that neither a football club steward nor a football club safety officer was responsible for opening that gate at the Leppings Lane end.

CHAPTER 6

FIGHTING TALK: CHALLENGING RACISM IN FOOTBALL

Seven million pounds is a lot to pay for a nigger.[1]

INTRODUCTION

The sad reality is that there is far more to 'racism in football' than the occasional utterance emanating from a poorly educated dullard on the terraces. There is little that can usefully be added to the various texts on this aspect of racism that have appeared over the past decade (see, for example, Garland and Rowe, 2000 and Power, 2000). These works have explored the phenomenon of fans' racism; legislative approaches to it; club-based initiatives; and the work of Kick-It (see below), the Commission for Racial Equality (CRE) and a host of other organisations that have an interest in the issue. This chapter seeks to adopt a different perspective. Its main emphasis is on racism in the boardroom and the changing room and the game's (inadequate) response to it. The one point that might be worth making on the subject of fans' racism is that the general opinion among stewards and the police seems to be that the most effective response is for other fans to turn round and say, 'I'm not prepared to put up with that'. Understandably, relatively few supporters are willing to do so; it is far easier to leave such situations to the police, the stewards or someone (anyone!) else, but fans' intervention is certainly a more effective response to racism than another dose of ill-penned legislation.

WHICH SIDE ARE YOU ON, BOYS?

Some folk would suggest that the racism peddled by jovial Georgie Best in an unguarded, off-the-cuff remark during an 'Evening With' event at the Fairfield Halls in Croydon does not bear comparison with 'proper' racism. Certainly (they would probably argue), what George Best said was unacceptable, but surely it is a world away from the vitriolic abuse, banana throwing and monkey chants that Arthur Wharton, 'Dixie' Dean, Clyde Best and others have endured for decades?

---

1   George Best (on Manchester United's signing of Andy Cole) (see Thorpe, 1995).

It is not. Best's racism was no different to 300 Everton fans chanting 'Niggerpool' during Merseyside derbies when John Barnes was at Anfield, but the football industry, and the media frenzy that feeds off it, scarcely concerns itself with racism. When it does, it demonises terrace racism because it is a far softer target than the racism of players, managers and club officials. Best's comments were little different to those peddled by former Everton player and Wales international Kevin Ratcliffe, which led to the industrial tribunal case of *Hussaney v Chester City FC* (1997). But, like Best's comments, neither the sports press nor the mainstream media paid Hussaney much attention. It gets some attention here in an attempt to redress the balance.

James Hussaney played as an associate schoolboy for Chester City FC between June 1995 and June 1997. He played a number of games for their youth and reserve teams. In January 1997, he was due to play in a game against Oldham Athletic reserves. Kevin Ratcliffe, Chester City's manager, was also due to play in that game. As part of his duties, Hussaney was required to change the studs on Ratcliffe's boots, but, despite being told what to do, he fitted them wrongly. Ratcliffe angrily shouted, 'Where's James, the black cunt?'.

Hussaney was not present, but two of his friends were and Ratcliffe's words were relayed to him. Hussaney telephoned his father to tell him what had happened and, during the game, Hussaney senior came to the ground, looking for Ratcliffe. A confrontation was avoided by the intervention of the youth team coach and although, later in the day, Ratcliffe offered what was later claimed to have been an apology, Hussaney said that Ratcliffe was smiling at the time and tried to minimise what he had said. Ratcliffe never denied uttering the words attributed to him.

Soon afterwards, Hussaney's mother spoke to a director of the club and arranged a meeting with the director, Ratcliffe and the youth team coach. By that time, Ratcliffe was genuinely apologetic; it was agreed that the club would issue a formal written apology to Hussaney and a disciplinary warning would be issued to the manager. However, at this meeting, the youth team coach considered it prudent to get involved in the affair. The tribunal found that he had behaved aggressively towards Mrs Hussaney and that both he and the director unjustifiably accused her son of 'having a bad attitude'. Hussaney never received his formal apology and Ratcliffe's 'warning' was nothing of the sort. Five months after the incident, Chester City told Hussaney that it would not be offering him a professional contract, following discussions between Ratcliffe, the youth team coach and the assistant manager about his merits as a player. Hussaney brought an action before an industrial tribunal that both the words used and the failure to offer him a contract were acts of direct racial discrimination and, as such, contravened the Race Relations Act 1976.

The industrial tribunal held that the words 'black cunt' were racially specific and were an express, undisguised racial insult. Uttering them was a clear act of racial discrimination. There was much to be said for Hussaney's claim that the failure to offer him a contract so soon after the incident, coupled with the baseless allegation of bad attitude that preceded it, had been discriminatory. But, after careful consideration, the tribunal decided that the decision to release Hussaney was made purely on the basis of his potential as a footballer, justified by the knowledgeable observation of the manager, his assistant and the youth team coach. The tribunal stated that it was important not to underestimate the effect of any racial insult, even one uttered on an isolated occasion. 'While not in the highest order of gravity, the discrimination here was bad enough,' said the tribunal chairman.

The tribunal was particularly scathing of the way in which the injury to Hussaney's feelings had been exacerbated by Chester City's approach to his grievance. He made a justifiable complaint and, in the discussions that arose from it, had been unjustly accused of having a bad attitude. Ratcliffe never stood before him and said he was sorry; and, despite its promises, the club had never sent him a letter to that effect. In the words of the tribunal chairman:

> The disciplinary letter to the second respondent was not the letter of an employer who has formed the view that a senior manager had gravely misconducted himself. There is not a word in it about the likely consequences of a repetition on the second respondent's employment; its tone is too mild. The respondents' treatment of the complaint aspired to the appearance of proper action, but it was neither authentically determined nor indignant.

The club was more concerned with maintaining a cosy relationship with its manager than with dealing effectively with a clear incident of direct racial discrimination.

In the circumstances, the tribunal decided that Hussaney's treatment merited an award of £2,500 for injury to feelings, a head of compensation established under s 57 of the Race Relations Act 1976. It is payable in cases where the applicant knows, at the time of the incident complained of, that she or he has suffered an act of discrimination. The amount that should be awarded for injury to feelings can be difficult to quantify. The Court of Appeal in *Alexander v Home Office* (1988) said that the award should not be so minimal as to trivialise the public policy issues behind anti-discrimination law. But neither should awards be on a par with those given for bodily injury, which are far more serious and have longer term implications. In the wake of *Alexander* (1988), *North West Thames RHA v Noone* (1988) and the provisions of the Unfair Dismissal (Increase of Compensation Limit) Order 1991 (SI 1991/466), the minimum award will normally be in the region of £500 and the maximum will usually be £4,000 (Pitt, 1994, p 79).

When the industrial tribunal decision was announced in November 1997, the Football Association (FA) sought to pre-empt criticism by announcing that it would be holding an inquiry into the incident. Six weeks passed with no mention of the outcome of this inquiry in the media, so, in the middle of January 1998, the FA was contacted to find out the state of play. An official in the Association's Press Office opined that an enquiry had indeed been held, but the results of it would not be public. 'There isn't a disciplinary issue here, so we'll just communicate the results [of the enquiry] to the club and leave it at that,' he said. This response confirmed the existence of a policy of paying lip service to initiatives that challenge racism on the terraces while seeking to minimise public awareness of racism *within* the game. One doubts whether even the FA would have been able to maintain its silence if the tribunal had found that the failure to offer Hussaney a new contract had been motivated by his having complained of Ratcliffe's racism. From reading the tribunal's judgment, it seems that they were within an ace of doing so. The ultimate irony is that, in May 2000, newly demoted Chester City were ordered by a Football League tribunal to pay Ratcliffe £200,000 compensation in bizarre circumstances. Ratcliffe had terminated his own contract, jumping the sinking ship that was Chester City to join Shrewsbury. However, a clause in his contract entitled him to compensation if the ownership of Chester City changed hands, which it did before Ratcliffe left. After an eight hour hearing, the tribunal ruled that the terms of that clause entitled Ratcliffe to compensation totalling £40,000 a year for the duration of his five year contract. Chester have a right of appeal.

Aside from the incident of racism itself, the point that needs to be made in relation to *Hussaney* was that there seemed to be no one in authority whom the player could have aired his grievance to. As his parents' attempts to instigate a formal investigation and obtain an apology illustrated, the relationship between the manager, coaches and directors of Chester City FC was too close to allow for a proper, dispassionate consideration of the facts. As the tribunal noted, Chester City's response was 'neither authentically determined nor indignant'. Hussaney was let down by the club, he was let down by the FA and there was no organisation within the game to whom he could turn for advice and guidance. The only avenue that was realistically open to him was to pursue his complaint via an external body such as a local race equality council, a law centre or the Commission for Racial Equality (CRE). In similar circumstances, most players would have said nothing.

In order to reduce the possibility of similar cases arising in the future, the sensible way forward would be for the clubs themselves to introduce codes of practice and equal opportunities policies voluntarily, to monitor their implementation and to revise them regularly in order to ensure their effectiveness. The problem, as mentioned above, is that the football business pays no more than lip service to such issues. The lip service paid thus far to the Football Taskforce's recommendations on racism and the lamentable level of support that most clubs have lent to the 'Kick-It' campaign does not instil one with confidence in their willingness to respond wholeheartedly to the concept of equal opportunities.

THE FOOTBALL TASKFORCE'S RESEARCH INTO RACISM

The clubs' and governing bodies' duplicitous approach to racism was precisely the kind of behaviour that the 'Football Taskforce' was charged with addressing. The Taskforce's creation had been mooted before the 1997 election, as New Labour sought to cash in on the populist political capital associated with the game, and it was duly established in July 1997 by the new sports minister, Tony Banks. Banks' appointment in preference to long standing Shadow Sports Minister Tom Pendry had ruffled a few feathers in the earliest days of the Labour Government; his decision to appoint David Mellor, the former (Conservative) Home Secretary, as Taskforce Chairman caused even more surprise.

Bodies such as the Football Taskforce are just one element of New Labour's 'Quangocracy'. Over 500 people – ranging from trade union leaders to former athletes – have been appointed to ministerial taskforces and departmental review bodies since the 1997 election. Within a few months of coming to power, Tony Blair's Government had established 18 taskforces, 80 review bodies and 69 advisers. Labour justified the plethora of new organisations on the grounds that, after 18 years of one-Party rule, everything was open to review. However, there are legitimate concerns that, when official channels that have at least some vestige of public accountability and transparency are bypassed, some important issues on standards and responsibility in public life are bound to be raised (Nolan, 1995; 1996). Few people are aware of what the precise remit of a particular 'taskforce' is; their rules of engagement often seem to be made up as they go along and it seems that their influence does not attract a concomitant level of accountability.

There is some serious money floating around, too; these advisers work throughout government at a total cost to the taxpayer of nearly £3 million a year. At the top of the pay league is Adrian Montague, a banker, who, as head of the private Finance Taskforce at the treasury, attracts a salary of £160,000. Keith Hellawell, the anti-drugs 'tsar', earns more than £100,000 a year. Whatever one's thoughts about David Mellor, it should be said that his post is unpaid and he actually makes a loss on his job, because the work takes up a day of his secretary's time each week. Mellor's estimated income of £200,000 a year stems from consultancy work and contacts in the Gulf States and elsewhere, but, of course, he has developed other business interests as a consequence of his role with the Taskforce. These have included, *inter alia*, book reviews, his Saturday evening phone-in on BBC Radio 5 and a weekly column in the *Evening Standard*.

It is probably too early in the game to say much about the Taskforce's various reports and the effect that they will have. Much of their work is still up for discussion within the game and within central Government, and there is a fear that many of the Taskforce's recommendations will end up gathering dust or will be watered down before being implemented. In particular, those aspects of its work which deal with the vexed question of precisely what role an 'Ombudsfan' should have – if, indeed, it should have any role at all – remain controversial. However, its work on racism represented its first report and its recommendations were published in the summer of 1998, so it is now possible to gauge responses to it.

As part of its inquiries into racism, the Taskforce solicited the views of various clubs, governing bodies, county football associations, academics, pressure groups, players' representatives and others, the following recommendations were made (Taskforce, 1998, pp 3–5).

Playing the game: eliminating racism

The FA should:

- issue new guidance to referees to make clear that an immediate red card should be shown to players making any racist comments on the field of play;

- amend FA disciplinary rules to recognise racist abuse on and off the pitch as a distinct offence, punishable by separate and severe disciplinary measures;

- instruct county FA disciplinary committees that incidents of racism on the field of play should be punishable by severe penalties;

- require county FAs to sign up to an anti-racism charter and pledge positive action to encourage wider participation in all aspects of the game;

- establish a unit to monitor the implementation of the charter and to which all FA-affiliated teams can report suspected breaches of its provisions.

Local authorities should:

- exclude local football clubs with a record of involvement in racist incidents from council owned playing facilities.

*The Professional Footballers' Association and the
League Managers' Association should:*

- recommend inserting an anti-racism pledge in players' and managers' contracts, with breaches incurring severe sanctions (fines or dismissal).

Playing the game: encouraging wider participation

Local authorities should:

- promote special community coaching schemes with the specific aim of encouraging wider participation in football from all sections of the community.

The Government should:

- make efforts to ensure that all schoolchildren – particularly those in inner city schools – have access to playing fields (preferably grass) on a regular basis.

*Professional football clubs and
conference clubs should:*

- review scouting activities to ensure that teams from all sections of the local community are regularly watched.

The FA should:

- set targets for increasing the number of black and Asian qualified FA coaches and referees;
- take positive action to meet those targets.

Watching the game: eliminating racism

The Government should:

- amend the Football Offences Act 1991 to make racist abuse by individual spectators at football matches a criminal offence.

*The Football Trust (and bodies awarding grant
aid to football clubs) should:*

- require recipients of grant-aid to implement the nine point plan of the Kick-It campaign on a regular and ongoing basis.

The FA Premier League and the Football League should:

- prepare written guidance for member clubs on action to counter racism.

All professional clubs and conference clubs should:

- amend ground regulations to recognise racist abuse as a separate offence – distinct from the use of foul language – and set out the penalties involved;

- set up a confidential freephone 'hotline' through which supporters can report incidents of racist abuse to club officials;

- implement measures in the Kick-It campaign on a regular basis, including the broadcasting of a clear anti-racist message prior to kick-off at all home games.

The FA, Football Licensing Authority and Football
Safety Officers' Association should:

- ensure that football stewards are trained to deal with racism at football matches as part of a mandatory NVQ or equivalent qualification;

- agree a simple procedure to deal with incidents of racism at football matches, to be made standard at all grounds in England.

Watching the game: encouraging wider participation

All administrative organisations in football should:

- adopt a comprehensive written equal opportunities policy to cover the recruitment and treatment of all staff.

Professional clubs and conference clubs should:

- adopt a comprehensive written equal opportunities policy to cover the recruitment and treatment on non-playing staff;

- form partnerships with local organisations – supporters' groups, local authorities, community groups and police – to market the club to a wider audience;

- use innovative ticketing schemes to reach sections of the community not currently attending matches;

- offer club facilities for community events and encourage players to visit schools.

Wider aspects of the game

The FA should:

- ensure that the FA Council – and county FA councils – are more representative of the game and the communities they serve;

- require all work to tackle racism in football to be co-ordinated under the banner of the Kick-It campaign;

- create a Charter Mark, to be awarded to clubs and football organisations making substantial efforts to tackle racism and encourage wider participation.

The Government should:

- set a clear timetable for any future work which arises out of this report and carry out a follow-up report to determine progress.

Racism is still a blot on the game, and, while nobody would doubt the Taskforce's good intentions, committees are better at deploring it than doing anything about it. The Government responded by drafting and supporting the Bill that became the Football (Offences and Disorder) Act 1999, which, as previously mentioned, changes the law on racist chanting. That was the easy bit: the real challenge lay in persuading the clubs and the game's authorities to do their part and, in particular, to do more than mouth platitudes about racism on the terraces.

THE GOVERNING BODIES' RESPONSES
TO THE TASKFORCE REPORT

The FA

In June 1998, the FA wrote to the Minister for Sport, outlining the steps it had already taken in respect of the Taskforce's recommendations and indicating how it intended to develop its anti-racism policies in the near future. It pointed out that racist remarks on the field of play already constituted a dismissable offence under law 12, and the Instructions to Referees sent out in May 1998 reminded them that this was the case. In response to the Taskforce's recommendation that the FA should 'instruct disciplinary committees that [such incidents] should be punishable by severe disciplinary measures', the Association merely commented that any offences under law 12 'are by nature serious offences and therefore carry a significant penalty ... All on-field offences carry fixed penalties'.

The FA also said that, as from 28 May 1998, 'any act, statement, conduct or matter which is discriminatory by reason of sex, sexual orientation, race, nationality, ethnic origin, colour, religion or disability shall constitute behaviour in contravention of [the Rules of the Association]'. Racist behaviour off the field of play is covered by this rule. In response to the suggestion that it 'sets targets to increase the number of black and Asian qualified FA coaches', the Association's Technical Department 'is currently taking this matter forward' and has appointed 'a respected Asian coach under the auspices of the Asians in Football Working Party'. Its adoption of a written equal opportunities policy for the recruitment and treatment of all staff is particularly welcome, as is the fact that it has requested the county associations to take it on board, too. The vexed question of racism awareness training for stewards as part of 'a mandatory NVQ or similar qualification' is presently under discussion by the FA and other governing bodies, in conjunction with the Football Licensing Authority and the Football Safety Officers' Association.

While only time will tell whether these initiatives have the effect of challenging discriminatory behaviour within the game, the fact that the FA has at least responded positively to the Taskforce's recommendations is certainly to be welcomed, but the fact remains that its response to *Hussaney* was lamentably inadequate.

The Football League

Unfortunately, the League has been less proactive to date. In its response to the Minster, it contented itself with saying that the recommendations of the Taskforce had been passed on to the clubs 'via the League's guidance note', which is no more than a synopsis of the Taskforce's recommendations insofar as they apply to the clubs. The following recommendations as to action that clubs should take are all mentioned in this 'guidance note': ensure that teams from all sections of the community are regularly watched; set up confidential 'hotlines' so fans can report incidents; adopt written equal opportunities policies; form partnerships with relevant local organisations; and devise more innovative ticketing policies. But there is no indication of how the League intends to put pressure on the clubs to comply; this is probably an area where any 'Ombudsfan' will have to be particularly proactive.

For there is strong evidence that many clubs pay mere lip service to anti-racism initiatives and to their obligations to be equal opportunities employers. Clubs' active involvement in the Kick-It campaign is largely confined to the Football in the Community office. In the light of all the circumstances, suggesting that clubs should be left to their own devices to deal with employees' legitimate concerns does not strike one as a credible option. When dealing with cases of alleged discrimination, employment tribunals *will* be more sympathetic towards an employer who has a written and properly implemented equal opportunities policy, but this is not something that clubs seem willing to introduce voluntarily.

Hussaney v Chester City FC (1997) confirms (not that there was any doubt) that racism in football is at least as virulent in the bootroom and the boardroom as it is on the terraces. The FA's unwillingness to intervene in *Hussaney* was unforgivable and undermines any exhortations that it might make about its desire to challenge racism within the game.

THE KICK-IT CAMPAIGN

Throughout its report, the Taskforce commented favourably on the work of Kick it Out, a body which was initially funded by the CRE and various organisations within the game and which has specific responsibility for challenging racist practices. In particular, the Taskforce drew attention to its campaign, 'Kick Racism Out of Football' ('Kick-It'). This had initially been launched by the Commission for Racial Equality and the Professional Footballers' Association (PFA) in August 1993, and provided the impetus for the establishment of the independent body, Kick it Out. Although there had been anti-racism initiatives in the game before (which had mostly been instigated by the fans themselves), Kick-It was the first campaign to get the backing of the PFA, the FA and most of the clubs. Kick it subsequently developed as an independent organisation and does outreach work with clubs, local authorities, ethnic minority communities and supporters' groups. It does a lot of good work and merits more support from the game's higher echelons than it actually receives.

At the time of its launch, every professional club except York City voiced their support for Kick-It. Approximately 75% of the clubs agreed to display anti-racist posters at their ground and to print a joint statement from the PFA Chief Executive and the Chairman of the CRE in their match day programmes. That statement condemned both those who are responsible for racist behaviour at football grounds and those who condone it by doing or saying nothing.

The Kick-It campaign also called upon clubs to take the following steps to help tackle racism:

- issue a statement saying that the club will not tolerate racism, spelling out the action it will take against those engaged in indecent or racist chanting. The statement should be printed in all match programmes and displayed permanently and prominently around the ground;

- make PA announcements condemning racist chanting at matches;

- make it a condition for season ticket holders that they do not take part in this or other forms of offensive behaviour;

- take action to prevent the sale of racist literature inside and around the ground;

- take disciplinary action against players who engage in racial abuse;

- contact other clubs to make sure that they understand the club's policy on racism;

- encourage a common strategy between stewards and police for dealing with abusive behaviour;

- remove all racist graffiti from the ground as a matter of urgency;

- adopt an equal opportunities policy in relation to employment and service provision.

However, anyone who regularly travels to watch football matches at different grounds will be aware of the wide differences in clubs' support for Kick-It. Some clubs undoubtedly do more than others, and regular attenders will be aware that clubs who use perimeter adverts or PA announcements to show their support for Kick-It have always been the exception, rather than the norm. The research that is discussed here was carried out in order to document the level of support that Kick-It was enjoying in 1996/97, four seasons after its introduction.

This survey was particularly concerned with the extent to which the clubs that had agreed to support 'Kick-It' had implemented three specific anti-racism strategies which required little or no expenditure on their part. As outlined above, clubs have been asked to issue a statement that the club will not tolerate racism, spelling out the action that it will take against those engaged in indecent or racist chanting. The clubs had been asked to print this statement in their match programmes, display it permanently and prominently around the ground and make PA announcements condemning racist chanting at matches.

Given that many clubs had developed anti-racism initiatives of their own that went beyond what Kick-It had asked them to do, the survey also gave clubs the opportunity to talk about their own efforts. In addition, at least one club had introduced a telephone 'hotline' which fans could use to report instances of racist behaviour. This research sought to ascertain whether other clubs intended to follow suit.

On 11 June 1997, a questionnaire (see below, Appendix 1) was sent to the chairmen of the 91 clubs which had played in the Premier League or the Football League in 1996/97 *and* which would be playing in one of those leagues in 1997/98. Clubs were invited to make comments about their own anti-racism initiatives, were asked for their opinions on hotlines and were invited to indicate whether they had implemented the Kick-It campaign's three low cost strategies with which this research was primarily concerned. By the end of July 1997, and following the despatch of a 'reminder' letter, a total of 65 clubs had responded, giving a participation rate of 71%. The most pertinent aspects of that survey are summarised here. (For a more detailed analysis, see below, Appendix 1.)

The extent of respondent clubs' participation in Kick-It

Of those 65 respondents, 16 had played in the Premier League in 1996/97 (80% of clubs in that league), 18 in the First Division (75%), 16 in the Second Division (67%) and 15 in the Third (65%). Sixty of the 65 clubs that responded (92% of all participants) stated that they had implemented, in whole or in part, the low cost anti-racism strategies in accordance with the commitment that they made to the campaign in August 1994. However, of those 65 clubs, only 10 had implemented all three aspects – the programme statements, the perimeter adverts and the PA announcements. Twenty one had introduced two of the three, and 29 had introduced one. Five respondents had not implemented any of the three elements.

Given that 75% of all league clubs had pledged their support for the Kick-It campaign back in August 1993, it was disappointing that only 10 used all three of the Kick-It strategies in 1996/97. Very few Premiership or other 'big name' clubs were leading the way in this respect. With two exceptions, the clubs implementing all three strategies were in the First and Second Divisions and had average gates of between 6,000 and 12,000. The two exceptions were Premier League clubs based in London. In all, five out of the 10 clubs using all three strategies came from London. Of the other five, only one could be considered to be based in a multi-racial community, and none could be regarded as a 'big club'.

Twenty one clubs had introduced two elements. They were all using programme inserts, but 17 (82% of this group) used them in conjunction with PA announcements and four (18%) used them in conjunction with perimeter advertising. Of the 29 clubs that had introduced one element, 27 had chosen 'inserts in match day programme' as their sole way of supporting Kick-It. The other two used PA announcements alone.

Anti-racism 'hotlines'

The decision to look at 'hotlines' in the context of football stemmed from research into the use of hotlines in other industries – especially the health service and local government – and trade unions (Lewis and McArdle, 1997). As mentioned above, in the course of attending a number of games in 1996/97, it had become apparent that one lower division club had a 'hotline'. Although their use has since been supported by the Taskforce, when this research was carried out, there was no firm idea of how many others existed or whether clubs were considering introducing them. They were not something that the clubs had been asked to consider introducing as part of their support for the Kick-It campaign.

It transpired that two clubs had operated hotlines in the 1996/97 season and four clubs said that they were seriously considering introducing one. Of the two already possessing such a system, one was a Second Division side in the West Midlands and the other was a First Division London club. Of the others, 33 clubs said that they did not believe that 'hotlines' were necessary at their ground because they either had no history of racial abuse or believed that their existing methods of enabling fans to complain about abusive behaviour were adequate. Sixteen clubs did not give reasons for not introducing a hotline; two cited lack of resources; and two said that it was something they would look at again when their new ground was complete. Six clubs were interested in the concept of 'hotlines' but felt that they needed more information about their cost and effectiveness before deciding whether to introduce one.

The London side had introduced their hotline at the beginning of the 1996/97 season and its existence was made known to fans by way of a message in the match day programme and other club literature. The hotline number was manned during office hours only and was reached through the internal switchboard. The club said that it had been used more than a dozen times during the season and some fans had been informally warned about their future behaviour.

The West Midlands club had introduced its hotline after the start of the 1996/97 season. Fans could similarly telephone the club's main switchboard during office hours and be asked to put through to a named individual. The club used a number of means to advertise its existence – PA announcements, messages in the programme, adverts in the local newspaper and perimeter advertising. By the end of the season, this hotline had been used by fans on between three and six occasions. As a result of those calls, some fans had been informally warned as to their future behaviour, while others had been permanently banned from the ground and/or reported to the police. Both clubs kept their hotlines in 1997/98 and, it seems, still have them.

Although both of those sides are 'big city' clubs, neither would be regarded as being a 'big club' in terms of history or present league position. However, both have had high profile problems with racism in the recent past – one of them being particularly notorious for the ease with which it has been possible to buy far-Right publications within the environs of the ground on match days. Similarly, the four clubs that intended to introduce hotlines in the 1997/98 season are all based in cities with large black and Asian populations, and two of them were notorious hotbeds of racism and hooliganism in the 1970s and 1980s.

Of the 65 clubs surveyed, 27 (41%) said that they used other methods of discouraging racially abusive behaviour, either in addition to or instead of hotlines or the campaign's three strategies. However, 16 could do no more than vaguely identify their 'other means' as using the local media, stewards or displaying posters around the ground. These clubs did not reveal much detail about how those systems operated or whether they considered them to be effective.

The other 11 members of this group have developed sophisticated anti-racism or 'Football in the Community' programmes. The most innovative of these community initiatives rightly received due credit in the Taskforce's report. Some clubs are working closely with the CRE and their local authority. One was the first (and, it seems, is still the only) club to implement a fully comprehensive equal opportunities policy for all its employees. Others have worked closely with their supporters' groups and their respective local authorities to develop anti-racism initiatives that extend beyond football and reach into the wider community.

The innovative taken by a very small number of clubs illustrates the contradiction between the high profile, commercialised, globalised game as played by a handful of élite sides (and to which most others aspire) and the community-oriented, localised arena in which some others see their future. However, most clubs could do a lot more – particularly those that are based within multi-racial communities. In urban areas other than London, the response to the Kick-It campaign from some of the country's biggest clubs is lamentable. Indeed, the efforts of the country's top teams have generally been less than wholehearted. Few élite Premiership sides had decent community initiatives or had shown a willingness to engage in wholehearted support of 'Kick-It'. A club's decision on whether or not to participate actively in the Kick-It campaign depended on whether a chairman, the local authority or other influential individual felt that it was something that the club should get involved in. Geographical location, on-field success, level of support and a history of racism were far less significant than whether individuals within the club were willing to make the effort. Most clubs are doing far less than they agreed to do when they signed up to the Kick-It campaign in 1993, even allowing for the significant minority that have taken the issue seriously and are doing a lot of worthwhile work. While the putative move towards 'Supporters' Trusts' as a means of 'giving a voice' to 'ordinary fans' may have some merit, most of the individuals who will get involved in them – white, middle class professionals who, a decade ago, would probably have gone nowhere near a football ground – are not going to have equal opportunities at the top of their agenda. The FA's anti-discrimination policy (reproduced in Football Taskforce, 1998, p 53) falls short of what is needed, not least because it does not commit signatories to taking effective disciplinary action against players or managers who engage in racist behaviour. The following may help to fill the gap.

CONCLUSION: A DRAFT EQUAL OPPORTUNITIES CODE OF PRACTICE FOR FOOTBALL CLUBS

(a) Equal opportunities policies

- In order to demonstrate their commitment to equal opportunities, clubs should have a written policy document and should establish monitoring mechanisms which ensure that the policy is implemented across the board.
- The policy document should be widely distributed and publicised. For example, it could be reproduced (wholly or in part) in match programmes.
- The equal opportunities policy should be consistently applied to:
  o the recruitment of managers, players, stewards and other staff (whether employed, self-employed or agency workers);
  o their terms and conditions (in relation to training and promotion, as well as pay, holidays, sickness and pension arrangements, etc);
  o their discipline and dismissal.

- All staff should be encouraged to report breaches of the club's equal opportunities policy. They should be told how to report concerns and be given a written assurance that they will not be victimised for doing so.

- Clubs would have an obligation to act upon any information received about breaches of the equal opportunities policy. This may require an investigation and disciplinary action, where appropriate.

(b) Training

Clubs should pay particular attention to the training of players, stewards and other staff in equal opportunities matters. For example, it should be made clear that:

- racism includes discrimination on the grounds of nationality, ethnic and national origins and religious beliefs, as well as colour;

- racist incidents will be systematically recorded and dealt with firmly;

- a failure to adhere to or enforce the club's equal opportunity policy will be treated as a breach of discipline.

(c) Public statements on racist behaviour

- Clubs should also issue a public statement to the effect that people will only be admitted to their ground on condition that they refrain from racist behaviour.

- As with the club's equal opportunities policy, the public statement should be widely addressed and publicised. For example, tickets, the PA system and posters inside and outside the ground (in addition to posters detailing ground regulations) could all be used to draw attention to the entry condition.

- Clubs should establish a means by which members of the public can report their concerns about racism at matches, for example, by setting up a telephone hotline. In order to encourage its use, the hotline should be free to the user and, most importantly, confidential. Resources would need to be devoted to publicising and staffing the hotline, investigating the concerns, taking action where appropriate and reporting back to the informant (and possibly the police). In order to show their support, the FA or the Football League should be willing to make these resources available.

- If racist behaviour is established, a club must be prepared to impose sanctions, even when this goes against its interests, for example, by disciplining staff members (including players and managers) or prohibiting offending spectators from attending future matches.

CHAPTER 7

SEX DISCRIMINATION, EMPLOYMENT LAW AND THE PROFESSIONAL GAME

INTRODUCTION

The legislation that seeks to limit an employer's power to discriminate on the basis of sex or ethnicity has existed for nearly 30 years. The passing of the Sex Discrimination Act 1975 and the Race Relations Act 1976 (hereafter the 1975 Act and the 1976 Act respectively) had been necessary to ensure Britain's accession to the European Economic Community, but their enactment had not been without legal or political controversy. The Acts represented a departure from the common law position, under which an individual was entitled to enter, or not enter, into contractual relations with whomever he or she wanted, on whatever terms the parties agreed, and the terms of their contract were sacrosanct. As Lord Davey had put it in *Allen v Flood* (1898):

> ... an employer may ... refuse to employ a man from the most mistaken, capricious, malicious or morally reprehensible motives that can be conceived, but the workman has no right of action against him.

It was not for the law to enquire into the motives behind one person's refusal to contract with another, and it was certainly not the law's role to interfere with the agreed terms and conditions of it.

This purpose of this chapter is to consider how the 1975 and 1976 Acts have impacted upon discriminatory employment practices within sport in general, and within football in particular. It does not consider recent anti-racism laws or other initiatives which are football-specific. These have been dealt with exhaustively by other writers (see, for example, Giulianotti, 1994; Garland and Rowe, 2000; Osborn and Greenfield,1998) and there is little that one can usefully add to their endeavours, although Chapters 6 and 11 of this book do contain some thoughts on 'Kick-It' and the relevant work of the Football Taskforce. Instead, this chapter concentrates on a number of recent and relevant discrimination cases which merit greater consideration than they have received hitherto. Particular attention is given to those cases in which sex discrimination was established but the organisations responsible argued that their discriminatory behaviour was still lawful because Parliament had specifically exempted sex discrimination in sport from the provisions of the 1975 Act. In other words, sports bodies were arguing in these cases that the law allowed them to adopt discriminatory practices that would be unacceptable in virtually every other area of employment.

Those defendants' arguments have been based on the provisions of s 44 of the 1975 Act, the details of which are considered below. However, analysis of the relevant case law shows that the courts and (more frequently) the employment tribunals have consistently interpreted s 44 as narrowly as possible. By doing so, they have denied discriminating sports organisations a legal escape route that Parliament could have left open to them. Section 44 certainly limits the rights of women in sport so far as participation is concerned, but to far less an extent than might have been the case.

A BRIEF OVERVIEW OF ANTI-DISCRIMINATION LAW

The 1975 and 1976 Acts were the product of a Government-sponsored Report into anti-discrimination legislation in other jurisdictions (Street Report, 1967). From the early 1960s, successive governments had taken steps towards joining the European Economic Community (now the European Community (EC)) and the authors of the Report were charged with devising anti-discrimination legislation that conformed with the fundamental requirements of EC law. The Report drew heavily on US anti-discrimination laws and recommended the establishment of an Equal Opportunities Commission (EOC) and a Commission for Racial Equality (CRE) to carry out certain advisory and education services. It recommended that these organisations should also be given responsibility for monitoring the activities of institutions, firms or industries whose practices gave cause for concern, and that individuals should have the right to take their complaints straight to an industrial (now employment) tribunal, if they elected to do so. Accordingly, the cases that are discussed here were all precipitated by a complaint from the individual concerned, although all were acting with the support of either the EOC or the CRE.

Under the 1975 Act, discrimination may be either direct or indirect in form. Direct sex discrimination consists of treating an individual less favourably than an individual of the other sex would be treated, and, if discriminatory treatment has been established, there is no defence – unless, within the context of sport, a s 44 defence can be made out. Certainly, it is no defence for an employer to argue there was no malice or deliberate prejudice behind the discriminatory conduct (*James v Eastleigh BC* (1991)). Indirect discrimination arises when employers impose requirements or conditions which seem to be applied equally to both sexes, but which actually result in members of one sex being less likely to be able to comply with it. Indirect discrimination *can* be justified, although the domestic courts and the European Court of Justice are both wary of 'objective justification' defences (*Jenkins v Kingsgate (Clothing Productions) Ltd* (1981); *Bilka-Kaufhaus GmbH v Weber von Harz* (1986); see, also, Hervey, 1991).

Direct discrimination

Section 1 of the 1975 Act provides:

(1) A person discriminates against a woman in any circumstances relevant for the purposes of this Act if –

    (a) on the grounds of her sex he treats her less favourably than he treats or would treat a man; or

    (b) he applies to her a requirement or condition which he applies or would apply equally to a man but –

        (i) which is such that the proportion of women who can comply with it is considerably smaller than the proportion of men who can comply with it; and

        (ii) which he cannot show to be justifiable irrespective of the sex of the person to whom it is applied; and

        (iii) which is to her detriment because she cannot comply with it.

The most straightforward examples of direct discrimination concern the use of racist or sexist language in the workplace, as peddled by the second defendant in *Hussaney v Chester City FC* (1997), but direct discrimination law covers far more than the use of hate speech by an intellectually challenged employer. It seeks to prevent employers from relying on stereotypes of sex or race by rendering unlawful any decisions that emanate from an employer's reliance on them. This means that it would be direct discrimination for an employer to refuse to interview any woman who applied for a job that required heavy lifting (for instance, bar staff or fitness instructors), by adopting the attitude that 'women are the weaker sex and I won't consider employing one'. The employer *can* reject the application of any woman who simply does not have the physical strength required for the task, just as he could reject a man for the same reason, but he has to consider the individual, not the stereotype.

A discriminatory act that resulted from an employer's introduction of 'quotas' or 'affirmative action' programmes would similarly be unlawful, even if their motives for introducing them were ostensibly laudable (Potter and Regan, 1997). However, EC law now provides for the possible introduction of positive discrimination by Member States – an important development, considered at length below, Chapter 8. At the moment, recruiting a woman or a person from a particular ethnic group – for example, in an effort to ensure that the composition of a leisure centre's workforce reflects that of the broader community – would be direct discrimination against male applicants or those from other ethnic groups. Employers have to tread a fine line between encouraging applications from underrepresented communities and engaging in unlawful discrimination. The 1975 Act does not prevent the adoption of measures that do not involve preferential treatment but which aim to encourage a greater degree of equality of opportunity – these are acceptable.

Incidentally, evidence that a firm has monitored its recruitment patterns and has taken positive steps to remove barriers to the recruitment of women and ethnic minorities is invaluable evidence in a discrimination case, and the EOC and CRE encourage their use by employers.

The effect of direct discrimination law on sports employers is best illustrated by consideration of the landmark judgment in *James v Eastleigh BC* (1991). The council allowed free admission to its swimming pools for women over the age of 60 and men over 65, and a 63 year old male argued that this policy amounted to direct discrimination on the ground of his sex. The policy should have been scrapped when the Sex Discrimination Act 1986 (which sought to ensure that English law was in line with EC law) came into force on 7 November 1987, after which it became illegal to have different retirement ages for women and men.

Indirect discrimination

The provisions on indirect discrimination were incorporated into the 1975 Act following the US Supreme Court's decision in *Griggs v Duke Power Company* (1971) on the illegality of rules that are equally applied to both sexes but which have an unequal effect on one of them. Ironically, the Act then became law just before the Supreme Court ruled, in *Washington v Davis* (1976), that, under the equal protection clause (as distinct from the employment provisions of the Civil Rights Act 1964), a plaintiff (now claimant) had to show a discriminatory purpose on the part of the defendant. However, the 1975 Act was not amended in the wake of this decision, and proving a discriminatory *animus* is not necessary under either domestic or EC law. Under s 1(1)(b), it is enough for the claimant to show the existence of a *requirement or condition* that is applied equally to all, but that the *proportion* of members of one sex who can comply with it is smaller than the proportion of members of the other. In addition, the fact that the applicant cannot comply with that requirement or condition must be *to his or her detriment*. As mentioned above, it is a defence for the employer to show 'objective justification' – that is, that their reasonable needs justified the application of the discriminatory provision.

DIRECT DISCRIMINATION IN NON-COMPETITIVE SPORTS EMPLOYMENT

The cases that have concerned direct discrimination in sport are *Bennett v FA* (1978); *Greater London Council v Farrer* (1980); *British Judo Association v Petty* (1981); *Hardwick v FA* (1997); and *Couch v British Boxing Board of Control* (1998).

Bennett and *Couch* concern women's rights to participate in sport as competitors and establish the limits of s 44. The other cases concerned women whose participation was not competitive. They establish that s 44 is of no relevance in such circumstances.

Section 44 of the 1975 Act provides that:

> Nothing in Pts II to IV [of the Act] shall, in relation to any sport, game or other activity of a competitive nature where the physical strength, stamina or physique of the average woman puts her at a disadvantage to the average man, render unlawful any act related to the participation of a person as a competitor in events involving that activity which are confined to competitors of one sex.

Section 44 was discussed in *Greater London Council v Farrer* (1980), although it did not prove central to the ruling in that case. It concerned a decision by the council to issue entertainment licences to certain premises on which their owners wished to hold wrestling bouts. The council would only issue licences on the condition that female wrestlers were not allowed to compete, regardless of whether they wrestled against men or against other women. A female wrestler who was denied the opportunity to compete as a consequence of that policy sought a declaration from the industrial tribunal that the council had acted unlawfully by aiding an employer (namely, the bout's promoter) to discriminate against her on the ground of her sex. The council contended that her application should be refused, arguing that the London Government Act 1963 allowed it to impose such conditions when granting licences and that s 51 of the 1975 Act permitted discrimination that was necessary to ensure compliance with earlier legislation. The council also mounted a s 44 defence almost as an afterthought, in case its first line of argument failed.

The industrial tribunal upheld the ban on s 51 grounds, and that decision was upheld on appeal. However, in the Employment Appeal Tribunal, Slynn J said, *obiter*, that the way in which s 44 had been drafted meant that it could never be applicable to sporting events in which all the competitors were female. Its ambit was limited to situations in which it was proposed that women and men should take part in the same event:

> It does not seem to us that this section is dealing with the situation where it is desired that a girl should play a game against a girl, or where teams of girls should play other teams of girls [*Greater London Council v Farrer* (1980), p 272].

Since *Greater London Council,* the scope of s 51 has been significantly restricted and the defence which the council successfully relied upon in that case is no longer available. Section 51 gave a blanket exemption for discriminatory acts that were necessary to comply with a statute that had come into force before the 1975 Act received royal assent. This was deemed necessary in order to avoid conflict with the provisions of the Factories Act 1961 and other industrial safety legislation that gave special protection to women (for example, by restricting night working or the number of hours that they could work in a factory). Many of those restrictions contravened the Equal Treatment Directive (76/207/EC) and were removed by the Sex Discrimination Act 1986. Section 3(3) of the Employment Act 1989 further restricted its scope after the European Commission expressed the opinion that the amended s 51 still contravened the Directive.

The brief consideration of s 44 in *Greater London Council* was expanded upon in *British Judo Association v Petty* (1981). A woman who was a qualified coach and referee was banned from refereeing men's national level tournaments, which were far more remunerative for referees than lower level tournaments. The Association argued that Petty would lack the physical strength to intervene and separate the competitors, should the need to do so arise. It also argued that the élite-level males had made it clear that they did not want a woman referee under any circumstances. It supported the men's stance and argued that s 44 allowed them to ban Petty from officiating if they wanted to, regardless of their motives for doing so.

The tribunal ruled that the Association's conduct contravened the 1975 Act. It approved of Slynn J's *dictum* in *Greater London Council* and went on to affirm that referees were not 'participants' for the purposes of s 44. Accordingly, they were entitled to the full protection of the anti-discrimination laws:

> We think that the words [of s 44] should be given their obvious meaning and not extended so as to cover any discrimination other than provisions designed to regulate who is to take part in the contest as a competitor [*British Judo Association v Petty* (1981), p 666, *per* Browne-Wilkinson J].

DISCRIMINATION IN COMPETITIVE SPORTS EMPLOYMENT

British Judo Association established the inapplicability of s 44 in the context of women who work in non-playing capacities within sport. *Bennett* and the recent decision in *Couch* (1998) establish that the section does have relevance to the legal position of women who actually *compete*, but that its application is restricted to very specific circumstances. Indeed, *Bennett* is the only case where a s 44 defence has been successful.

In *Bennett*, a schoolgirl (aged 11 at the time of the hearing) who played football with the boys at school wanted to join a boys' side that played in a local league. The rules of both the regional football association and the national governing body did not permit mixed teams in league competition, so they banned her from playing for the boys' side. The ban was upheld at first instance and Theresa Bennett appealed. The Court of Appeal heard medical evidence that the strength, stamina and physique of pre-pubescent girls is not markedly different to that of pre-pubescent boys (see Dyer, 1992), and that there are at least as many physiological differences within the sexes as there are between them. However, while accepting that the main purpose of the 1975 Act was to prevent the application of sex-based stereotypical assumptions, the Court of Appeal ruled that s 44 had been drafted in a way that obliged it to take these very stereotypes into account. Football was a sport in which the strength of the *average* woman put her at a disadvantage to the *average* man and Bennett's individual attributes could not be taken into account. Neither could s 44 be interpreted as meaning that the court should consider the attributes of the 'average female' at 11 years of age.

Lord Denning MR accepted that Bennett 'used to run rings around the boys' and said that, without the existence of s 44, the county football association would have had no defence to her claim. However, 'the average woman is at a disadvantage to the average man because [the average woman] has not got the physique to stand up to [the rigours of mixed football]'. The court sympathised, but allowing Bennett to play would require it to stretch the bounds of judicial creativity beyond breaking point.

Given the spectacular growth of women's soccer in the UK over the past decade, a latter day Theresa Bennett would have little difficulty finding a team. Mixed sex soccer up to the age of 12 is commonplace. Thereafter, girls can play for under 14s, under 16s and under 18s teams before moving on to adult women's teams. However, this was certainly not the case in the mid-1970s. Yet, s 44 established that the extent to which sports bodies can discriminate is actually very limited. *Couch v British Boxing Board of Control* (1998) illustrates that s 44 is limited to situations where a woman wants to compete against men. If she seeks to compete only against other women, the section is irrelevant.

Couch needs to be considered in conjunction with *Hardwick v FA* (1997). It is not a 'football case', but, when taken together, the two cases illustrate the consequences of conservatism and prejudice within sport's governing bodies. The applicant was, at all material times, the holder of the World Women's Welterweight title. She had successfully defended her title in the US on two occasions in 1997, but the British Boxing Board of Control had refused her application for a professional boxer's licence, which she needed in order to box professionally in the UK. Indeed, the Board had never granted a licence to any female boxer. Couch argued that the Board had failed to give proper consideration to her application and had, therefore, contravened the provisions of s 13 of the 1975 Act (which prohibits discriminatory treatment by a qualifying body).

At the tribunal hearing, John Morris, the Secretary General of the Board, stated that 'the British Board is very definitely not in favour of women's boxing at this time', adding that the particular dangers that boxing posed to women's health was the sole reason for its stance. He confirmed that the

Board had not even considered Couch's application because it was not willing to take any steps that could be seen as encouraging the spread of women's boxing. In defending its position, the Board argued that s 44 meant that its action was entirely lawful, regardless of the merits of the rationale behind it.

The Board purported to rely on numerous medical arguments in support of its contention that boxing posed special dangers to women. In its notice of appearance, it claimed that there was medical evidence that, *inter alia*:

- hormonal changes occurring monthly can result in increased fluid retention prior to a period and that can result in a weight gain of anything up to 4–6 lbs. This raises the difficulty of weight categories. Under no circumstances can any artificial means of weight reduction be adopted;

- unfortunately, many women suffer-pre menstrual tension, when they are more prone to accidents. They are emotionally more labile and this may also have relevance to a boxer's performance and tendency to injury;

- dysmenorrhoea (painful periods) is not an uncommon occurrence and is treated with powerful painkillers. This would not be allowed in professional boxing;

- the taking of contraceptive pills to prevent pregnancy or to delay or avoid periods are strictly contra-indicated in professional boxing, as no drugs or medication whatsoever are allowed (*Couch*).

Unfortunately for the Board, in *James v Eastleigh BC* (1991), the House of Lords had already established that neither chivalry nor paternalism justifies sex discrimination. Even if there were any truth to the medical arguments, a desire to protect women from the consequences of an informed choice about consent and the voluntary assumption of risk provided no defence to a discrimination claim. In any event, the tribunal decided that the medical evidence was just a smokescreen for the Board to hide its double standards behind. It accepted that some of the rules of boxing pertaining to weight categories banned substances and clothing might have to be changed for the purposes of women's boxing. However, those issues had already been dealt with in those countries where women's boxing was more widely accepted, which included the US, Denmark, Germany, Belgium, Holland and Hungary. The inconvenience to a governing body of having to change its rules was no reason for allowing it to flout the law of the land:

> The Board has no medical evidence that it is more dangerous for women to box than men, or indeed vice versa ... Her application was rejected allegedly on medical grounds, although she was never medically examined. The real reason for her refusal was on the ground of sex ... The 'medical grounds' are all gender-based stereotypical assumptions [and are] not capable of amounting to valid defences to a claim of discrimination [*Couch v British Boxing Board of Control* (1998), p 2].

The failure to give Couch a medical also amounted to discriminatory treatment on the basis of her sex, because even the most hapless male applicant for a boxer's licence would have been given the medical.

So far as the Board's mounting of a s 44 defence was concerned, the tribunal confirmed that s 44 'can only be relied upon where a female, if allowed to participate, would be involved in a game or sport where the other players were male; for example, a woman wanting to join a men's football or rugby team'. Couch was not seeking to fight against other men. The tribunal concluded by saying that it was 'difficult to recall a more outrageous defence being proffered in a sex discrimination case'. In September 1998, three months after the judgment, Jane Couch was granted a licence to box in the UK. She fought in south London, with little fuss, in November 1998 and is still World Champion.

THE *HARDWICK* CASE

The scope of s 44, as established by the whole series of cases from *Bennett* to *Couch*, should be enough to make British sports organisations aware of their obligations under the 1975 Act. *Hardwick v FA* (1997) shows that there is still a long way to go before professional football's governing body can claim to be an equal opportunities organisation. Vanessa Hardwick was a schoolteacher who taught soccer to 12–16 year old girls, coached women's teams in her spare time and held an intermediate coaching licence, awarded by the FA (the domestic game's governing body). In the summer of 1996, she participated in the FA's advance coaching licence course, in an attempt to get the highest qualification available, but at the conclusion of the course she was deemed to have failed. She claimed that the manner in which she had been treated on the course and the decision to fail her amounted to direct discrimination under s 1(1)(a) of the 1975 Act. She also claimed that her treatment amounted to discrimination by a body that awarded qualifications, contrary to s 13(1)(b) of the 1975 Act, and discrimination by a body that provided vocational training, contrary to s 14(1)(d). The FA claimed that its coaching courses were open to men and women equally, and that Hardwick was treated no differently to how a male candidate with the same marks would have been treated.

To refute this, Hardwick told of her experience in the final and most important aspect of the course, in which candidates who had performed relatively poorly in the earlier parts could still pass if they performed particularly well. This aspect involved coaching a full 11 vs 11 match on a full size pitch and being assessed on the way in which the candidate coached the players in that situation. The first three parts of the course had taken up the first half of the two week course, but the whole of the second week was devoted to the final exercise. There were 72 candidates on the course and, because each match was of 90 minutes' duration, it took four days to complete this part. The candidates knew that the most successful of them (that is, those with fewest failures in the first three parts of the test) would sit the fourth part on the first or second days, while the least successful would have to wait until the end. In percentage terms, only 14% of candidates who had taken the 11 vs 11 test on the first day of the second week had ever failed the course. Of those who had taken the test on the second, third and fourth days, the daily failure rates were 33%, 50% and 64% respectively. The industrial tribunal said that this daily increase in the failure rate was irrefutable evidence that the later one took this test, the more likely one was to fail it:

> We are satisfied that the order of appearance was important and represented a clear indicator as to the coaches' expectations about who would pass and who would fail.

Although Hardwick had failed some aspects of one of the first three tests, her results from other two had been among the best of the 72 candidates – good enough to mean that, had the usual criterion been applied, she would have done the 11 vs 11 test on the second day. In fact, she did not do the test until the final afternoon, and was actually the penultimate candidate.

Hardwick failed some aspects of the 11 vs 11 (partly because she had acted on bad advice from her supervisor, according to the tribunal), so, at the end of the course, she had no failures in two of the parts but a number of failures in the other two. According to two of the coaches on the course, these results placed her in the 'borderline' category and her performance should have been given careful consideration at the formal assessment meeting held at the end of the course, where a final decision on all the candidates was made. This did not happen. Discussion of Hardwick's performance was limited to a rubber stamping of the head coach's decision to fail her. She argued that both the decision to make her wait until the final afternoon rather than follow the normal procedure and the failure to consider her results properly had been motivated by reason of her sex.

Hardwick obtained evidence that, out of over 140 men who had participated on advanced certificate courses in the spring of 1995 and 1996, nine of them had passed the course despite having worse results than her. The FA's technical co-ordinator explained that this discrepancy was due to the fact that, since 1994, the assessment criteria for the spring and summer courses had been different. He freely admitted that the effect of the different criteria was that one was more likely to gain the most prestigious soccer coaching qualification in the country if one attended the spring course than if one attended the summer course.

The spring course was particularly popular among ageing professional players, while the summer course (held during the school holiday) was dominated by teachers – a highly significant piece of evidence, and one that was not lost on the industrial tribunal. The existence of different criteria enhanced the employment prospects of retired professional soccer players at the expense of the humble teacher, but the different criteria were not revealed to those who applied for places on the summer course:

> This explains how [nine players who had attended courses in the spring] were accorded passes and Hardwick, with much better marks overall, had failed ... If the spring criteria had been applied to the summer course, she would have passed notwithstanding her failures at the 11 vs 11 [*Hardwick v FA* (1997), p 11].

The FA compounded its error by arguing, ridiculously, that Hardwick had failed, not because she was a woman, but because she had done the wrong course: if she had attended the spring course she would certainly have passed, they said. Effectively, the game's governing body was arguing that it was merely guilty of duplicity in offering preferential treatment to professional players rather than being guilty of sex discrimination. Indeed, the FA's director of coaching asserted that 'the fact that candidates passed in spring with inferior marks to the applicant was due to misdirection and mismanagement within our coaching scheme. It had absolutely nothing to do with sex discrimination'.

Be that as it may, Hardwick had shown that she had been treated less favourably than the nine men who had passed the spring course despite having worse grades than hers. This meant that the defendants had to prove that, on the balance of probabilities, the differences in her treatment had been for reasons other than sex, and that this was indirect discrimination which was objectively justifiable. The FA failed to discharge this burden. It was unable to rebut Hardwick's assertion that her 11 vs 11 test had taken place on the last day for no reason other than the fact that she was a woman. Neither could it convince the tribunal that a male candidate with the same results would have failed without the matter being properly considered at the final assessment meeting.

Another important aspect was whether it was permissible to compare Hardwick's marks with those of male candidates who had attended a spring course, or whether comparisons could only be made with men who had also participated on the same course as her. The law provides that a comparison 'must be such that the relevant circumstances in the one case are the same, or not materially different, in the other' (s 5(3) of the 1975 Act). The FA had wanted to compare Hardwick with a candidate on the same course who had achieved very similar results and who had also failed. However, the tribunal held that the two courses were substantially the same and the choice of comparator was Hardwick's alone, in accordance with *Bullock v Alice Ottley School* (1991). She was awarded a total of £5,000 to compensate her for injury to her feelings.

Although not a case in which s 44 was relevant, the recent case of *Cummins v Kingstonian FC* (1998) is worthy of note. *Cummins* concerned a sex discrimination claim by a woman who had commenced employment as an office administrator with the club in August 1997, initially on a two month trial period. She worked under the supervision of two permanent members of staff and assisted a number of voluntary workers who helped out at the club in various capacities. Kingstonian play in the Premier Division of the ICIS League and, as the tribunal chairman noted, they are 'a typical football club in the league to which it belongs', in that they depend on volunteer workers 'to oil the works of the machine'. In June 1999, Hardwick was awarded £16,000 compensation. The tribunal also ruled that the FA should present her with her advance coaching licence within 28 days ((1999) *The Guardian*, 29 June, p 5).

The case arose out of alleged instances of sexual harassment by the club's finance director, who was one of the club's volunteer workers. The applicant gave evidence that the individual concerned had 'made verbal approaches towards her and on one occasion simply put his arm around her in a fashion which she found to be unacceptable'. She had informally discussed the matter with a friend and another volunteer worker, and was dismissed within a couple of days of mentioning the matter to the other volunteer. She claimed that her treatment contravened the terms of the 1975 Act, s 1 of which states that sexual harassment amounts to discriminatory behaviour on the grounds of sex. She also alleged that the club had contravened s 4 of the Act by victimising her through dismissal once she had made an allegation of harassment.

In response, the club made 'a blanket denial of all the applicant's main allegations'. It asserted that she had 'become extremely emotional and had appeared to overreact in an uncontrolled fashion' over the death of the Princess of Wales and said that the Chief Executive had decided to dismiss her on the ground that the standard of her typing was unsatisfactory. He had not discussed the possibility of dismissing her with the other employee or with any of the volunteer workers. However, there had still been three weeks left of the applicant's two month trial period when she was dismissed. While the tribunal accepted that there was certainly room for improvement so far as her typing was concerned, 'this is just the sort of thing that can easily be dealt with by a firm oral or written warning if it is a matter of concern'. It did not amount to grounds for dismissing the applicant three weeks before the end of her trial period, especially as she had not even been given an oral or written warning regarding the need to improve beforehand.

The real reason for her dismissal was that, after the volunteer worker had taken the entirely proper step of informing the Chief Executive that the applicant felt that she was being harassed, the Chief Executive had taken a unilateral decision to sack her because she was a troublemaker. Indeed, the club's other permanent and salaried staff member (the finance director) 'only discovered the applicant's departure by chance, he thinking that she had apparently gone on holiday'. The applicant had been the victim of sexual discrimination and had been victimised. Had the matter been dealt with sensibly, 'it might never have been more than a distant memory for any of the parties ... There was no actual physical sexual misbehaviour and, although the language used was unacceptable, it was by no means at the top of the bracket for that type of unacceptable language'. She was awarded £3,500 damages for injury to feelings and compensation for loss of earnings of £7,200.

CONCLUSION

On the basis of these judgments, it seems possible to formulate a three stage test that can be used in order to determine whether sex discrimination is lawful within a particular sports context:

(a) is the applicant seeking to participate in a sport, game or physical activity?;

(b) is she seeking to participate as a *competitor* – as opposed to acting as a coach, referee or in some other capacity?;

(c) is she seeking to compete in the same event as men (that is, by playing with or against them)?

Unless the answer to all three of these questions is 'yes', s 44 will have no application and will not provide a defence against discriminatory treatment. There are no legal grounds for discriminating against women who apply for positions as managers, coaches, stewards or other non-playing roles, because such people are not 'competitors' for the purposes of that section. Employers would be better advised to take adequate steps to safeguard the rights of their employees (and, by doing so, safeguard their own legal position), for the relevant case law has limited the applicability of s 44 to such an extent that it is, effectively, 'dead law'.

The limited scope of s 44 makes it all the more important for sports employers to introduce effective equal opportunities policies. Their existence, and their proper implementation, can help to persuade an employment tribunal that equal opportunities are being taken seriously in the particular workplace. They can also reassure employees that their workplace rights are being respected. Employers can avoid discriminatory practices by giving proper notification of vacancies (something that seems to be an anathema in the nepotistic world of sport) and promotion or training opportunities, and by monitoring their recruitment procedures. Sports bodies still have a long way to go before they can legitimately claim to be equal opportunities employers. *Hardwick* (1997) and *Couch* (1998) mean that the extent of sports bodies' obligations under discrimination law, and the steps they could take to ensure their compliance with them, should be sufficiently clear, both to the bodies themselves and to their legal advisers.

CHAPTER 8

PLAYER VIOLENCE AND INJURIES

INTRODUCTION

This chapter will examine the law that applies when players inflict injury upon each other whilst playing in a football match (for coverage of this area of the law as it applies to all sports, see Gardiner *et al*, 1998). There are no specific 'sports laws' that cover this area. The general law of the land applies to any such incidents. The laws apply whether the game in question is a Sunday league park game or the World Cup Final. All that is required for the law to operate is a non-consensual touching of the opponent. The more serious the injury caused, the more serious the punishment or the higher the award of damages. In this chapter, the main criminal law, compensatory law and some new legal developments with potentially far reaching consequences will be examined. It commences with a theoretical perspective.

SPORTS VIOLENCE, THE 'MANLY VIRTUES' AND THE LAW

The purpose of this part of the chapter is to place the law on violence and consent in football within the context of the House of Lords' decision in *R v Brown* (1992), which determined that one cannot consent to the infliction of injury upon oneself in the course of homosexual, sadomasochistic activities. The decision affords protection from the full rigours of the criminal law for those who commit violent acts on the field of play and highlighted the law's ambivalent approach to sports violence at a time when there was concern about the supposed increase in the use of violence in sport. It raised the fundamental question of whether the courts should intervene at all in the case of injuries inflicted during the course of sporting activities. It also raised concerns in sporting circles that, if injuries inflicted consensually and in private were now unlawful, would injuries inflicted consensually but in public – that is, injuries inflicted on the sports field – be treated any more leniently? Of the two, public violence is far more likely to lead to a breach of the peace, and the question of implied consent to the risk of injury is at least as problematic in a sports context as it was in the peculiar circumstances of *R v Brown*.

In the event, a close reading of the majority judgments averted those fears. Their Lordships' majority decision amounted to little more than an exercise in queerbashing. The persistent use of the word 'victim' in both the Court of Appeal and the House of Lords illustrates the courts' presumption that they were dealing with abusive relationships. 'The use of "victim" could be contrasted with "receiver", which has none of the connotations of lack of consent, misuse, abuse, etc [Moran, 1995].' It indicates the courts' lack of awareness of the realities of sadomasochistic relationships, where the limits of consent are more clearly marked than in sporting contexts and are more stringently adhered to – those who overstep the boundaries quickly discovering that nobody else will play with them anymore (Thompson, 1995).

Brown concerned the appeals against conviction of a group of sadomasochistic homosexuals who, over a 10 year period, had willingly participated in the commission of acts of violence against one another for the sexual pleasure which those individuals gained from the giving and receiving of pain. Lord Lane CJ said in the Court of Appeal that 'it is, unhappily, necessary to go into a little detail' about the men's activities (p 555). Although he delivered a detailed, blow-by-blow account of what occurred, a brief synopsis will suffice for the purposes of this chapter, lest readers' sensibilities be offended. The torments included hitting another man's penis with a ruler while holding his testicles with a spiked glove; the application of stinging nettles to the genitals; the dripping of hot wax into someone's urethra; and multitudinous incidents of branding, hitting, whipping and flogging. Remarkably – but crucially – none of the participants required hospital treatment, nor did they suffer permanent injury; these players were true professionals.

In the course of their investigations into the murder of a teenage prostitute, Jason Swift, in East London, the police had uncovered video recordings of sadomasochistic activities that some of the men had in their possession. The police initially thought that they had stumbled across a 'snuff' video, but quickly realised that the defendants had simply used camcorders and home video apparatus to record their 'happy times', as others might record family weddings or holidays by the sea. Assault charges were proffered against the 10 defendants, most of whom had played a starring role in the production and some of whom – let it not be forgotten – had been, or were subsequently, convicted of sexual offences against children. After viewing the videos, the trial judge ruled that the activities were so violent that a defence of consent to the infliction of the injuries should not be available. Faced with that ruling, the defendants entered guilty pleas in a desperate but futile bid to avoid imprisonment.

The appellants' activities had been conducted in secret. Code words were adopted so that the participants could make it clear if the pain was too much, and the instruments used were sterilised. However, so far as the courts were concerned, the precautions that they had taken paled into insignificance alongside those that they had failed to take. Tellingly, 'there was, of course, no referee present, such as there would be in a boxing or a football match' (*R v Brown* (1993), p 85, *per* Lord Jauncey), which further negated the consent defence. The absence of a referee leaves the violence of sadomasochistic activities unchecked. Blood will flow; 'wounds can easily become septic ... an inflicter who is carried away by sexual excitement or by drink and drugs could easily inflict pain and injury beyond the level to which the receiver consented' (p 91). There was no one who could intervene and save the 'victim' from further punishment. The defendants were convicted of either assault occasioning actual bodily harm, contrary to s 47 of the Offences Against the Person Act 1861, or unlawful wounding, contrary to s 20 of that Act.

The convictions were upheld by the Court of Appeal, which referred the matter to the House of Lords by certifying the following point of law as a matter of general public importance:

> Where A wounds or assaults B, occasioning him actual bodily harm in the course of a sadomasochistic encounter, does the prosecution have to prove lack of consent on the part of B before they can establish A's guilt under [ss 20 and 47 of the 1861 Act]?

By a majority of 3:2 (Lords Mustill and Slynn dissenting), the House of Lords affirmed the decisions of the other courts by answering that question in the negative. The majority felt that 'public policy requires that society be protected against a cult of violence which contains the danger of proselytisation and corruption of young men and the potential for the infliction of serious injury' (p 75).

The judgments indicate that, for public policy reasons, the majority in the House of Lords wanted to proscribe consensual, homosexual, sadomasochistic acts. None of the judges who dealt with the case during the trial or the two appeals missed out on any opportunity to comment upon the homosexuality of the men involved. Those comments ranged from the perceived likelihood of older gay men corrupting younger men (*per* Lord Lane in the Court of Appeal, p 560) to the inevitable, ill-informed comments about sadomasochism and AIDS (Lord Lowry obliging in the House of Lords, p 100).

The problem that faced their Lordships was that there was no established legal principle that rendered the men's activities unlawful. This difficulty was illustrated by Lord Jauncey's failed attempt to establish a common thread through all the relevant consent cases in the hope of finding a constant factor which could then be used to guide their Lordships in the present one. Ultimately, he was forced to declare simply that 'it would not be in the public interest that deliberate infliction of actual bodily harm during the course of homosexual sadomasochistic activities should be held to be lawful' (*R v Brown* (1993), p 85). Despite his best endeavours, his decision could not be justified on the basis of the existing case law and he was forced to rely instead on a vague 'public policy' argument.

In his dissenting judgment, Lord Mustill adopted a different, humane approach. He thought that the wrong law was being used to prosecute the men involved, arguing that the 1861 Act was designed to deal with public outbreaks of unruly violence and was not the proper vehicle to deal with sexual relationships between consenting adults: 'In my opinion, it should be a case about the criminal law of private sexual relations, if about anything at all'. He accepted that sadomasochism was a new challenge for the court but did not want to repeat Lord Jauncey's failure to create a workable analogy between sadomasochism and the earlier consent cases, including the prizefight cases and a number of Canadian ice hockey cases such as *R v Ciccarelli* (1989). Instead, Lord Mustill placed each case in which the defence of consent had been successfully used into one of a number of different categories. He then analysed the principles that governed each of those categories and finally tried to ascertain 'whether the decided cases teach us how to act to this new challenge' (p 105). He gave brief consideration to those instances that were not relevant to the case in hand (such as surgery and lawful correction) and dealt at greater length with those which were. Sports and games fell into the latter category.

His Lordship recognised that 'some sports, such as the various codes of football, have deliberate contact as an essential element' (p 109). He reviewed the earlier cases in an attempt to ascertain where the boundary between acceptable and unacceptable levels of violence was to be drawn. Yet, he was forced to conclude that one could not say where that dividing line lay. Ultimately, the crucial factor was not so much the degree of violence but the context in which that violence had occurred, so, in effect, the consent of those involved becomes superfluous in the face of the more significant notion of public policy.

The implication for sports violence is that the full force of the criminal law will only be unleashed if the violence which has occurred poses such a threat to social order that it constitutes a breach of the peace. Alternatively, it the violence goes so beyond the pale in its severity that a 'consent' defence could not possibly be available, then the courts might also intervene. However, this would probably mean that a defendant would have had to have been involved in a fight or a similar situation which clearly took the incident outside the parameters of the game. A vicious and pre-meditated kick that was made to look like a clumsy or ill-timed tackle, for example, is unlikely to lead to a prosecution under the 1861 Act, although it could, of course, precipitate a civil action.

The case of *R v Aitken* (1992) provides an illustration of this. In that case, Cazalet J had declared that one could actually consent to being set fire to (and seriously injured) as part of military initiation ceremonies, because such 'robust games' and 'horseplay' were part of 'the Royal Air Force ethos' (*passim*). Such violent conduct is privileged because it helps to build 'real men' and exemplifies 'the popularity and social acceptance of homosocial bonding ... which goes on long after the majority of men have become engaged in "secure" heterosexual relationships' (Collier, 1995, p 105). The contrast between this approach, as exemplified in some of the sports cases, and the 'harsh, punitive laws [which exist] in relation to homosexuality' (Collier, 1995, p 105) and which were unleashed in *R v Brown* (1992), is all too evident.

THE INCREASE IN THE USE OF THE LAW

Wherever modern sport is played, the law is becoming increasingly involved. This has been especially noticeable where sports injuries are concerned. Whether players are being prosecuted for headbutting an opponent, as in *Ferguson v Normand* (1995), or sued for ending their careers, as in *McCord v Cornforth* (1998), the law is taking a much greater interest where one player injures another in the name of sport. As has often been said by Edward Grayson (1994), the law of the land does not stop at the touchline.

However, this does not mean that every injury inflicted on the field of play will automatically lead to a legal action. There are a number of factors that will stop this from happening, not least of which is most players' general reluctance to use the law against a fellow player. But football cannot rely on this goodwill alone in the hope that the law will not involve itself. The severity of the injury, the consequent loss of earnings or a general feeling of malevolence towards the perpetrator can all lead to an injured player using the law against another footballer.

Not only can such incidents be unlawful – they are also, invariably, contrary to the rules of football. The argument that injuries are 'part of the game' does not always hold true, especially where the injury is caused by anything other than accidental contact. By deliberately acting outside of the rules, a player cannot truly be said to be playing the game. If that is the case, then the injuries have not been caused as part of the way that the game is played. In other words:

> [As] cheaters make moves not recognised by the constitutive rules of the sport, not only do they fail to prove themselves better players than their fellow competitors, but they have not even succeeded in playing the game in the first place [Simon, 1991, p 15].

The argument, then, runs thus: if a player is not (technically) playing by the rules, then his opponent cannot consent to the injuries inflicted outside of the rules of the game. If consent does not operate, then the challenge is an unlawful assault, which can lead to either a civil or criminal action.

Where the opposite occurs, the fact that the challenge is within the laws of football does not automatically bring it within the law of the land. In *R v Bradshaw* (1878), a manslaughter case which followed a challenge on the goalkeeper that caused him to die from internal injuries, the judge explained to the jury that:

> There is no doubt that the prisoner's act caused the death and the question is whether the act was unlawful. No rules or practice of any game whatever can make that lawful which is unlawful by the law of the land; and the law of the land says that you shall not do that which is likely to cause the death of another ... Therefore, in one way, you need not concern yourselves with the rules of football ... [I]f a man is playing according to the rules and practice of the game and not going beyond it, it may be reasonable to infer that he is ... not acting in a manner which he knows will be likely to be productive of death or injury. But, independent of the rules, if the prisoner intended to cause serious hurt to the deceased, or if he knew that, in charging as he did, he might produce serious injury and was ... reckless as to whether he would produce serious injury or not, then the act would be unlawful ... and you must find him guilty.

From this extract, it can be seen that the rules of the game are not conclusive when considering whether or not an action was lawful. The rules can only be used for attempting to assess whether or not the player intended, or was reckless as to, the injuring of an opponent. In other words, it is easier for a jury to find that a player who was playing within the rules was not deliberately trying to inflict injury on an opponent but was in fact trying only to play the game, that is, making or attempting a tackle. On the other hand, if an incident was clearly a breach of the rules, then it is easier for the jury to infer that the injury was inflicted either intentionally or recklessly, in other words, a deliberate foul or punch. What is important is that the court is not supposed to treat injuries caused on the football field any differently from violent acts committed in any other setting. In theory, a footballer who commits an unlawful assault during the course of play should be no more surprised to find himself in court than a person who starts a fight in a pub.

It is for these reasons that a knowledge of the law becomes important. In most other areas of life, one cannot inflict harm upon another, so why is sport treated differently? What follows is an outline of the criminal law of assault, the civil law of assault and negligence and the defences to both. Within the discussions of law, the inherent problems of bringing legal actions for sports injuries will also be discussed.

CRIMINAL LAW

The criminal law is used in football in the same way as it is used when injury is inflicted in any other setting. It is used to protect players from harm, to uphold the values of society and to punish offenders in a way which will deter them and others from following a similar course of conduct in the future. Where player violence is concerned, the potential for provoking crowd disturbance, where appropriate, is also taken into consideration. The criminal law is supposed to treat all assaults in the same manner, whether they are committed on the field of play or in the street. However, as we shall see, this aim is rarely fulfilled where player violence is concerned.

Breach of the peace

A breach of the peace occurs where there is a threat to a person or his property (*R v Howell* (1982)). The powers arise under s 115 of the Magistrates' Courts Act 1980 and the Justices of the Peace Act 1361. After hearing a complaint, the magistrates can bind over the defendant to keep the peace. A bind over is a promise of good behaviour. A surety is paid into court, either by the defendant or on his behalf, where it is held for a specified period of time. If, during that time, the bind over is breached, either the surety is lost or the defendant can be sent to prison, or both.

In *Butcher v Jessup* (1989), several players became involved in a goalmouth fight during a Glasgow Rangers vs Glasgow Celtic Scottish Premier Division match. The history of sectarian violence between rival fans (Rangers and Celtic are traditionally Glasgow's Protestant and Catholic teams respectively) meant that the players' behaviour was likely to cause a serious breach of the peace, in the form of serious crowd disturbance. Two of the players were bound over. In this way, players' future conduct can, in theory, be controlled so that they do not repeat their behaviour, with its potential for causing major crowd disturbances.

Common assault

Common assault is governed by s 39 of the Criminal Justice Act 1988, which states that it is an offence triable only in the magistrates' courts. The offence can be committed in either of two ways: by a technical assault; or by a battery. Assault is an act which causes the victim to apprehend the immediate infliction of unlawful personal force. Battery is the actual infliction of unlawful force to the body of another (*Fagan v Metropolitan Police Comr* (1969)). These two offences are only used where little or no harm is caused to the victim. As a result, they are rarely used to control player violence and such an incident will usually be controlled by the sport's internal disciplinary system. However, these offences do form the bases for the more serious offences discussed below. For ease, 'assault' will be used to cover both assault and battery.

The *mens rea*, or state of mind, for common assault is intention or recklessness as to touching (*R v Savage; R v Parmenter* (1992)). Both of these words have specific legal meanings. Intention is obviously hard to prove without a confession. It can only be inferred from the evidence available. If a player claims not to have intended the assault, then the jury may only infer intent when the assault was a virtually certain consequence of the action (*R v Nedrick* (1986)).

'Recklessness' is defined as the situation where the perpetrator of the act appreciated that there was a risk involved with his act, yet nonetheless went on to take that risk (*R v Cunningham* (1982)). For the purposes of battery, the risk to be taken is the risk of touching the victim. This is a very problematical test to apply to football. Every footballer knows that there is a risk of touching an opponent almost every time a challenge is made. The degree of risk is not quantified by the law – it simply has to be an appreciable risk, or one which is foreseeable. Thus, a 50:50 challenge for the ball clearly carries an appreciable risk of making contact. The lawfulness of attempting such a challenge is not being doubted; however, a player will want to know whether an offence can be committed in these circumstances, where actual bodily harm or greater is caused to the victim. In theory, the answer would be yes. However, often, the only reasons why players are not guilty of offences every time they play are through the concept of consent and because little or no injury is inflicted.

Section 47 of the Offences Against the Person Act 1861

> Whosoever shall be convicted ... of any assault occasioning actual bodily harm shall be liable ... to be imprisoned.

The *mens rea* for s 47 is either an intention to apply force or recklessness as to whether force will be applied to the person of another. The unlawful consequence is that actual bodily harm be occasioned to the victim. Actual bodily harm is any harm that is calculated to interfere with the health or comfort of the victim (*R v Miller* (1954)). This is the most common charge for footballers and can cover a wide range of injuries; in addition, the requirement that the harm be only occasioned and not intended or foreseen can make it relatively easy for a participant to commit this offence.

For example, in *R v Birkin* (1988), following a late tackle, the defendant struck the tackler in the face, breaking his jaw in two places. The defendant pleaded guilty and, in mitigation, stated that it was a spur of the moment action and the degree of injury actually caused was neither intended nor expected. Despite this claim, the court would not tolerate such incidents and a sentence of six months' imprisonment was imposed by the Court of Appeal.

In *R v Lincoln* (1990), the victim stood in front of the defendant whilst the latter took a throw in. After taking the throw, the defendant ran past the victim and said, 'Nobody does that to me' and then punched the victim, breaking his jaw in two places. The defendant was convicted. The spur and heat of the moment nature of the act, and the fact that the defendant was of previous good character, had been provoked, would be likely to lose his job and had been banned from playing football for a year, were all to be taken into account when calculating the sentence. However, as this was a serious matter, the Court of Appeal decided that the sentence would only be reduced from four months to 28 days.

These cases demonstrate just how seriously the courts take this kind of injury when a case is brought before it. Although both of these cases involve off-the-ball incidents or fights, the law is equally applicable to injuries caused by on-the-ball challenges.

Section 20 of the Offences Against the Person Act 1861

Whosoever shall unlawfully and maliciously wound or inflict any grievous bodily harm upon any other person ... shall be guilty of ... an offence.

To be guilty under s 20, the defendant must intend that, or be recklessness as to whether, force is inflicted on the victim. Additionally, at the time of contact, the defendant must foresee some harm as the result of his action. He need not foresee serious harm or the degree or type of harm actually caused – just 'some harm' (*R v Savage* (1992)). The result of the contact must be either a wound, which is when the continuity of the skin is broken (*Moriarty v Brooks* (1834)), or grievous or really serious harm (*DPP v Smith* (1961)).

In *R v Chapman* (1989), the defendant's brother was involved in a scuffle with the victim, following a tackle. As the victim lay on the ground, the defendant kicked him in the head, causing a wound requiring five stitches. It was held that, in the light of the early plea of guilty, the sentence should be reduced from 18 to 12 months, with the balance suspended.

Again, this offence is more likely to involve fights than poor tackles. However, again, the law is equally applicable to both on and off-the-ball assaults.

Section 18 of the Offences Against the Person Act 1861

Whosoever shall unlawfully and maliciously by any means whatsoever wound or cause any grievous bodily harm to any person, with intent ... to do some grievous bodily harm to any person ... shall be guilty of an offence.

The difference between ss 20 and 18 is that, under s 18, the wounding or grievous bodily harm must be caused with the intent to wound or cause grievous bodily harm, whereas under s 20 there is no specific intention to cause grievous bodily harm. Cases involving s 18 will be unusual in sport, as, even where the players intend to criminally assault each other, it will be a rare case indeed where they also intend to cause the very high degree of injury necessary for this offence. Thus, a charge under s 20 is the more likely where player violence is involved.

The most well known football case involving a s 18 charge was *R v Blissett* (1992). During the course of a third division match, the defendant and victim both jumped to head the ball. In the course of the challenge, the victim sustained a fractured cheekbone and eye socket, which resulted in the victim being unable to play competitive football in the future. Although sent off for the challenge, the defendant was cleared by both a Football Association (FA) inquiry and the Crown Court. The court relied heavily on the evidence of Graham Kelly, the then FA Chief Executive, who claimed that this was the kind of challenge which, on average, would occur around 50 times per game. Accordingly, the defendant was acquitted.

The offences under ss 20 and 47 are most frequently used to punish player violence. However, all of the cases above show that the courts clearly consider player violence to be a serious breach of the law. They also highlight the conflict present in bringing such cases before the criminal courts. On the one hand, the courts are at pains to point out that player violence is just as serious as the violence committed anywhere else. However, evidence such as that put forward by Kelly seems to suggest that, if a certain type of act is committed regularly enough, it will become legitimised and, as such, it will become immune from the FA's internal disciplinary and criminal sanctions.

A further point worth noticing is that each of the cases, except *R v Blissett*, involved a fight. Although fighting is the most common form of violence that leads to a prosecution, *Blissett* shows that this need not always be the case. If injury is caused deliberately, even by a seemingly legitimate challenge, then, technically at least, the criminal law has been broken. This acknowledgment is partly behind the increase in sport and football related prosecutions. But, at the same time, the use of sports-specific mitigation such as a claim that the incident took place in the heat of the moment, or that the defendant experienced a degree of provocation from his victim, is also on the increase. This means that sports cases, despite statements of the judges to the contrary, will usually be treated less severely than non-sports cases, where such mitigation will generally not be looked upon so favourably. Yet, it is usually only assaults that are completely beyond the scope of the game itself, such as fights, which feel the full force of the law.

Homicide

Homicide is the unlawful killing of a living person under the Queen's peace (*Beckford v R* (1988)). It can be subdivided into two distinct offences – murder and manslaughter. The distinction between these two offences is that, for murder, there must be either the intent to kill or the intent to cause grievous bodily harm to one's victim (*R v Cunningham* (1957)); whereas for manslaughter there must be an unlawful act, generally an assault, which all sober and reasonable people would inevitably recognise must subject the victim to at least the risk of some, non-serious, harm (*R v Church* (1966)).

So far, there have been no sports related cases that have resulted in a conviction for murder. In football, it would be very hard to prove murder, unless something really out of the ordinary occurred.

For manslaughter, death must be neither intended nor even necessarily expected. All that must be foreseen for a charge of manslaughter is that some injury would occur to the victim as a result of the unlawful act, which in a sports situation will usually be the commission of either a s 47 or s 20 assault. If death results from a s 18 assault, the defendant will be charged with murder (*R v Cunningham*).

In *R v Moore* (1898), a goalkeeper in a football match was in the process of clearing the ball when the defendant jumped, with his knees up against the back of the victim, which threw him violently forward against the knee of the goalkeeper. The victim died a few days later from internal injuries. In summing up, the judge said that the rules of the game were quite immaterial and it did not matter whether the defendant broke the rules of the game or not. Football was a lawful game, but it was a rough one and persons who played it must be careful not to do bodily harm to any other person. No one had a right to use force which was likely to injure another and, if he did use such force and death resulted, the crime of manslaughter had been committed. A verdict of guilty was returned. In other words, in making the challenge, the defendant should have known that the force used by him would cause some injury to the victim and that, therefore, he should not have made the challenge in that way.

More recently, in *R v Hardy* (1994), following a ruck in a rugby union match, there was a brawl between players of both sides. During the fight, the defendant punched the deceased on the jaw. The deceased fell and hit his head on the ground, which was still very hard from a recent frost. The deceased died two days later. The defendant was acquitted on grounds of self-defence, as he claimed that he only threw the punch because he was being hit from behind.

These two cases, together with *R v Bradshaw* (1878), are examples of how difficult it is to succeed on a manslaughter charge. Only Moore was convicted. Bradshaw was considered to have caused the death by an accidental collision, while Hardy had acted in lawful self-defence to prevent further punches being landed on his unprotected head. The severity of the injuries caused in those cases is unlikely to be repeated, except in the most extreme circumstances.

However, the evidential problems surrounding cases based on tackles will mean that it is unlikely that the Crown Prosecution Service will proceed with such a prosecution in the first place. The difficulty in proving an intention to injure, or even make contact, is extremely difficult many months after the incident. Although recklessness is a sufficient state of mind for assaults, it is rarely used as the basis for a criminal charge in football cases, possibly because physical contact is too easy to foresee. With deliberate injury-causing contact less likely in football, few cases at present reach the courts. On other occasions, the players are content to accept that this is a part of playing a physical sport. Thus, many players will simply decide not to proceed with a prosecution in the first place.

DEFENCES

According to the provisions discussed above, technically, an unlawful assault is committed virtually every time a player touches a fellow player during a game. With recklessness being an acceptable state of mind for assaults, every time a player consciously runs the risk that an opponent may be touched by a tackle, an offence is committed. This is clearly an untenable situation. If this was the usual way in which sports assaults were dealt with by the courts, nobody would play football, as the risk of prosecution would be too great. The two defences most commonly used to charges of player violence are consent and self-defence.

Consent

The concept of consent is used to ensure that many minor assaults are never considered for prosecution. The theory behind the defence is that, if a 'victim' allows another person to make contact with or injure them, then the 'attacker' should not be legally responsible for the consequences. Although there are no cases giving direct and detailed guidance on this issue, the case of *R v Brown* (1992) (discussed above), which involved sadomasochistic behaviour, and two recent Law Commission Consultation Papers (*Criminal Law, Consent and Offences Against the Person*, No 134, 1994; *Consent in the Criminal Law*, No 139, 1995) do set out how the criminal law sees the role of consent in sport. In relation to sport and consent, the House of Lords in *R v Brown* (1992) said:

Some sports, such as the various codes of football, have deliberate bodily contact as an essential element. They lie at a mid-point between fighting, where the participant knows that his opponent will try to harm him, and the milder sports, where there is at most an acknowledgment that someone may be accidentally hurt. In the contact sports, each player knows, and by taking part agrees, that an opponent may from time to time inflict upon his body (for example, by a rugby tackle) what would otherwise be a painful battery. By taking part, he also assumes the risk that the deliberate contact may have unintended effects, conceivably of sufficient severity to amount to grievous bodily harm. But he does not agree that this more serious form of injury may be inflicted deliberately. This simple analysis contains a number of difficult problems, which are discussed in a series of Canadian decisions ... on the subject of ice hockey, a sport in which the ethos of physical contact is deeply entrenched. The courts appear to have started with the proposition that some level of violence is lawful if the recipient agrees to it, and have dealt with the question of excessive violence by inquiring whether the recipient could really have tacitly accepted a risk of violence at the level which actually occurred ... [In the present appeal,] what we need to know is whether, notwithstanding the recipient's implied consent, there comes a point at which it becomes too severe for the law to tolerate. Whilst common sense suggests that this must be so, and that the law will not licence brutality in the name of sport, one of the very few reported indications of the point at which tolerable harm becomes intolerable violence is in the direction to the jury given by Bramwell LJ in *Bradshaw* (1878) that the act (in this case a charge at football) would be unlawful if intended to cause 'serious hurt'.

Whatever the deeper theoretical and public policy difficulties lying beneath this decision, it can be seen that consent in sport need not be, and rarely will be, expressly given. Participants do not say before taking part in a game that they accept that they may be injured as a result of playing. Instead, consent is implied by a person's participation, as can be seen from the above quote, that 'each player knows and by taking part agrees that an opponent may from time to time inflict upon his body ... what would otherwise be a painful battery'. In football, this would mean that tackles, shoulder barges and general physical contact would all be legal because of the implied consent of the participants.

It is accepted by the law that, generally, players can consent to some degree of contact in the name of sport, but not to the deliberate infliction of actual bodily harm or greater. They can, however, consent to the risk that deliberate, legitimate contact may produce unintended injuries of a serious kind. This is because, although the courts have held (in *R v Lloyd* (1989), for example) that sport does not provide a licence for thuggery, they appreciate that some harm may occur accidentally in the normal course of many sports. This means that off-the-ball violence is rarely tolerated by the law (*Ferguson v Normand* (1995)), whilst on-the-ball violence is lawful if it is a legitimate part of the game and is not intended to cause harm.

However, the rules on consent fail to address several important issues. What do footballers believe they are consenting to? Is it as straightforward as the law considers, or should it pay more attention to the 'playing culture' (Gardiner, 1993) of a sport? The playing culture of a sport is important because it can define the particular types of conduct that players expect from participation. It extends not only to play which is within the constitutive rules of the game, but also to minor breaches of the rules which are accepted by the players as being part of the game. Thus, the playing culture could be used to define the limits of lawful conduct in a sport and the extent to which consent can legitimise certain common, non-dangerous types of foul play.

The 'playing culture' has been defined by the Australian courts, in *Rootes v Shelton* (1968), as the rules, conventions or customs of a sport, or as a frequent or familiar infraction of the rules of a game that can fall within the ordinary risks of the game accepted by all the participants (*Elliot v Saunders* (1994)). Although the playing culture has been tacitly accepted, English courts have not gone on to define it in any further than this. A more detailed and explicit definition of the playing culture of football would make it easier for both players and courts to determine in advance the kind of behaviour to which a player does not, and cannot, consent. In other jurisdictions, particularly the US and Australia, the definition of playing culture has been more fully developed.

The American Restatement of Torts (1965) states that:

> Taking part in a game manifests a willingness to submit to such bodily contacts or restrictions of liberty as are permitted by its rules or usages. Participating in such a game does not manifest consent to contacts which are prohibited by the rules or usages of the game if such rules or usages are designed to protect the participants and not merely to secure the better playing of the game as a test of skill. This is true, although the player knows that those with or against whom he is playing are habitual violators of such rules.

In the Australian case of *McNamara v Duncan* (1971), the court stated that:

> A footballer consents to those tackles which the rules permit and, it is thought, to those tackles contravening the rules where the rule infringed is framed to maintain the skill of the game; but otherwise if his opponent gouges out an eye or perhaps even tackles against the rules and dangerously ... Sports and games differ in their objects and in what is expected of the actors. In the game of Australian Rules Football, deliberate injury, in the sense of something done solely or principally with a view to causing sensible hurt, is not justified by the rules and usages of the game ... Hurt produced as a result of intentional acts is, on the other hand, an inevitable concomitant of ordinary play.

These two extracts show how the court can develop a broad general notion of 'playing culture', through the use of the terms 'rules and usages' and 'ordinary play', which can apply to all sports. The main problem concerns who should define the extent of the playing culture. Different parties involved with football, whether players, officials or administrators, will have differing ideas and priorities as to what is an acceptable way of playing the game. For example, if Kelly's views in *R v Blissett* are accepted, then deliberately leading with the elbow whilst going for a header is an acceptable part of the playing culture of football and is, therefore, lawful. In the light of FIFA's directives to referees for the France 98 World Cup, this view of the playing culture is unlikely to be accepted by the courts in this country. However, until the playing culture argument is more fully developed in English law, the courts and players are left without sufficient guidelines as to the precise nature of the consent given by a footballer.

Self-defence

A person who is being, or honestly (*Beckford v R* (1988)) believes that he is about to be, attacked can use reasonable force to repel the attacker. This defence can be relied upon by either the victim or somebody who is using force to protect the victim. The use of force must be necessary to prevent a sufficiently specific or imminent attack. The only limit on the force that can be used is that it must be reasonable in the circumstances. There is no further requirement of proportionality in the response (*Palmer v R* (1971)). As long as the victim uses only the force that he instinctively believed was necessary to avert the attack, that will be evidence of the reasonableness of the response (*R v Whyte* (1987)). Self-defence is a complete defence to a crime, resulting in the victim receiving no punishment for his actions, as it operates to legalise them.

In sport, self-defence is only likely to be an issue in off-the-ball incidents. If the incident is on-the-ball, the defence of consent, or a claim of accident, will usually be more appropriate. In *R v Hardy* (1994), the defendant was acquitted of manslaughter on the grounds of self-defence. He claimed that he was receiving repeated blows to the back of the head and neck and that the only way in which he believed that he could prevent further blows was to hit his assailant. The unforeseen consequences of the act did not affect the operation of the defence.

Thus, a player can use force to repel an attack which is being carried out on either himself or another player. The difficulty, however, is in trying to distinguish between genuine self-defence and retaliation. Retaliation would appear to be inconsistent with lawful self-defence. The former is an intentional battery for the purposes of attack, whilst the latter is a lawful act committed only because of the apprehension of danger to oneself. The problem for the criminal courts is to distinguish between the two. In the heat of the moment, it would be hard enough for a referee to do this, let alone a jury many months after the incident occurred. The argument then becomes whether the players are consenting to violent responses to violent play or acting in legitimate self-defence. Again, the problem is that, without a ruling on playing culture, it can be difficult to define the precise limits of a player's consent. In these circumstances, the courts are at present more at ease with the concept of self-defence.

TORT

In order to secure compensation for injuries received through the fault of another, the injured party must bring a civil action in tort. The most common cause of action is in negligence, where the injury is caused during the course of play or by a mistimed tackle. In other words, the claimant is claiming that, as a result of the negligence of the other player, injuries have been sustained. The claimant can claim for any losses foreseeably attributable to the injury, including loss of earnings and damage to property, for example clothes, medical expenses and pain and suffering.

The test for negligence comes originally from *Donoghue v Stevenson* (1932). This introduced the 'neighbour' principle. According to this concept, everyone must ensure that they take reasonable care to avoid acts or omissions which they can reasonably foresee would be likely to injure their neighbour. The 'neighbour' is any person who is so closely and directly affected by the act that they ought reasonably to have been in the contemplation of the defendant when the injury-causing act is performed.

This was applied to football in the case of *Condon v Basi* (1985), establishing that a footballer can sue for any injury caused by the negligence of another player. However, there are a number of problems with this test. Establishing who a player's 'neighbours' are is not a problem – they will be the other players. The problem is in defining how poor a player's standard of play must be before it is considered to be negligent. In *Condon v Basi*, the Court of Appeal approved of the trial judge's approach by holding that:

> It is not for me in this court to define exhaustively the duty of care between players in a football game. Nor, in my judgment, is there any need, because there was here such an obvious breach of the defendant's duty of care towards the plaintiff. He was clearly guilty, as I find on the facts, of serious and dangerous foul play which showed a reckless disregard of the plaintiff's safety and which fell far below the standards which might reasonably be expected in anyone pursuing the game.

In other words, because the act was so clearly negligent on its own particular facts, it was unnecessary for the court to lay down detailed guidelines. The test has not been developed significantly since. The court did try to say that a different standard should apply in professional games as compared to non-professional games, but this has since been expressly rejected in *Elliot v Saunders* (1994). Instead, a judge should simply take into consideration all of the relevant circumstances of an incident, of which the standard of play will be one such factor.

Despite all of these developments in the law of negligence, it was not until December 1996 that a professional footballer finally won a case for injuries caused by the negligence of a fellow professional. *McCord v Swansea City FC and Cornforth* (1998) has shown that it is possible for a player to recover damages for injuries sustained through a poor tackle.

The facts were simple and of the kind that can be seen on almost any football pitch on any day of the year. McCord, a player with Stockport County, and Cornforth, of Swansea City, both went for what was described as a 50:50 ball. McCord got to the ball first, with Cornforth arriving only a split second later. However, Cornforth's leg was adjudged to have been some 18 inches off the ground, which was eight inches over the ball. He made contact with McCord's leg, which was broken so badly that he was unable to continue his career as a professional footballer.

The evidence presented in court demonstrates the difficulties that can arise with actions of this nature. The referee had been unsighted and so could offer no opinion. His assistant believed that there was no intention to injure, but that a foul had been committed. Bobby Gould, the former Welsh manager, claimed that it was a dreadful tackle – one of the worst he had ever witnessed – with the player having no intention of going for the ball. If this latter opinion was true, then both civil and criminal actions for assault should have been brought against Cornforth.

Instead, Kennedy J found that there was a duty to take such care towards an opponent as was reasonable in all of the circumstances; that the challenge was dangerous and a serious mistake or misjudgment; and that it was not a deliberate act but was an error inconsistent with taking reasonable care. In other words, despite the facts of this case being based on a 50:50 challenge, the defendant was still held liable for negligence because of his mistaken, or misjudged, effort in challenging for the ball.

As mentioned above, this was the first time that a professional footballer had succeeded in obtaining damages for injuries resulting from a negligent tackle. In *Elliot v Saunders*, Paul Elliot lost, whilst, in the other recent high profile case concerning John O'Neil and John Fashanu, the parties settled. However, no new law was made or used in *McCord*. It was a simple application of the existing law of negligence – the breach of a duty of care causing foreseeable harm – to professional football. However, despite this, it is still an extremely important decision. It demonstrates that bad tackles, and not just fights and intentional kickings, are actionable. It reinforces the duty of care and the fact that such a duty can be breached, despite defences that are claimed to be based upon such injuries being part of the game; that it was a split second decision, made in the heat of the moment; that it was a 50:50 ball; or that the game is hard, fast and, by definition, includes a certain degree of physical contact. The reasoning in this judgment has recently been extended to cover the situation where an injured player has been able to resume his career following a serious injury. Thus, a player who suffers a career interrupting, rather than a career ending, injury can now also sue for losses incurred by the injury (see *Watson v Gray* (1998), below).

However, there was again no reference to the playing culture of football. So the sport is once again left with no significant guidelines as to what is, and what is not, lawful conduct. All that a player, or a court, must look for is negligence on the facts and in the circumstances of each situation. This can be a particular problem when it comes to deciding whose opinion should be relied upon in each case. In *McCord*, the judge took the middle line between the opinions of Mr Gould and the assistant referee. In *Elliot v Saunders*, a case with substantially similar facts, a large number of experts – both past and present players and coaches – gave their opinions as to whether the challenge was negligent or not. Finally, in *R v Blissett*, the opinion of the FA's Chief Executive was what swayed the court to acquit. With no definition of what the 'playing culture' is, and no decision as to who is a football expert or who should define 'playing culture', the judge at trial and the players on the pitch are left with very little indication as to when they are running the risk of making an unlawful challenge.

In *McCord*, the judge held that, because of Cornforth's previous good character in the game, he would find the challenge negligent, as opposed to intentional. For his career ending injury, McCord received £250,000.

The one confusing issue that remains is over the meaning of 'reckless disregard', a term often used to describe the state of mind of the defendant towards the safety of the claimant. Some have tried to argue that this introduces the US standard of playing with a reckless disregard for the safety of the other players. This would mean that footballers would have to be more careless before a legal action based on reckless disregard could be successfully brought than is the case when using negligence as the standard. Again, this has been expressly rejected by the courts in *Elliot v Saunders*; however, the judges have usually insisted on repeating the phrase when discussing liability of footballers.

The argument in favour of using reckless disregard as the standard states that, because of the greater degree of carelessness required for liability, less pressure is put on the players to change their style of play simply because of the threat of a civil action hanging over them. It is only very rarely that players intend to commit acts of violence, and, because most injuries come about through actions committed in the heat of the moment, with no thought of the outcome of the act apart from, for example, who is going to gain the advantage or win the game, they should have to adhere to a lower standard of care than other people. In other words, instead of having to fall below the standard of the ordinary reasonable sports participant, they must act with reckless disregard to the safety of their fellow players.

Reckless disregard is possibly the more workable test for sports cases, as it concedes that players are often more intent on playing the game than on wondering about the possibility of a legal action. If they are playing to win, it is unlikely that they are fully considering the consequences of their actions. Reckless disregard gives more leeway to players, punishing only a high degree of negligent and dangerous play, as opposed to simple negligence, which can be too easy to satisfy, especially in contact sports. However, in reality, there is unlikely to be much practical difference between reckless disregard and negligence in all the circumstances. If the latter test is applied, taking into account the playing culture, accepted styles of play and the heat of the moment as relevant circumstances, then sports participants are likely to receive just as effective protection as they would under the doctrine of reckless disregard.

Volenti non fit injuria

Volenti non fit injuria means that no harm is done to a person who has assumed the risk. As a modern defence to negligence, it sits somewhat uncomfortably and confusingly between contributory negligence and consent. In order to be able to raise this defence, a defendant must show that the claimant voluntarily assumed a risk that was known about in advance. In *Rootes v Shelton* (1968), the court held that *volenti* operated to exclude the duty of care. This cannot be the position. Instead, *volenti* operates to exonerate a defendant from liability for what would otherwise have been an actionable breach of duty.

In football, it is hard to say convincingly that a player voluntarily runs the risk that an opponent will play the game with such a high degree of negligence that injury may be caused. Instead, the more likely position is that a player will run the risk that injury may occur from a challenge that is either within the rules or, perhaps, is within the accepted playing culture of the game. For example, a player may run the risk that a late tackle may injure him, but he is not giving the opposition a licence to challenge him without reference to the ball or without regard to his health and safety. In the majority of sports situations, consent or contributory negligence will be more appropriate defences.

Trespass to the person (battery) and self-defence

Where harm is deliberately inflicted on another player, a civil action for battery can be brought, as opposed to a negligence action. The tortious form of battery is almost identical to its criminal counterpart, differing only slightly in the mental requirement. Where, for the crime, intention or recklessness as regards contact is required, for the tort, intention alone is sufficient (*Letang v*

Cooper (1965)). Where only less than intention can be proved, an action should be brought in negligence.

Battery is much more difficult to prove than negligence where on-the-ball challenges are concerned. It is generally only a cause of action where the injuries have resulted from a fight or other deliberate injury-causing act. As was discussed above in relation to criminal assaults and batteries, the evidential difficulties in proving intent will mean that negligence, rather then battery, will usually be pleaded. A further, practical problem is that, if the defendant is insured, the policy will not cover intentionally caused harm. As the insurance company will usually be in a better position to pay the compensation than the defendant, a claimant will usually plead negligence, except in the most extreme cases.

The defence to civil battery, as in the criminal law, is consent, with the same basic rules applying to both. Consent is, again, implied from a player's conduct, rather than being given expressly. There is no direct authority on the degree of injury to which one can consent for the law of tort. However, it is possible that a player may be able to consent to more injury being inflicted on him under the civil law than the criminal law; that is, a participant may be prosecuted for an act that could not result in a civil action for compensation because of the victim's consent. In *R v Coney* (1882), Hawkins J said that it may be that consent can, in all cases, be given so as to operate as a bar to a civil action on the ground that no man can claim damages for an act to which he himself was an assenting party. It is possible that this may have been overruled as a result of *R v Brown* (1992), on the ground that public policy may find this situation difficult to uphold.

One final area in which trespass to the person may be developed has recently been tested in court. In *Watson v Gray* (1998), the second claimant, Watson's employer (Bradford City FC), claimed against Gray's employer, Huddersfield Town FC. The basis of the claim was unlawful interference with contract, with Huddersfield Town being vicariously liable for the actions of Gray. For such a claim to succeed, it must be proved that the person causing the injury knew that there was in place a contract of employment and that that contract was deliberately interfered with.

Although there was some considerable confusion over the precise application of this tort in the judgment, the judge made two important points. First, an action for interference with contract would be sustainable in a football injury case where the above criteria were fulfilled. Secondly, in this particular case, there was no intention to injure and, therefore, there was no unlawful interference with Watson's contract of employment. In the future, therefore, where injury is caused by a battery rather than through negligence, an employer may be able to sue for any loss caused to his business by an injury to an employee player.

Waiver clauses

In many States of the US, it is possible for a player to contractually opt out of the right to sue for compensation for sports related injuries. This can be done through either of two similar methods – waivers and releases.

A waiver is a pre-participation contract that protects the potential defendant from liability. As its title suggests, a potential claimant signs a contract, waiving the right to take legal action for injuries received during the particular activity. In effect, it denies that it is possible to breach the duty of care owed to the claimant by the defendant. Releases, on the other hand, are post-injury contracts which state that the injured party will not pursue an otherwise legitimate cause of action against the person and/or organisation that has caused their injury.

Throughout the US, each State of which has its own separate legal system, there is a near total lack of uniformity as to how these contracts should be worded. Some have virtually no control over the wording of such clauses, as long as the defendant's liability is excluded in some way. Others require much more formal wording, which must set out exactly the kind of injury-causing incident that is being excluded.

In this latter group of States, the courts take a much more rigorous approach. The waivers and releases must either expressly exclude negligence, or it is strongly urged that the word 'negligence' is used in the waiver. If 'negligence' is not used, a description of the behaviour being excluded could be used as an alternative. The criteria are extremely strict and are construed against the party trying to rely on the clause. In this way, there is a measure of control over the operation of these clauses. This ensures that the party who is waiving his rights knows exactly what it is that he is waiving. However, many States have little such practical guidance. Public policy ensures that, in the vast majority of States, gross negligence and intentional injury cannot be waived.

This type of contract, or clause within a contract, is unlawful in this country. Under s 2(1) of the Unfair Contract Terms Act 1977, a person cannot, by reference to any contract term or notice given to persons generally or to particular persons, exclude or restrict his liability for death or personal injury resulting from negligence. Further, where a contract term or notice purports to exclude or restrict liability for negligence, a person's agreement to, or awareness of, the contract is not enough to be taken as indicating his voluntary acceptance of any risk (s 2(3)). In other words, even if a player waives his rights, it does not automatically bar him from a legal action to recover damages for his injuries at a later date.

LIABILITY OF OFFICIALS FOR
INJURIES TO PLAYERS

The liability of a player for causing injury to another player has long been established. However, before 1996, little, if any, judicial thought had been given to the potential liability of match officials for injuries suffered by players under their control. By a simple extension of the neighbour principle, it is possible to extend liability to referees and, possibly, to coaches. The reasoning is very straightforward. The referee owes a duty to the players under his control to ensure that, by his application of the rules, they do not suffer any harm. If, by his negligent application of the rules, one of the players is injured, then the referee will be liable for the resulting harm. The case that finally established this rule, *Smoldon v Nolan and Whitworth* (1996), has the potential to create a massive new area of liability for officials and, in all probability, coaches as well.

The plaintiff was playing in the front row of the scrum in an under-19s colts rugby fixture. During the course of the game, the scrum had collapsed far more frequently than one would normally expect. In colts fixtures, a special procedure for engaging the scrum was part of the rules. This was supposed to ensure greater safety for the players involved in scrums at junior levels. It was found by the court that the referee had not enforced the correct procedure for engagement and that this was one of the reasons for the high number of collapsed scrums. In one of the collapsed scrums, the plaintiff suffered a broken neck, leaving him paralysed.

The court held that the law was as stated in *Condon v Basi* (1985) and *Elliot v Saunders* (1994); namely, that the standard of care is that of negligence in all the circumstances. The duty imposed on the referee is to exercise that degree of care for the safety of the players which is appropriate in the circumstances. This is an active duty on the referee to ensure the safety of the players. There are no grounds of public policy which operate to exclude liability in the case of sports officials.

The role played by the rules of the game, especially by the special rules relating to the engagement of scrums, was only evidence from which the inference could be drawn that the referee had breached his duty. The court held that the referee had failed to exercise reasonable care and skill in the prevention of collapses by sufficient instruction to the front rows and in the use of the special engagement procedures for colts. In other words, he had fallen below the standard of a reasonable, competent referee. *Volenti* was not applicable as a defence, as a player can only voluntarily run the risk of incidental injury. He cannot consent to the possibility that the referee will fail in his duty to apply the safety rules of the game.

Following this decision, a previously unexplored area of liability has been opened up. Although the judge explained that his was a decision that should be confined to the particular facts of the case and should not be of general applicability in other levels of the sport, the effect of the decision could be that, if a referee negligently allows breaches of the safety rules of a game, as opposed to merely the playing rules, then a player who is injured as a result of those breaches may bring a civil action against the referee. The distinction between a playing rule and a safety rule is that a playing rule is only enforced so that the game can be played efficiently, for example, the offside rule and the rules relating to when the ball is out of play. A safety rule is there to protect players, such as the restrictions on high kicking and tackles from behind.

The consequences of this decision are potentially very far reaching. For example, if a referee failed to send a player off for an offence and that player later caused an injury to another, the referee could be held partly liable for the defendant committing the foul, as, if he had followed the rules correctly, the defendant would not have been on the field of play to commit the foul in the first place. A further problem for referees could arise from the state of the playing surface. If a pitch was too wet, too hard or too uneven and the referee should not have allowed the game to proceed, any player injured by the referee's negligently allowing the game to be played on an 'unplayable' or otherwise unsafe surface could again find himself able to sue the official for the consequent injuries.

The full extent of this decision will only be seen over time, when other cases are brought before the court. However, this area of liability could be the most devastating for sport. There are a number of problems associated with this decision. It could stop parents, teachers and other casual referees from taking control of junior games. It could lead to defensive refereeing, such as stopping the game for any minor infringement; more red and yellow cards may be shown, which could change the nature of how the game is played; and this could, in turn, lead to sporting isolation: if the courts describe how the game ought to be played, rather than FIFA, England and Wales could be excluded from international competitions. Insurance may become compulsory, which leads to a degree of elitism if only those who can afford insurance can play or referee. Finally, it could also lead to compulsory certification of referees, which again could lead to increased expenditure and fewer qualified officials to go round.

On the other hand, defensive refereeing is currently being encouraged by FIFA, as can be seen from the instructions to officials for France 98. Certification and proper training are to be encouraged, rather than discouraged, especially by the FA. Finally, insurance is the only guarantee of a compensatory payout. Even if a legal action is brought, there is no guarantee that the defendant will be able to pay. In *Smoldon* (1996), the defendant could only cover the £1 million damages because of the Rugby Football Union's insurance policy. He could never have met that high level of damages out of his own salary. Without that insurance cover, Smoldon would have received very little.

The immediate outcome of the decision is that referees will start to want to be insured before taking to the field. Others may see the risk as too great to run, or too expensive to run, just to be involved with sport. The consequent knock-on of this could be a lack of referees at the non-élite and non-competitive levels of the game. The problem then could be that, with part of the fun element removed from football, people may become less interested in officiating in games in the first place.

A further, as yet unexplored, area of liability which could grow from the *Smoldon* decision is the liability of coaches. If a referee can be liable for the negligent application of the rules of a game, then, by analogy, a coach could be liable for the negligent supervision of a player or for inappropriate training methods or tactics. Liability for the negligent supervision of players is most likely to occur at junior and school levels. If the players are left unsupervised and, as a result, injure themselves or others, the lack of adequate supervision could lead to liability. This, again, is a simple application of the rules of negligence. The coach would owe a duty to the players to adequately supervise them. If, by not supervising them, a player is injured, liability could be imposed.

Liability for inappropriate training methods could occur in a number of different situations. If a coach over-trains a player to such an extent that injuries occur, or forces a player to train or play whilst not fully fit, an action may lie against the coach. Again, this is a simple application of the law on negligence. The coach owes the player a duty to take reasonable care to ensure that he will not be injured whilst training or playing. If the training regime leaves the player at risk of injury, or if a pre-existing injury is exacerbated by being forced to train or play before it has properly healed, the *Smoldon* principle could be extended to include coaches.

This line of argument could be further extended to inappropriate training techniques and inadequate equipment. If a particular technique is found to be injury-causing but is persisted with, or if, for example, an unbalanced weights programme is used that places too much stress on the joints or muscles, then the coach could be found to be negligent for the resulting injuries. Similarly, if the coach uses unsafe, out of date or dangerous equipment and a player is injured through its use, again, the coach could be liable for the injuries caused. Although this type of liability may be considered to be far fetched, the speed with which the law is developing in this area may mean that coaches find that they are exposing themselves to liabilities that they did not know existed.

This area of liability could also be extended to cover the teaching of tactics that cause injury to the player or an opponent. For instance, if a player is taught to tackle dangerously and injures himself or another, the coach may be at least partially responsible. This could also be extended to the 'psyching up' of a player, or even to the idea of tackling an opponent hard and early. Although this would be difficult to prove evidentially, there is no reason, legally, why this concept, coupled with vicarious liability, could not apply in these situations.

In Australia, the potential liability of a coach for the 'over-psyching up' of a player has been accepted, but it has not yet led to a successful claim. In *Bugden v Rogers* (1993), a high tackle from an opponent injured a rugby league player. Damages were claimed against the club, partly on the grounds that the coach had excessively psyched up the players, highlighting which of the opposing side should be targeted for physical abuse. Although the lack of evidence of this 'over-psyching up' meant that this claim failed, the court clearly acknowledged that the risk that this kind of motivation would, in some players, lead to the adoption of illegitimate means was plain. In such a situation, a coach who encouraged action close to the limits of lawfulness would, in an appropriate case, have to bear the consequences of overstepping that line. If evidence was available, the court said that the coach, or his club, could expect to have to pay a substantial amount in damages to the injured player.

Thus, if a player is taught to hit hard and early, the coach runs the risk that he may be liable for any injury caused by such an instruction. If, however, the injury is caused by the player going clearly beyond what can be expected of him as a footballer, the club and coach will not be liable. An example of a situation where the employing club was not liable for the actions of one of its players was when Eric Cantona of Manchester United kicked Matthew Simmonds ((1995) *The Times*, 26 January). This was clearly not an act authorised by his contract of employment with the club. As the court had said in *Warren v Henleys Ltd* many years previously, the act of assault by the employee was done by him in relation to a personal matter affecting his personal interests.

Thus, a participant is authorised to play the sport according to the rules, or, more likely, to play within the playing culture of the particular game. Certain elements of foul play will be tolerated as falling within the course of employment if they are committed in the furtherance of the employer's goals, in other words, with a view to winning the game. However, if the act was of a purely personal nature, then the employer will not be liable. For example, if a participant commits a tort during a tackle, whether or not that tackle is within the rules of the game, the employer will be vicariously liable for the damage, as the act is for the benefit of the employer and within the course of the employment. That is merely an improper method of performing an authorised act. If, on the other hand, a participant simply punches or attacks an opponent, he will be acting outside of the scope of his employment. The act is unauthorised and the employer is not responsible for it.

These are all situations where the law can be imposed on coaches for the injuries caused by, or to, their players. It is by no means certain that the law will in fact develop along these lines, but it would not take any great extension of the law for coaches to find themselves increasingly liable where injuries are caused to players. Potentially the greatest area of growth could be where players are asked or, at the élite and professional levels, even forced, to play whilst still recovering from injury. Any exacerbation of the injury could be at least partly the fault of the coach, especially if the true nature of the injury is, for instance, kept from the player to encourage him to play on.

Finally, it is now possible to sue a governing body for its failure to implement adequate safety procedures for the benefit of its participants (see *Watson v British Boxing Board of Control* (1999)). Where a governing body knows that there is a risk of injury from a particular act that occurs within its sport and it negligently fails to act to bring about the reduction or eradication of that type of injury, it can now be sued. Thus, for example, if it were considered by a court to be too dangerous to allow players to lead with the elbow when going in for a header, and that the FA had been aware of the risk of injury by such challenges and had done nothing about it, then they could find themselves liable to any injured player for failing to change their playing and safety rules to take account of this risk. Once the law is involved in football, as it now is, it will become increasingly hard to control its application to new situations.

CONCLUSION

The law described in this chapter exists to protect players, not to bring about a legal revolution that will forever change the nature of football. Those who play, coach and officiate the game according to its rules and customs (or playing culture) will never find themselves having to defend their actions in court. Not all fouls are actionable. Not even all injuries will result in a legal action. If less than actual bodily harm is caused, which will usually be the case, then the laws on consent will generally operate to legalise the act. In this situation, the players will then be subjected only to the penalties handed down by the referee or disciplinary tribunal, depending on the incident's seriousness. On top of this filter, in general, most players do not want the law to be involved when they are injured.

However, attitudes can change. If the FA does not take any action to stop the further encroachment of the law, then the law will continue to develop apace, whether or not that is beneficial to football as a whole. At present, players can be fined, sent to prison or sued for inflicting injuries on other players. The operation of the law can no longer be ignored as an anomaly; it is a fact of modern football. The FA may develop its disciplinary tribunals and the Professional Footballers' Association can develop its insurance cover to render the law unnecessary or obsolete. But, as yet, they have not done so.

It has also been argued that the law is already unnecessary because these alternative mechanisms are in place. It is said that this is exposing the players to the risk of double jeopardy; that is, they can be punished twice for the same act. In the words of the Everton Chairman, Peter Johnson, following Duncan Ferguson's unsuccessful appeals, 'Even muggers don't get punished twice' ((1995) *The Guardian*, 9 November). However, it is not unusual for members of other professions to run this risk. Doctors and lawyers, to name but two, can be punished by both the law and their respective professional associations.

The use of the law to secure punishments and compensation for playing injuries is a growing phenomenon. All participants in the game would benefit from knowledge of the law in this area. However, it is perhaps those who are in charge of the game who should take the closest interest in the operation of the law. They are the people who can develop the alternatives which will obviate the need for recourse to the law. However, until then, this area of the law will remain very much a part of modern football.

CHAPTER 9

JUDICIAL REVIEW, 'PUBLIC AUTHORITIES' AND THE DISCIPLINARY POWERS OF GOVERNING BODIES

INTRODUCTION

This chapter is concerned with the extensive disciplinary powers ordinarily possessed by sports governing bodies, and in particular with the absence of effective external supervision of how these bodies exercise those powers. It reconsiders the ramifications of the several failed applications for judicial review which were brought against governing bodies after *R v Panel on Takeovers and Mergers ex p Datafin* (1987) had, ostensibly, provided the courts with the opportunity to extend judicial review to the decisions of these bodies. The courts' subsequent refusal to do so attracted comment (Morris and Little, 1998) but, after *R v Disciplinary Committee of the Jockey Club ex p Aga Khan* (1993) and the other 'sports cases', the issue appeared to be of academic interest only. However, this situation may be in need of reappraisal in the light of Parliament's decision not to provide a definition of 'public authority' for the purposes of the Human Rights Act 1998. That decision means that the sports cases may now have a new relevance, for Parliament has entrusted the courts with the task of defining 'public authority' and has charged them with deciding, on a case by case basis, whether a particular body is a 'public' one for the purposes of the Act. If the courts were to adopt a broader interpretation of 'public authority' than they adopted for judicial review purposes, then sports bodies could fall within the ambit of that broad interpretation and some restrictions might be placed on the extent of their disciplinary powers. Accordingly, the future relevance of the sports cases lay not in their contribution to analysis of the law on judicial review, but in how they might influence the courts' deliberations over the meaning of 'public policy' for the purposes of the 1998 Act.

This chapter briefly discusses the basics of judicial review and the application of the *locus standi* provisions. It provides some examples of sports bodies' disciplinary powers and the ramifications of their having such wide ranging powers are discussed. Given that most of the salient judicial review cases have concerned horseracing, it explains how that sport's governing body was able to develop its wide ranging disciplinary powers while remaining free from legal intervention. The relevant judicial review cases are analysed within the context of the phrase 'public authority', as used in the Human Rights Act 1998, and arguments for extending the 1998 Act to them are advanced.

THE JUDICIAL REVIEW PROCEDURE

The discretionary High Court remedy of judicial review emanates from the courts' inherent jurisdiction over how public bodies or public officers exercise their authority, those bodies being under a duty to act fairly and not to exceed or abuse those powers. 'Public bodies' usually connotes bodies set up under statute or those which have been given statutory powers. In limited circumstances, the courts will also review the exercise of the Crown's prerogative powers (see *Council of Civil Service Unions v Minister for the Civil Service* (1984) (the *GCHQ* case)), although the Crown's prerogative powers of entering into treaties and the defence of the realm are among those that are not justiciable. The decisions of non-statutory tribunals may also be reviewed if they exercise a public function. For this reason, decisions of the Criminal Injuries Compensation Board are reviewable, even though the rules governing its determination of compensation claims are wholly non-statutory (see *R v Criminal Injuries Compensation Board ex p Lain* (1967)).

In contrast, judicial review is not available in respect of non-statutory bodies such as private clubs and other voluntary associations that operate in the private sphere. Grievances against bodies located within the realms of private law should be pursued by recourse to private law remedies. Such was the case in *Nagle v Fielden* (1966), in which a female trainer of racehorses successfully challenged a quaint Jockey Club rule that training licences could not actually be granted to women – the name of their 'head lad' had to appear on the licences. The Court of Appeal, overturning the decisions of the Master in Chambers and the appeal judge, granted Nagle leave to proceed with her statement of claim for private law remedies of a declaration and injunctive relief. The Court of Appeal's decision ultimately obliged the Jockey Club to award Nagle a trainer's licence in her own name.

If the High Court determines that the decisions of a particular body *are* subject to judicial review, it may, in limited circumstances, issue the writ of habeas corpus, grant injunctions or make declarations. However, the most important power of judicial review is the power to grant orders of certiorari, prohibition and mandamus. These orders are collectively called 'prerogative orders'. They are available solely in judicial review proceedings and are not available in respect of the decisions of private tribunals. The scope of the various prerogative orders is as follows.

Certiorari

This can be used to quash a decision made by a public body on the ground that it was reached illegally, was an irrational decision or was underpinned by procedural impropriety. In order for the remedy to be available, there has to be a 'decision' that is capable of being quashed – that is, a decision that has some legal effect (see *R v Criminal Injuries Compensation Board ex p Lain* (1967)). In addition to being applicable to 'ordinary' public bodies, certiorari is usually available to quash the decisions of inferior courts. This normally includes (amongst others) magistrates' and coroners' courts, county courts and ecclesiastical courts. The remedy is also available in respect of certain Crown Court decisions under s 29(3) of the Supreme Court Act 1981.

Prohibition

An order of prohibition is used to prevent a public body from acting, or continuing to act, in a way that abuses its power or offends against the principles of natural justice. It differs from certiorari, in that there is no need to wait for the review body to reach a decision capable of being quashed before a judicial review application can be made. However, it is similar to certiorari so far as the grounds for obtaining relief and the bodies whose decisions can be challenged are concerned. In other words, both remedies are available against any public body or inferior court that has acted outside its powers. Prohibition may also be granted on a contingent basis, in order to prevent the body from exercising its powers until a condition that will permit those powers to be exercised lawfully has been satisfied (*R v Liverpool Corp ex p Liverpool Taxi Fleet Operators' Association* (1972)).

Mandamus

This order obliges a public body to perform the public law duties entrusted to it. It can be used to force inferior courts to adjudicate on matters before them or to force public bodies to reach a decision within a reasonable period of time (*R v Secretary of State for the Home Department ex p Rofathullah* (1989)). It will not lie in respect of a discretion that has been exercised against the applicant or in breach of the duty to act fairly. Duties that are enforceable by mandamus are those where the duty in question gives the applicant an express or implied right to complain. For example, in *Arsenal FC v Smith* (1977), a ratepayer was able to seek mandamus to challenge an assessment on another ratepayer because the relevant legislation empowered him to do so. In contrast, the Court of Appeal in *R v IRC ex p National Federation of Self-Employed and Small Businesses Ltd* (1981) held that the statutory terms under which the Inland Revenue operated meant that there was no such right to challenge that body's decisions. The court's discretionary power to refuse to make a prerogative order may be wider in respect of mandamus than in the case of the other remedies.

The conferment and regulation of these prerogative orders is governed by the Ord 53 of the Rules of the Supreme Court 1977 (see Rules of the Supreme Court (Amendment No 3) Ord 1977 (SI 1977/1855)) and s 31 of the Supreme Court Act 1981. The Act placed some, but not all, of the provisions of Ord 53 on a statutory footing and has resulted in a unified and simplified judicial review procedure. Of course, in the event of any conflict or ambiguity between the Act's provisions and those of Ord 53, the Act applies.

The *locus standi* provisions

Leave of the High Court to bring a judicial review application will not be granted unless the court is satisfied that the applicant 'has a significant interest in the matter to which the application relates' (s 31(3) of the Supreme Court Act 1981). There is little doubt that the Football League had a significant interest in the Football Association's (FA's) desire to establish the Premiership, or that Stevenage Borough's interest in the Football League's stadium provisions became particularly pertinent once they became serious challengers for (and eventual winners of) the Conference title. But could the supporters of Stevenage or Flint Town United have used the judicial review mechanism to secure their day in court if those clubs had been unable or unwilling to bring their respective cases? The authorities suggest that they would not.

In *R v IRC ex p National Federation of Self-Employed and Small Businesses Ltd* (1981), the House of Lords considered whether s 31(3) prevented a taxpayer from having *locus standi* to challenge a decision by the Inland Revenue not to examine the tax affairs of another taxpayer before a certain date. The House of Lords ruled that the statutory requirement of confidentiality in the Inland Revenue's dealings with individual taxpayers meant that its decisions could not possibly be open to review. However, Lord Wilberforce went further, stating that the rationale behind s 31(3) of the Supreme Court Act 1981 was to prevent the courts' time from being wasted by busybodies with misguided or trivial complaints. This leads one to wonder how such a complaint might be identified and whether a fan with no financial stake in a club or the game as a whole would inevitably be reduced to the rank of mere busybody. The decision in the New Zealand case of *Finnigan v New Zealand RFU* (1985) suggests that a broader interpretation of s 31(3) would not be completely out of the question.

This case arose out of the Union's acceptance of an invitation to tour South Africa in the spring of 1985, contrary to the Gleneagles Agreement, which prohibited sporting contacts with South Africa during the darkest days of apartheid. Two club players sought judicial review of that decision. They argued that the decision violated the Union's own rules, which oblige it to promote, foster and develop the amateur game in New Zealand, and that the decision to tour tarnished the image of New Zealand rugby to such an extent that it was incompatible with those objectives. They also claimed that a decision to tour could only be taken at a full meeting of the whole Union, not by the Union Council meeting in isolation, as had been the case here.

The application was struck out at first instance on the ground that the plaintiffs, being mere club players, lacked *locus standi*: only members of the Union could challenge the council's decision. On appeal, the Court of Appeal agreed that the council could make a decision on whether to go ahead with a tour. But Cooke J stated that the question of whether the plaintiffs had a sufficient interest to challenge that decision had to be judged in relation to the subject matter, rather than being viewed in isolation. The question of whether a tour of South Africa compromised the development of the amateur game was too important to be dismissed as a matter of internal management or administration. If persons such as the applicants were denied standing, it would effectively mean that there was no way of establishing whether the Union had acted lawfully or not. The applicants were not to be dismissed as mere busybodies and their appeal on the question of *locus standi* would be allowed. The court said that 'standing to claim that an unincorporated association controlling a sport has acted beyond its powers may be accorded to a person, even though that person is not a member or in a contractual relationship with the body' (*Finnigan v New Zealand RFU* (1985), p 178). Unlike its English counterpart, the New Zealand Court of Appeal was 'not willing to apply to the question of standing the narrowest criteria that might be drawn from private law fields. [This case] falls into a special area where ... a sharp boundary between public and private law cannot be drawn' (p 179).

Nevertheless, even if applicants were able to convince the court that they had a sufficiently strong interest in the matter at hand, the court could only intervene if the decision it was being asked to overturn had been made in the course of the exercise of a public law function. Judicial review is only available against public bodies. Local authorities, police authorities and government departments are obvious examples of bodies whose decisions would be open to review. The remedy would thus be available in respect of stadium safety decisions taken by the Football Licensing Authority (FLA) or any local authority exercising its function as a certifying authority under the Safety at Sports Grounds Act 1975 or the Football Spectators Act 1989. However, the reported cases on the actions of sport's governing bodies such as the FA appear to have established conclusively that such organisations are *private* bodies, to which the remedies of judicial review are not available.

SPORTS BODIES' DISCIPLINARY POWERS

All governing bodies have the power to impose sanctions on 'participants' whose behaviour is deemed to fall outside that which is acceptable. For the purposes of this chapter, 'participants' includes players, owners, trainers and the like. It also covers individuals such as stewards, race starters and timekeepers who require licences from the sport's governing body in order to compete, participate or otherwise offer their services at a sporting event that is sanctioned by the governing body in question. A participant who transgresses in this way will usually be asked to answer charges of 'bringing the game into disrepute', with their case ordinarily being heard by a specially constituted disciplinary committee. In football, for example, the 'disrepute' provision has famously been invoked against George Graham in respect of 'unsolicited gifts' received in connection with player transfers ((1995) *The Guardian*, 22 February, p 18) and against Eric Cantona for his kung fu style attack on the racist and failed armed robber, Matthew Simmonds ((1995) *The Guardian*, 1 April, p 1). UEFA fined Robbie Fowler for wearing a tee-shirt outlining his sympathy for striking dockworkers in a UEFA Cup match ((1997) *The Guardian*, 28 March, p 26). Sports other than football have 'disrepute' provisions, too. In rugby league, record fines of £15,000 were levelled on each of England's two most prestigious clubs after their players were involved in a 'mass brawl'. Cricketers have been fined and banned under similar provisions for talking to the media and for using 'recreational' drugs. Even the governing body of professional darts has found it necessary to take disrepute action against players who misbehave (through the making of 'offensive hand gestures') on the oche (McArdle, 1999b).

Although the law is playing a greater role in sporting matters than ever before, these incidents are for the most part dealt with by the relevant governing body rather than by the magistrates or the judiciary, even when criminal conduct or civil wrongs have resulted. Entrusting this task to domestic tribunals reflects the essentially domestic, private nature of sports bodies and the domain in which they operate. Its main benefit is that it prevents matters that have little relevance beyond the confines of the sport in question from taking up the courts' time, eating into scarce public resources and creating a state of affairs in which, as in the Diane Modahl case (McArdle, 1999a), the parties' lawyers are the only winners.

However, the benefits of allowing these bodies to exercise unfettered disciplinary powers are dependent upon governing bodies carrying out their duties properly and exercising their powers in good faith. Football's governing bodies' powers to punish managers who speak rashly to the press ((1996) *The Guardian*, 26 September, p 22) or players who criticise their former managers ((1992) *The Guardian*, 20 February, p 18) are a cause for concern. Sports bodies may impose sanctions that can destroy an individual's reputation or terminate their career (McArdle, 1999b). Concern also arises because of the double standards which those organisations are wont to exercise: in addition to deciding whom to punish and the length of ban or severity of fine to be imposed, they can also decide whose behaviour will attract nothing more than a blind eye – most notoriously so in respect of athletes' use of performance enhancing drugs. 'Disrepute' allows the governing body to use its discretion to ignore incidents that it would prefer not to draw to people's attention.

When the governing bodies themselves have committed discriminatory acts, the courts have taken the opportunity to force those bodies to comply with anti-discrimination law, for example in *Couch v British Boxing Board of Control* (1998) and *Hardwick v FA* (1997). There have also been occasions when the courts have reviewed the procedural fairness of football's internal decision making processes (*R v Stevenage Borough FC ex p Football League* (1996)). However, the prevailing judicial attitude, so far as the scope of these bodies' powers are concerned, is that 'justice can often be done ... better by a good layman than by a bad lawyer' (*Enderby Town FC v FA* (1971), p 605, *per* Lord Denning MR). The courts will not review the merits of disciplinary decisions so long as the governing bodies have not departed from the basic requirements of natural justice.

The consequence of this policy of non-intervention is that:

A well regulated sport will ensure that an athlete who faces disciplinary proceedings is entitled to independent representation, prior notification of the charges he or she faces, the right to confront witnesses and the right to present his or her case in defence or in mitigation. In addition, burdens and standards of proof often reflect those that operate in legal proceedings with the standard in serious disciplinary cases approaching that of proof beyond reasonable doubt [McCutcheon, 1999, p 41].

As a result, those who attract the wrath of a governing body will have little chance of mounting a successful challenge to any disciplinary action that may follow, so long as the procedures that have been deployed at the disciplinary hearing are legally watertight. If sports bodies adhere to their own disciplinary procedures, ensure that the alleged miscreants are given a fair hearing and generally fulfil their duty to act fairly, they will have little reason to fear judicial intervention. Given the number of specialist 'sports lawyers' and the tendency of governing bodies to recruit legal people to draft their rules and regulations and serve on their disciplinary committees, there should be small likelihood of a sports organisation failing to conduct its proceedings to the required standard. *Hardwick* and *Couch* show that one should never be too surprised at the arrogance and incompetence that domestic sports bodies are wont to display. The fact remains, though, that disciplinary provisions such as 'bringing the game into disrepute' are so broadly drafted as to confer an unduly wide margin of discretion on decision makers. A well drafted and properly executed disrepute provision allows governing bodies to discipline miscreants for just about anything.

The origins of sports bodies' disciplinary powers

Because these organisations are a law unto themselves when it comes to disciplinary matters, it is worth considering how they have managed to secure such wide ranging powers while remaining free from legislative and judicial scrutiny. For the most part, the disciplinary powers that are vested in contemporary governing bodies are little different to those that they possessed in the Victorian era, by which time the vast majority of them already had exclusive control over the affairs of their particular sport.

Enough has been said about football – it is worth making some comparisons with other sports. The history of the Jockey Club will suffice to illustrate how these bodies became ever more powerful, accruing wide ranging disciplinary powers without having to relinquish the privileged legal status which allowed them to regulate their sport as they saw fit.

Established in 1752, the Jockey Club's founders were those members of the aristocracy who bred the horses, employed the riders and owned the land on which races were held. They devised the Rules of Racing partly to standardise conditions, but primarily to provide a 'level playing field' in order to facilitate gambling among themselves and the sport's other wealthy patrons. As their sport grew more complicated and gambling became more lucrative in the early 19th century, allegations of corruption and cheating – and of gamblers refusing to settle their debts – became too numerous to ignore. The task of settling these disputes fell to the Jockey Club and, throughout the 19th century, it was called upon to consider the activities of scurrilous individuals who were accused of doping horses, throwing races or otherwise engaging in underhand activity. However, the Club's philosophy was that a gentlemen's word was his bond. Owners and gamblers got away with sharp practice simply because of the social class to which they belonged, but the Jockey Club would brook no opposition over how it regulated racing matters and would use all the power and influence that was at its disposal to safeguard its independence.

Some changes were unavoidable: concerted pressure from social reformers eventually led to the passing of the Gaming Act 1845, which was ostensibly concerned with betting among all social classes but merely strengthened the Jockey Club's hand because the Act's provisions were only targeted at the dissolute working poor. So far as the wealthy followers of the turf were concerned, the Act simply meant that their gaming debts were unrecoverable in law and only the stigma of being reported to the Jockey Club might force the debtor to pay up. When a Bill that could have significantly undermined the Jockey Club's power over the Rules of Racing (by proposing that no horse should carry less than seven stone) came before the House of Lords in 1866, the Club successfully used its influence to ensure that it was defeated (Birley, 1993, p 229). Finally, the Metropolitan Racecourses Act 1879 (which provided for minimum standards of amenities at race venues) also improved the lot of the Jockey Club because it was empowered to introduce a licensing system for courses and was allowed to close certain metropolitan tracks that had been run on purely commercial lines. This meant that it was able to close courses that had attracted the 'wrong sort' (namely, the undeserving poor, who would probably have attended professional football matches, had they been able to afford the admission), or at least persuade the owners to take measures to attract a higher class of punter. The powers given to the Jockey Club under the Act indicated that its right to run racing's affairs had been accepted by the legislature, and the Act placed no fetters on how the Club should exercise the licensing power that was granted under it.

'PUBLIC BODIES', SPORTS BODIES AND THE HUMAN RIGHTS ACT 1998

In 1990, the 59 racecourses in Great Britain attracted some five million spectators to more than 7,000 races at over 1,000 meetings. As Lord Bingham MR said in *R v Disciplinary Committee of the Jockey Club ex p Aga Khan* (1993), 'it has been estimated that over 100,000 people depend for their livelihood on racing and betting. There are some 19,000 owners, 6,500 stable lads, 550 trainers and 1,000 jockeys registered with, or licensed by, the Jockey Club'. The Club exercises an enormous degree of control over all of these individuals and it can take away their ability to earn a living from racing by revoking or suspending those licences. Those who participate in football at whatever level are in a similar position: they have no choice but to submit to whatever disciplinary terms their governing body chooses to impose, regardless of how capricious they might be in the exercise of those terms. For example, players who fall foul of their governing body do not have the luxury of plying their trade under the auspices of another body, because that organisation would incur FIFA's wrath.

If there are to be any new restrictions placed on the extent of these powerful bodies' disciplinary powers, they may arise as a consequence of applicants persuading the courts that a sports governing body is a 'public authority' for the purposes of s 6 of the Human Rights Act 1998. If that hurdle can be been cleared, an applicant will then have to show that the disciplinary power that has been exercised against them amounts to a violation of a right that is protected under the terms of that Act. This would still leave governing bodies free to exercise an extensive array of powers, including the right to punish individuals who take recreational or performance enhancing drugs. However, their freedom to take action against those who, for example, write books or newspaper articles that are critical of the sport's authorities, or appear in videos extolling the virtues of 'soccer's hard men' ((1992) *The Guardian*, 3 October, p 17), would be open to challenge.

Section 1 of the Human Rights Act 1998 states that those rights covered in Arts 2–12 of the European Convention on Human Rights, Arts 1–3 of the First Protocol and Arts 1 and 2 of the Sixth Protocol are protected rights, subject to 'any derogation or reservation' in the Act itself (s 1(2)). This means that Art 10 of the Convention – the right to freedom of expression – has been a protected right since 2 October 2000, when the Act came into force, and, under s 6(1), it is unlawful for 'public authorities' to act in a manner which violates a protected right. As mentioned above, 'public authority' is not defined in the legislation and it has been left to the judiciary to determine whether a particular organisation amounts to a 'public authority' for the purposes of the Act. This means that, while the decision to regard sports organisations as private bodies for the purposes of judicial review might seem to prevent them from being seen as public bodies for another purpose, they could still fall within the scope of the Human Rights Act. The idea of sports bodies being subject to human rights legislation may seem far fetched, but, if the courts interpret the phrase as meaning 'pertaining to people generally or collectively', rather than narrowly defining it as 'governmental' or 'official', then most sports bodies would be covered. Stephen Greer (1999) believes that the broader definition should prevail, contending that 'individual rights are most seriously threatened by concentrated individual power, whether or not this power is exercised by an organ of State or of civil society'. He also points out that the broader interpretation would be more in keeping with the spirit of the Convention.

EX P DATAFIN, LAW AND THE 'PUBLIC' NATURE OF MONOPOLY SPORTS BODIES

Even under a broad interpretation of the phrase 'public authority', only those sports bodies that are true monopolies could fall within the scope of the 1998 Act. However, it should be remembered that the vast majority of sports bodies are true monopolies that possess wide ranging disciplinary powers. In fact, the extent, scope and nature of most sports bodies are not dissimilar to those enjoyed by the Panel on Takeovers and Mergers (PTM).

The PTM has absolute authority over devising, interpreting and amending the rules of its own particular game – to wit, the City of London's various Codes of Practice that relate to company mergers and takeovers. Its remit is to ensure that takeovers and mergers are conducted in accordance with the provisions of those Codes. The case of *R v Panel on Takeovers and Mergers ex p Datafin* (1987) concerned the PTM's rejection of a complaint made by Datafin about another company's activities during a takeover battle. Datafin sought judicial review of the PTM's rejection of their complaint. Leave to apply for judicial review was refused at first instance. Hodgson J accepted that the PTM wielded extensive power in an area of great public significance but said that it was not susceptible to judicial review because its powers were not derived solely from legislation or from the exercise of the royal prerogative.

However, the Court of Appeal held that the PTM *was* a body whose decisions were subject to judicial review, notwithstanding the unusual source of its powers. The fact that the source of a body's powers was not to be found in the traditional public law sources would not necessarily mean that public law remedies would be unavailable. The Court of Appeal felt that the courts should consider the nature of a body's powers, as well as the source of them, when deciding whether that body was subject to judicial review (*R v Panel on Takeovers and Mergers ex p Datafin* (1987), p 577, *per* Sir John Donaldson MR). The PTM operated in the public domain, was performing a public duty and was exercising public law functions. It would be subject to public law remedies if it acted in breach of the principles of natural justice, even though it was completely self-regulating and had not been created by statute or under colour of public law (p 579).

In the wake of *ex p Datafin*, it seemed that judicial review could be available in respect of other bodies which operated under agreements that fell short of being contracts and which could, additionally, be regarded as performing a public function. In the subsequent 'sports cases', this was not the case. However, the 'public domain' issue could be crucial to any applications that arise under the 1998 Act, particularly if the courts choose not to follow *Law v National Greyhound Racing Club* (1983) and decide instead to give a broad interpretation to the phrase 'public authority'.

Law concerned a decision by the stewards of the National Greyhound Racing Club (NGRC) to suspend the plaintiff's training licence for six months after one of his dogs failed a doping test. The plaintiff sought private law remedies, issuing an originating summons seeking, *inter alia*, a declaration that the stewards' decision was *ultra vires*. He claimed that the decision to suspend him was in breach of an implied term of his contractual agreement with the NGRC, under which any actions taken by the NGRC which could result in a trainer losing his licence would be fair and would be made on reasonable grounds. The NGRC applied to have the originating summons struck out for want of jurisdiction, claiming that the plaintiff's application should have been made by way of judicial review. The NGRC argued that, although the case concerned a decision made by a domestic tribunal (namely, the NGRC), its decision had adversely affected a member of the public (the trainer) and only public law remedies could be used to challenge it.

Both the court at first instance and the Court of Appeal held that the activities of the Club were of a purely private or domestic nature. Its decisions were not open to judicial review and the plaintiff had been correct to proceed by way of originating summons. In reaching that decision, the Court of Appeal paid particular attention to the provisions of r 2 of the Club's Rules of Racing. This stipulates that:

> Every person who is an owner, authorised agent, holder of a licence or the
> holder of a temporary appointment ... shall be deemed to have read the Rules
> of Racing ... and to submit him or herself to such rules and to the jurisdiction of
> [the Club].

So far as the Court of Appeal was concerned, r 2 was incontrovertible
evidence that 'the authority of the stewards to suspend the licence of the
plaintiff derives wholly from a contract between him and the defendant'.
There was no public element in the relationship between the two parties, even
though the NGRC was a body whose decisions might be of public concern.

This notion of the 'private or domestic body' was of crucial importance in
the judicial review sports cases that succeeded *Law*. In these, the Jockey Club
and the English and Welsh FAs (in *R v FA of Wales ex p Flint Town United FC*
(1991)) have been held to be private bodies rather than public ones, even
though they operate in fields which are of immense public significance and
exercise monopoly powers. For example, in *R v FA ex p Football League* (1993),
the FA was held to be a private body whose powers and obligations were
rooted in private law only. This meant that judicial review was not available,
particularly at the suit of the Football League, which was in a contractual
relationship with the FA:

> The source of [the FA's] power is in its memorandum, articles, rules and
> regulations. It has no authority, save by contract. Its position is
> indistinguishable from the other sporting bodies whom the courts have held
> not to be susceptible to judicial review [*R v FA ex p Football League* (1993), *per*
> Rose JJ].

In *R v Disciplinary Committee of the Jockey Club ex p Massingberd-Mundy*, the
court suggested that the Jockey Club's disciplinary dealings would have been
reviewable were it not for *Law*. In *R v Jockey Club ex p RAM Racecourses Ltd*,
Stuart-Smith LJ felt that the decision not to assign fixtures to a new course
may have been reviewable, had the matter been 'free from authority'. In the
highest profile case, *R v Disciplinary Committee of the Jockey Club ex p Aga Khan*
(1993), the Court of Appeal held once again that *Law* meant that the powers
exercised by the Jockey Club gave rise to private rights and private law
remedies only by way of declarations and injunctions. The Jockey Club was in
no sense a governmental body and there was no public law element that
would justify 'extending the frontiers of judicial review' to it (p 867, *per*
Farquharson LJ).

However, the crucial point so far as the 1998 Act is concerned is that the
FA, the Jockey Club and most other sports bodies are fundamentally different
to the NGRC. Their origins, and the monopoly powers that they possess,
would bring them within the scope of a broad definition of 'public authority'.

In *Law*, the Court of Appeal had referred to the earlier greyhound racing
case of *Fisher v National Greyhound Racing Club* (1981), a restrictive practice
case. In *Fisher*, the court pointed out that there are 107 greyhound racing

stadia in Great Britain, of which 48 are licensed by the NGRC. The rest are not approved by that particular governing body. This represents a fundamental difference between the powers of the NGRC and those of the other sports bodies. If the NGRC only licenses 48 dog tracks out of 107 in the whole of the UK, there are 59 others that are outside NGRC control. A person who is aggrieved by NGCR deciding to revoke their trainer's licence, for example, could remain involved in the sport by patronising the other 57 tracks (Parpworth, 1995). There are big differences in the quality of stadium facilities, the provision of medial care for injured animals and the amount of prize money at NGRC licensed premises as compared to unlicensed ones, but the fact remains that the NGRC does not have the same monopoly powers as most sports bodies. Those who find themselves in dispute with the Jockey Club are not able to use other facilities, or align themselves with another governing body, in the way that greyhound trainers are able to. Similarly, every football club, at whatever level, is obliged to affiliate to the FA and abide by any rules that the FA chooses to impose if it wants to participate in the game. As Farquharson LJ observed in *ex p Aga Khan* (1993), the invitation to consent to the disciplinary rules of most sports organisations is very much on a 'take it or leave it' basis.

CONCLUSION

The FA and the Jockey Club are true monopolies. As such, they have more in common with the PTM than they have with the NGRC. The source of their powers might not be located in public law, but their influence is pervasive and they operate in areas that have considerable public significance. Football and horseracing are part of the fabric of national life and are also big businesses. Yet, even the decision of the old First Division football clubs to break away and form the Premier League was viewed as a private matter, despite its effect on the general public and on organisations in the public domain, such as public service broadcasters, the police and the emergency services.

The courts should act with restraint before interfering with the decisions of sporting bodies, however wide ranging their powers may be. However, *Hussaney* (1997), *Hardwick* (1997) and *Couch* (1998) give the distinct impression that some sports bodies are incapable of being left to their own devices and cannot be trusted to run their affairs properly. Football is a lot better than most in this respect, which does not say a great deal. A broad interpretation of 'public authority' which would bring sports bodies within the ambit of the Human Rights Act 1998 would place at least some limits on the unfettered degree of disciplinary power that they have enjoyed hitherto, as well as being true to the spirit of the legislation. Their authority in relation to performance enhancing drugs, recreational drug use and a range of other forms of misbehaviour that fall under their 'bringing the game into disrepute' provisions would remain unaffected. Their power to silence athletes who express political views, in the way that Robbie Fowler did, or to otherwise interfere with rights that are guaranteed under the 1998 Act, would not.

The courts' refusal to extend judicial review to sport's governing bodies should not be regretted. The explosion in the number of judicial review applications that has occurred over the past decade has eaten into scarce public resources and has caused untold delay and frustration to applicants whose grievances are of far more significance than the travails of Mr Massingberd-Mundy or the Aga Khan. However, this ought not divert attention from the fact that sports bodies can regulate their fiefdoms in whatever way they consider appropriate, through the exercise of limitless disciplinary powers and backed up by the imposition of fines or lengthy bans that can effectively spell the end of an individual's career. In the wake of the Diane Modahl affair, the treatment of James Hussaney and others and attempts to stymie individuals' freedom of speech, the arguments in favour of extending the Human Rights Act 1998 to them seem certain to be raised before the courts in the near future.

CHAPTER 10

PARTICIPATION AND THE LAW OF EQUAL OPPORTUNITIES

There has been a long history of excluding women from sports which require a lot of power, aggression and body contact. But women have been excluded also from such sports as golf, angling, snooker and darts, which require very little muscular energy but which have traditionally been male leisure preserves and important sites for collective male behaviour. Sport thus reinforces traditional male and female gender identities by supporting the idea that the existing division of labour – at work and at home – is the 'natural' state of affairs.[1]

INTRODUCTION

The early chapters of this book looked at how football, along with other sports, expanded through all sectors of the male population in the middle and late 19th century. This concentration on the times, places and people who have contributed to the development of the game has been at the expense of considering the bigger picture, and the purpose of this chapter is to redress the balance somewhat. Sports develop from, and contribute to, change in the fabric of the wider society. They have played a vital part in the maintenance of repressive forms of social and sexual control (Brohm, 1978; Vertinsky, 1990) and the philosophies and perspectives that contributed to their development in the late 19th century perspectives still influence sports participation within the wider community. The sex-based distinctions that continue to pervade sport have proved notoriously difficult to shift, despite the best endeavours of many well meaning people, but it is doubtless the case that the football industry has done more than most to break down barriers. The challenge now is to provide the unprecedented numbers of women who play and watch the game with the opportunity to make careers in football.

Chapter 9, above, showed that the UK's anti-discrimination laws provide no defence to discriminatory employment practices within the game, and only a limited defence to discriminatory provision of the opportunity to play it. The emphasis here is on the recent explosion of women's participation in football. It looks specifically at the promotion of girls' participation in schools and the provisions that have been made for women who want to continue playing, or take up the game for the first time, after leaving education. While the national curriculum's provisions on physical education and the work of the 'Football in

---

1   Rojek, 1989, p 141.

the Community' scheme are acknowledged as being fundamental to the growth of women's football, the discriminatory practices that are entrenched in the game place a glass ceiling on women's employment opportunities within it. The dearth of employment opportunities for women in sport has led some to suggest that affirmative action in sports employment would be appropriate. Given that European Union law now provides Member States with the opportunity to introduce positive discrimination in areas of employment where women have traditionally been underrepresented, it seems opportune to consider that particular issue within the sporting context. With that in mind, the US experience with Title IX of the Education Amendments 1972 is considered.

THE WOMEN'S GAME

The 'cult of masculinity', as espoused in the teachings of Charles Kingsley (Bloomfield, 1994), stood in opposition to what has been called the 'cult of domesticity'. The middle class ideal of the wife and mother who eschews physical exercise was celebrated by middle class women themselves. Sport reinforced distinctions based on sex as much as those based on class. The growth of football in working class communities, under the auspices of local employers and the Church, did not meet with the universal approval of the middle classes. Sir Robert Baden-Powell, for instance, lamented the popularity of 'this vicious game ... thousands of boys and young men, pale, narrow-chested, hunched up, miserable specimens smoking endless cigarettes ... hysterical as they groan and cheer in unison with their neighbours' (Birley, 1995, p 230).

Women's participation was anathema, for, although some middle class women were participating in golf, tennis or cycling by the 1890s (Blue, 1987), sport was a man's world and there was scientific evidence to justify the continuation of this state of affairs. From the late 1700s, 'anatomists had been representing the female form with a small skull (less ability for deep thought), short trunk and narrow ribs (since a sedentary lifestyle required less ability to breathe vigorously) and a wide pelvis (to better represent women's procreative functions)' (Vertinsky, 1990, p 155). Skeletal variations certainly did exist, but, as an ironic forerunner to the 'average man/average woman' provision in s 44 of the Sex Discrimination Act 1975, the differences *between* the sexes were exaggerated, while the differences *within* them were largely ignored. This gave credence to what Foucault (1980) called 'political anatomy' and Parsons (1937) termed 'sociobiology'. Men and women had different physiques, roles and behavioural traits – physical and intellectual strength for men, passivity and motherhood for women. These were 'natural', inherent and justified inequality. It was the same cod physiology that would be espoused by the Football Association (FA) in *Bennett* and the British Boxing Board of Control in *Couch* 200 years later.

Bennett (1978) and *Couch* (1998) showed how sports still give credence to the argument that natural, biological qualities determine social practices, even though that argument 'is precisely the wrong way around' (Connell, 1987, p 66). The behaviour of individuals is not determined by their biological sex; rather, the natural qualities of individuals are negated by the social practices (such as sport) through which gender relations are constructed. The sociobiological presumptions around which most sports practices are based are proving hard to dismantle, and the history of women's football illustrates this.

The first recorded game between women took place in London in 1895, with a North of England team defeating Southern England 7-1. A women's game in Newcastle later that year attracted a crowd of over 8,000 and, in 1902, the FA felt obliged to advise member clubs not to play matches against women because it was not a suitable game for women to play. There was the inevitable concern that playing football could damage women's reproductive organs, but fears about their physical frailty did not stop women from working in the mines and factories during the First World War, and it was at this time that the women's game took off in England. A number of factory teams were formed, the most famous of which was Dick, Kerr Ladies (named after the founders of an engineering works in Preston where the women were employed). On Christmas Day 1917, Dick, Kerr Ladies played a match against another women's factory team in front of a crowd of 10,000 in Preston. They raised over £600 for wounded soldiers, and thereafter raised thousands of pounds for charitable causes by playing against men and other women's teams in front of huge crowds. In 1920, they played St Helens Ladies at Goodison Park in front of 53,000, with 14,000 others unable to get into the ground (Lopez, 1997, p 5). By 1921, there were around 150 women's teams in England, attracting large crowds and raising huge sums for charities.

But their success continued to excite jealousy and resentment at the FA. In 1921, the FA Council followed up its 'advice' of 1902 by categorically prohibiting affiliated clubs from letting women's teams use their facilities. Again, they stated that football was an unsuitable game for women, but also alleged that too much of the money raised was being siphoned off in 'expenses' rather than going to worthy causes.

That ban was to remain in place for 50 years and, although the English Ladies' FA was founded shortly after it was imposed, the women's game struggled to find places to play because most grounds were, and are, used by clubs affiliated to the FA. It was also difficult to find referees and coaches who were willing to incur the wrath of the FA by getting involved. By 1947, there were only 17 registered teams in England, and the game remained in the doldrums for the next 20 years: 'The Dick, Kerr Ladies had given women's football a great start, but in truth the FA ban had squashed the life out of the game [Lopez, 1997, p 10].'

In the late 1960s, those involved in women's football recognised the need to introduce a proper administrative structure in order to help the game to develop. A governing body was established and the first meeting of the Women's Football Association (WFA) in November 1969 attracted representatives from 44 professional clubs. The Association drew up a proper development plan and lobbied the FA to rescind its ban on affiliated clubs giving their support to the women's game. In the following year, the FA lifted the ban and steps were taken to implement a coaching structure and a league competition. In 1971, a national cup competition was inaugurated.

The success of the men's team in winning the 1966 World Cup has been identified as an important factor in stimulating women's interest and involvement, but the impact of wider social changes also need to be taken into account. Increased affluence, more employment opportunities for women (particularly in physical education) and their improved access to university education all contributed to new opportunities to play the game. At least for middle class women. After the demise of factory teams such as the Dick, Kerr Ladies, it seems that working class women's participation came to an end. In any event, the FA's decision to overturn its ban had been forced upon it by international developments, rather than being a consequence of more enlightened attitudes. UEFA had noted the success of the women's World Cups in Italy and Mexico (in 1970 and 1971 respectively), and in 1971 passed a motion calling on all member countries' associations to bring the women's game in those countries under their control and to devote resources to developing it properly. The first European countries to completely integrate were Sweden, Denmark, Norway and Germany, and it is no coincidence that those nations have dominated the women's game in Europe ever since.

While their governing bodies were busy integrating, the English FA was still prevaricating over whether to recognise the women's game at all. In the meantime, the WFA did little to promote the game successfully. It was beset by petty squabbles and internal rivalry, it failed to send an England team to the 1971 World Cup and it missed out on the chance to host that event in 1972 and 1973, which would have been a golden opportunity to promote the game in this country. From its inception, financial difficulty and administrative incompetence plagued the organisation. Although levels of participation in women's football continued to increase throughout the 1970s and 1980s, the WFA proved incapable of carrying out the tasks assigned to it and the national side was unable to compete with the world's best. It was not until 1983 (in response to a FIFA edict) that the FA took the limited step of allowing the WFA to affiliate to it. This meant that the WFA agreed to abide by the FA's rules and regulations and, in return, the FA recognised it as the sole governing body of the women's game. The relationship between the two remained on this basis until full assimilation in 1993 – more than 20 years after the passing of a UEFA resolution.

Under the new structure, the FA took over responsibility for the WFA's debts and the existing league and cup competitions were revamped. The FA's official support meant that the the WFA was in a stronger position to approach funding bodies, such as the Football Trust, for financial support grants. Lopez (1997, p 71) cites the improved structure for the national team, better coaching and medical education, improved funding and media coverage as being the main benefits of the merger to the women's game.

The infrastructure that has been established as a consequence of these developments has helped to provide ample opportunities for women to play the game, regardless of their age, experience or ability. However, although women are well catered for as players, they remain invisible in most other aspects of the game. According to Lopez, research interviews that were conducted with fans as part of the Popplewell Report into Bradford and Heysel surveyed over 1,000 individuals, but not one of those interviewed was a woman, although they comprised between 10 and 15% of football crowds during even the darkest days of the 1980s. Female fans still comprise between 10 and 15% of those who attend Premiership matches, with almost half of these being aged under 30. The Football Taskforce has carried out some worthy research into racism, ticket prices and access for the disabled, but women's involvement seems to have been outside their remit. Even the most die-hard football misogynist could hardly fail to appreciate the marketing opportunities that women's interest in football represents, even if they are unmoved by the concept of equality of opportunity. The commercial benefits of this new market cannot be denied, but most professional clubs are not in a position to exploit them.

This chapter is concerned not with helping football clubs to make money, but with helping to ensure that women have opportunities for employment or participation in the game other than as players. As *Hardwick v FA* (1997), *British Judo Association v Petty* (1981) and the other discrimination cases have shown, forcing sports bodies to take these issues seriously can be achieved within the existing legal framework, although there have been calls for a new legislative framework to facilitate this.

FOOTBALL AND THE NATIONAL CURRICULUM

The steps that have been taken to ensure the non-discriminatory provision of sport and physical education in schools have contributed to the decline in the provision of most traditional team games, although the paradox is that football has done exceptionally well out of this change in the law. Many people were concerned about the decline in the amount of time that was being given over to team sports before the national curriculum's introduction in the mid-1980s. They believed that this decline could be arrested if provision was made for them under the new framework. The opposing argument was that making the provision of team sports a legal requirement under the national curriculum would simply reaffirm the traditional approach. Boys would play football and cricket, girls would play hockey and netball – and most youngsters would stop playing any sport at all, once they left school.

A National Physical Education Working Group (NPEG) was set up in order to determine the way forward and to oversee the provision of physical education in schools. In doing so, it was required to give specific consideration to how sex discrimination and gender stereotyping in schools sport could be overcome – a remit that seemed to be fundamentally at odds with the suggestion that more time should be given over to team sports. Furthermore, during the 1980s, the amount of curriculum time given over to physical education had fallen from 10% of the total to 5%. There was also a 25% reduction in the number of physical education specialists in teacher training over the same period. The number of teachers of other subjects willing to supervise sports also fell, partly as a result of changes to teachers' contract and the effect of industrial action in the 1980s, but also because of uncertainty about teachers' legal position in the event of accidents at school. A sympathetic interpretation of the teacher's duty of care in relation to sports injuries had been adopted by the High Court (and affirmed on appeal) in *Van Oppen v Clark and the Bedford Charity Trustees* (1989). This decision might have given teachers more confidence in their legal position and may have made them more willing to contribute to schools' sport, but the unwelcome and unnecessary hysteria that followed *Smoldon v Whitworth and Nolan* (1996) has probably changed that for good. Whatever the reasons, the provision of physical education in general (and team sports in particular) continued to fall down schools' and the Government's lists of priorities.

The national curriculum was introduced by the Education (Reform) Act 1988, which now provides that pupils must have a minimum of one hour's physical education per week. The arrangements for physical education are laid down in the Education (National Curriculum) (Attainment Targets and Programmes of Study in Physical Education) Order 1992 (SI 1992/603), with the provisions themselves being detailed in the Department for Education and Science's publication, *Physical Education in the National Curriculum* (1992). Its introduction has certainly not heralded an increase in the amount of time given over to physical education in state schools. In 1994, the number of schools that were providing 14 year old pupils with less than the then recommended minimum of 2 hours' physical education per week was twice what it had been in 1990. In 1999, a survey carried out on behalf of the Secondary Heads Association found that 'one-fifth of secondary schools and more than 40% of primary schools said physical education provision had decreased significantly' in the previous two years ((2000) *The Guardian*, 11 January, p 4). It seems that physical education, along with other foundation subjects such as art and music, are still being squeezed as a consequence of schools' need to make adequate provision for the core subjects.

So far as the mechanics of physical education are concerned, schools are obliged to develop programmes that concentrate on the development of knowledge, co-ordination and spatial awareness, rather than specific skills which enhance a child's ability at a particular sport. These targets can all be achieved through the medium of football, which lends itself to them better than most other sports. Schools still have a lot of leeway in determining precisely how the attainment of those targets is to be measured and what sorts of physical activity will be used to achieve them, and all physical education teachers have at least a grasp of the basics of the game. Football has done well out of these changes. It is cheap and relatively simple, children can quickly become familiar with its basic concepts and most can learn the requisite spatial and motor skills by learning the basics. But this certainly is not what the Secondary Heads Association or the Central Council for Physical Recreation had in mind when they started to lobby for more emphasis on team sports. The nation's dismal sporting performances on the world stage will continue until the lack of opportunities for children to play sport (rather than merely receive physical education) are addressed. A child's wish to play a 'real' sport seems to be at odds with the tenets of the national curriculum.

But NPEG's view was – rightly – that providing equality of opportunity and helping all children to develop physically has to be the paramount concern in the provision of physical education. Coaches and physical educators need to be aware that 'the game is *not* the thing – the child is'; and, in any event, most state schools simply do not have the resources to identify and develop youngsters who are capable of playing sport at a higher level. That has to be the role of local clubs, sports centres and initiatives such as the Football in the Community scheme. The activities that are taught under the rubric of 'physical education' should allow all children – regardless of sex, athletic ability, educational need or cultural or ethnic background – to attain the same motor skills and spatial awareness. The role of schools has to be to encourage more children (and girls in particular) to continue their participation in some form of physical activity once they become adults, rather than limiting their experience to unwilling participation in team games. There are also some worthwhile initiatives involving the use of football in other aspects of the curriculum, notably the 'Working Through Football' scheme and 'Football: Approaches to Cross-Curricular Topics' (Evans, 1991) – an educational programme that uses football to address various topics covered in maths, geography and history. The development of initiatives such as these means that there is more scope for the football industry generally, and particularly for Football in the Community officers and others working with schools, to get involved in a wider variety of activities than has traditionally been the case – simply teaching the technical and tactical aspects of football is no longer enough. If a more enlightened approach is taken, it should herald unprecedented opportunities for more women to gain employment in the football industry.

WOMEN, SPORT AND AFFIRMATIVE ACTION

In its most recent research into women's sport participation, the Sports Council for Wales (SCW) asserted that 'the long standing, general association of sporting endeavour with masculinity rather than femininity still persists'. Discriminatory attitudes continue to be widely held, and it was stated that significant steps towards reversing such views could be achieved by implementing a programme of positive discrimination. Its rationale was that such a programme would automatically lead to an increase in women's participation levels, and would also act as a challenge to the gender divisions that pervade the wider society.

The SCW's suggestions are problematic, for there is no history of positive discrimination, quotas or similar provisions in the UK's anti-discrimination laws. However, affirmative action has been fundamental to sport in US since 1972, and European Union law now makes provision for the introduction of similar policies among the Member States. The arguments in favour of positive discrimination in sport remain unconvincing, but the issue is on the agenda and it needs to be considered.

As is presently the case in the UK, attempts to challenge sex discrimination in sports in the US were restricted to using 'ordinary' employment law to oppose discriminatory practices. The most important provisions were the Equal Pay Act 1963, which concerned discrepancies in salaries paid to people working in the same company; and Title VII of the Civil Rights Act 1964, which dealt with discriminatory hiring and firing practices. However, these laws only applied in respect of organisations employing more than 15 people and the courts had interpreted their provisions broadly, so as to avoid interfering in employers' decisions unless it was clear that they had been made in bad faith.

From around 1970, attempts were made to change the law in order to deal with the discriminatory practices which restricted women's access to sport and physical education. In schools, the belief that girls should not participate in the same sports as boys, and should not participate competitively at all, was widely held. Invariably, girls were not afforded the same amount of curriculum time for physical education as boys and less money was spent on their programmes. Attempts to ameliorate the situation by recourse to the law as it then stood met with little success, with sex-based stereotypes remaining at the fore even in 1972, when Title IX was going through the legislative process. In *Bucha v Illinois High School Association* (1972), the court accepted that physical and psychological differences between women and men represented 'sufficient reason for prohibiting interscholastic competition between them' (p 71, *per* Austin J). The learned judge cited 'the fact that at ... the Olympic Games the men's times at each event are consistently better than the women's' (p 74) as justification for the different approach to boys' and girls' participation at school. Accordingly, the court upheld the Illinois School District's prohibition on organised cheering at sports, its $1 bar on the value of prizes and its ban on overnight trips to athletic events – prohibitions that only applied to the girls. In *Ritacco v Norwin School District* (1973), it was said that 'sound reason dictates that "separate but equal" in the realm of sport competition is justifiable ... the rule has a rational basis in the physiological and psychological differences that exist between males and females' (p 932, *per* Gourley J). In *Brenden v Independent School District* (1972), the court found that giving boys priority in terms of access to facilities, curriculum time and other resources did not violate the 14th Amendment: 'Physiological differences ... render the great majority of females unable to compete as effectively as males [p 1233, *per* Lord J].'

However, in *Brenden*, the court went on to say that these generalities could not be used to prevent élite-level schoolgirl athletes from competing in boys' teams. The plaintiffs were nationally ranked participants in their respective sports of running and cross-country skiing, and this justified their being allowed to participate in the boys' competitions: 'because of their level of achievement, they have overcome these physiological disabilities.' This case was cited with approval in *Haas v South Bend Community Schools Corp* (1972), which concerned a girl whose handicap was low enough to win her a place on the school golf team but who was denied that opportunity on the grounds of sex. De Bruler J ruled that it was unconstitutional to deprive a female who had 'made the grade' of the opportunity to participate. More importantly, he went on to say that no investigation into the relative athletic abilities of men and women could be carried out merely on the basis of evidence that, in general, women's records are 'worse' than men's. Such evidence 'cannot support a conclusion that the male sex is athletically superior' (p 503). This case was the first in which a court ruled that relying on stereotypes and on differences in athletic performance to justify discrimination was untenable. Along with the political furore which the debates over Title IX had fuelled, it led some schools and universities to introduce 'mixed competition' policies, in which one's ability to play to the requisite standard was the only criterion. However, these policies inevitably foundered because males benefited from their previous playing experience and access to training to such an extent that they continued to dominate in virtually every sport. There was a need for a regulatory framework which challenged discrimination in sports participation but which did not take an individual's playing ability into account. Such a framework was introduced under Title IX of the Education Amendments 1972, which sought to reverse the sexually discriminatory provisions that existed throughout the US education system.

THE LEGISLATIVE AND INTERPRETATIVE HISTORY OF TITLE IX

Title IX provides that 'no person in the United States shall, on the basis of sex, be excluded from participation in, be denied the benefits of, or be subjected to discrimination under any education program or activity receiving Federal financial assistance' (s 1681(a), 30 US Constitution, as amended). It did not specifically mention discrimination in sport, so the question of whether sport was covered at all gave rise to heated political debate and, subsequently, to legislative amendment and judicial confusion. But, if sport was covered, Title IX would only ever apply to educational programmes or activities, as community recreational leagues and programmes, such as Little League baseball, were not covered under the statute.

Title IX prohibits the use of Federal funds by discriminatory educational institutions and ostensibly protects those participating in educational programmes from the effects of discrimination. Although it was passed in 1972, the Regulations that were promulgated by the Department of Health, Education and Welfare (DHEW) and which ensured Title IX's applicability to sport did not become law until May 1975. Schools and colleges then had three years in which to comply with the Regulations, but, when this expired, educational institutions continued to protest that they were still unsure of what was expected of them. This was a stalling tactic on the part of the institutions that had made little attempt to comply with the law. In the first 10 days after the Regulations came into force, over 100 complaints were received against universities alone (Richardson 1994, p 165).

The Regulations (which were subsequently amended in 1992 in minor part) prohibit discrimination in the athletics program of any intercollegiate institution which receives Federal aid. Notwithstanding this general prohibition, they allow institutions to provide sex-segregated teams where selection is based on competitive skill, or where the activity in question is a contact sport, but it must still provide 'equal athletic opportunity' for members of both sexes. Institutions must, *inter alia*, effectively accommodate the interests and abilities of both sexes; provide equal access to coaching, equipment and training facilities; and ensure equality in the scheduling of games and practice times.

Rather than clarifying matters, these Regulations initially provided an opportunity to limit Title IX's effectiveness at a time when 'over-interference by the State' was high on the political agenda. In August 1981, Vice-President

Bush had revealed that the Regulations were being reviewed on the ground that universities had 'been going too far' with their anti-discrimination measures ((1981) *USA Today*, 13 August, p 1). And the National Collegiate Athletics Association's decision to present Ronald Reagan with the 1989 Theodore Roosevelt Award for his 'contribution to the cause of amateur sports' caused a great deal of anger amongst those who recalled his opposition to Title IX ((1989) *USA Today*, 21 December, p 2). The biggest challenge, though, came from the Supreme Court in *Grove City College v Bell* (1984). Here, a small, private college challenged the decision to terminate Federal funding in the shape of Basic Educational Opportunity Grants (which many students used to pay their college fees), on the ground that the college had failed to execute a Title IX Assurance of Compliance. The grants represented the only source of Federal funding for the College, which 'followed an unbending policy of refusing all forms of government assistance' (*Grove City College v Bell* (1984), p 576, *per* Powell J), but, at first instance, the court found that the grants constituted 'Federal financial assistance'. The fact that this 'assistance' reached the college indirectly (that is, via the students), rather than being paid directly, was immaterial.

The First Circuit Appeal Court affirmed this decision, but the Supreme Court overturned it. It agreed that the 'indirect' receipt of the grants was not relevant but held that the language of Title IX was 'program-specific': the grants assisted the college's financial aid programme and they could only be withheld if there was found to be discrimination in that specific programme. The fact that there may have been non-compliance in other areas of its program did not justify withholding the grants. So long as the college could execute an Assurance of Compliance with regard to its financial aid program, its students (and, therefore, the college) were entitled to receive those grants. If that were not the case, 'an entire school would be subject to Title IX merely because one of the departments received an earmarked Federal grant. This result cannot be squared with Congress' intent' (*Grove City College v Bell* (1984), p 531, *per* White J).

This decision, which 'effectively removed nearly every university athletic programme from the purview of Title IX' (Johnson, 1994, p 563), resulted from the Supreme Court's exclusive reliance upon the language of s 901 of Title IX. This appears to contain expressly program-specific language, in that it prohibits 'gender discrimination in any *education program or activity* receiving Federal financial assistance' (emphasis added). The court said that the restrictive language contained in s 901 indicated that Congress itself intended to limit Title IX's application to the specific programme or activity in which the discrimination occurred. Although it was obliged to give considerable weight to the DHEW's construction of the statute and the Regulations it promulgated, the court, following *Red Lion Broadcasting Co v FCC* (1969), ruled that it was not obliged to follow them if it believed that Congress' intent had not been followed. However, the court ignored the fact that, after Title IX was passed, several attempts were made by members of Congress to amend the legislation so that it was either applicable to inter-collegiate athletic programs or limited to programs or activities which received direct Federal funding. All of those amendments failed.

Those who supported the 'institution-wide' approach argued that the failure to pass any of those amendments showed that the Regulations had indeed reflected Congress' intent. However, the impact of the court's program-specific approach was to stymie female athletes' sex discrimination claims unless the athletic program itself received Federal aid, and most of them did not. In the wake of the judgment, at least 150 complaints of sex discrimination were withdrawn (Boutilier and San Giovanni, 1994, p 102). However, the Civil Rights Restoration Act 1987 now obliges the courts to adopt the institution-wide approach to Title IX. This provides a broader definition of 'program or activity', so that it covers all of the operations of a college, university or other post-secondary institution, or a public system of higher education, any part of which is extended Federal financial assistance.

Since the amending legislation came into force in March 1988, the question of whether a particular institution is in compliance has usually been answered after consideration of whether it passes the 'policy standard'. This test involves ascertaining whether the athletic interests and abilities of students are accommodated, what sports are offered and what levels of competition are available to the participants (44 Fed Reg 71,417 (1979)). In order to answer that question, the following issues have to be considered:

(a) whether participation opportunities for male and female students are provided in numbers substantially proportionate to their respective enrolments; or,

(b) where the members of one sex have been and are underrepresented, whether the institution can show a history and continuing practice of program expansion which is demonstrably responsive to the developing interests and abilities of the members of that sex; or,

(c) where the members of one sex are underrepresented, and the institution cannot show a continuing practice of program expansion, whether it can be demonstrated that the interests and abilities of the members of that sex have been fully and effectively accommodated (44 Fed Reg 71,418 (1979)).

The Title IX *Athletics Investigators' Manual*, established by the US Office of Civil Rights, assists investigators in assessing whether the policy standard has been met (see Johnson, 1994). The three factors are to be considered in the order given above, and investigators are not to consider the next 'step' in the test unless and until they are satisfied that its predecessor has been violated. Satisfaction of any part of the test constitutes compliance, but failing all parts of it automatically renders a university non-compliant (Johnson, 1994, p 567). With regard to the 'participation opportunities' test, there is no set ratio that constitutes 'substantially proportionate' or that, when it is not met, results in a violation. However, in *Roberts v Colorado State University* (1993), the 10th Circuit Court of Appeals rejected the university's claim that a disparity of 10.6% between women's academic enrolment rate and their athletic participation rate was acceptable. Guidance was also given in *Favia v Indiana University of Pennsylvania* (1993), where it was held that, in a college where 56% of students were female, 36.5% of athletes being female was an unacceptable figure. In *Cook v Colgate University* (1992), the court stressed that financial constraints were no justification for a failure to comply with Title IX. In *Cohen v Brown University* (1993), the university's plan to demote two men's and two women's teams from Varsity to club status in order to save money violated Title IX, because 75% of the money saved would come from the demotion of the women's teams.

This more liberal interpretation of the law persuaded a number of universities to amend their athletic programmes, rather than face a lawsuit: the threat of Title IX litigation prompted reinstatement of dropped women's teams at the University of Oklahoma (basketball), William and Mary College (basketball and swimming), the University of New Hampshire (tennis), the University of Massachusetts at Amherst (lacrosse, volleyball and tennis) and the University of California at Los Angeles (gymnastics). The settlement of Title IX litigation involving Auburn University and the University of Texas forced those schools to promote or create women's athletics teams.

Since the 1988 amendments, Title IX has resulted in much progress being made towards equality of funding and equality of opportunity for female athletes in educational institutions; however, many 'Title Niners' argue that, while formal equality may have been achieved, substantive equality remains elusive. While this raises the fundamental question of what anti-discrimination law can actually achieve in practice (McCrudden, 1990), it also highlights the fact that institutions continue to disregard the legislation for as long as possible and do little or nothing until they are 'at the door of the court'. A particular problem concerns the burden of proof, because 'it is the plaintiff rather than a particular college or university [that] is burdened with proving a shortfall in respect to full accommodation of student interests' (Richardson, 1994, p 178). By 1992, Washington State was the only university that seemed to be in full compliance with all aspects of Title IX ((1992) *Washington Post*, June 21, p 1), and that was as a consequence of the decision in *Blair v Washington State University* (1994). In October 1994, the University of Massachusetts reinstated three women's athletics teams in the face of a threatened lawsuit and proudly announced that *it* intended 'to become the first university in the country to come into full compliance with Title IX' ((1994) *USA Today*, 12 October, p 1). A survey carried out by the *Washington Post* in 1995 found no improvement since 1992 ((1995) *USA Today*, 5–11 October).

In addition to pointing out the inherent practical difficulties of affirmative action regimes, Richardson (1994) attributes the failure of Title IX to 'the statute's ambiguity, coupled with a confusing regulatory program', which served to thwart Congress' objective of reducing gender discrimination within sport (Richardson, 1994, p 161). So far as addressing women's participation in sport is concerned, there is a view, propounded by Boutilier and San Giovanni (1994), that Title IX's main shortcoming is not so much its 'confused regulatory framework' as the fact that it contains too many ingrained prejudices and assumptions about sport:

> The debate over Title IX and public policy has completely avoided questioning the long held belief that sport is a masculine domain. Women's alienation from sport, their indifference to it [and] their reluctance to enter into it stem in large measure from the fact that, as it existed historically, what sport celebrated, offered and rewarded does not reflect much of women's experience of the world. Title IX asks women to embrace the masculine model of sport [Richardson, 1994, p 107].

Whatever its drawbacks, the effect of Title IX on women's football has been enormous – not just in the US, but throughout the world. Its passing has been solely responsible for the explosion of women's soccer in the US over the last 20 years. The sport has low start-up costs, the basics can be grasped easily and there was no tradition of men's competition in the sport at school or university level. As such, it was ideally suited to those educational institutions that were looking to provide more opportunities for female athletes without incurring much expense beyond scholarships and running costs, and without (dare one suggest) treading on the men's toes. The consequence for the rest of the world has been that the US, along with Norway and China, still sets the standard for the women's game. In terms of training facilities, quality of competition, sponsorship and – crucially – media attention, the US is light years ahead of most other nations.

THE FUTURE OF WOMEN'S FOOTBALL: AFFIRMATIVE ACTION OR AN IN-HOUSE REVOLUTION?

FIFA President Sepp Blatter once said that the future of football is female. Any country that wants to be taken seriously as a potential host of the cash-cow that is the men's World Cup has to show that it takes the women's game seriously too. This need to impress FIFA by attempting to narrow the gap with the US is the sole reason why the English FA has thrown money at women's football since its merger with the WFA. But on-field success remains conspicuous by its absence, and those who agitate for affirmative action in sport in the UK argue that this will remain the case until more female coaches are given the chance to work alongside male coaches and be involved in the men's game. At the moment, too many of the best female players end up in administration or coaching children, whether as teachers or via the Football in the Community scheme, when their playing careers end. This is not a state of affairs that exists only in football, for there is plenty of research which shows that it pervades most sports; and the changes wrought by the national curriculum have done little to alter this state of affairs.

The way in which the national curriculum has been implemented, and the attitudes that remain within schools and amongst parents, have reinforced traditional attitudes about what is an appropriate sporting activity for members of each sex (see Hargreaves, 1994). The move towards mixed-sex physical education classes has not seen the demise of such concerns as boys getting more of the teacher's attention, taking up more space to practise or retaining possession of the ball in team games. Clarke (1995) suggests that there remains an attitude of 'benign apathy towards equal opportunities' within schools – especially among physical education teachers – and that the steps that have been taken to challenge discriminatory practices are inadequate. Before the national curriculum was even implemented, Campbell (1990) warned that attempts to challenge the culture of physical education and sports coaching would be undermined by the consequences of single-sex physical education colleges' becoming co-educational and merging with university courses and the move towards co-educational schooling. The pressure for physical education to become 'more academic' (resulting in what Flintoff called a 'move towards the scientific and measurable' (1990, p 18)) and the upgrading of courses to degree standard, saw women lose out:

> Men have gained positions of authority in the former women's colleges, but the opposite has not been the case in terms of women securing appointments in the former men's colleges. With only a few exceptions, women are vastly underrepresented in these institutions. This trend is set to continue, for it seems that fewer women than men now apply for posts in physical education teacher education and women are increasingly underrepresented in physical education's professional associations and committees. Similarly, many of the profession's academic journals are run and edited by men, contributing still further to a situation where men define the academic 'discourse' [Flintoff, 1990, p 18].

The difficulties that women face in accessing employment opportunities as a consequence of these developments are exacerbated by the continued preference for male coaches (Campbell, 1990). Schools, professional clubs, Football in the Community officers and others who are involved in employing and training coaches could help to break down discriminatory practices by giving women the opportunity to develop the skills, knowledge and experience they need to compete for positions of influence within football in general, not just within the women's game. But women's football is no different to most other sports where male coaches have been brought in to 'toughen things up' and 'professionalise the coaching'. This makes sense in the higher echelons of the game, but women who want to teach the sport need the opportunity to do so. If that means introducing affirmative action in sports coaching, then so be it, for governments are so desperate to be associated with sporting success that a law introducing a scheme it is not beyond the realms of possibility. It would be far more preferable, though, if Football in the Community was able to build upon its excellent work in this area by taking the initiative itself.

FOOTBALL IN THE COMMUNITY

The involvement of professional football, and professional footballers, in community schemes has its roots in the Chester Report. In 1978, the Government (under the auspices of the late Denis Howell, then Minister for Sport) had made over £1 million available to clubs who wished to instigate community-based projects, ideally in the most economically deprived areas. However, there was criticism that the money had been used to enhance existing facilities within the clubs 'while failing to involve the types of youngster intended' (Harding, 1991, p 351). But, in 1985, the Professional Footballers' Association (PFA) introduced a pilot scheme involving six clubs in the North West, providing a budget of £300,000 and employing over 60 people, many of whom were former professional players. By 1989, over 50 clubs were involved in the scheme, which was by then being jointly administered by the PFA, the FA and the Football League. By the mid-1990s, all professional clubs in England and Wales (and some semi-professional ones) had a Football in the Community officer ('Community Officer').

Broadly stated, the aim of the scheme was to re-establish the (supposed) links between the clubs and the local communities that many believed had been loosened and then lost altogether in the wake of media attention and hooliganism during the 1970s and 1980s. The idea was to take coaching schemes into schools, in the hope that more children would start to support their local side. There was a more ambitious element too. It was hoped that the scheme could somehow divert youngsters away from crime, drugs, anti-social behaviour and the other scourges of post-industrial Britain by providing suitable role models whom they could look up to, respect and emulate. In time, certain clubs began to offer both free training to the long term unemployed and support for those studying for vocational qualifications in the sport and leisure industries.

The benefits to the PFA were that the schemes offered employment opportunities to its retired members, and it was able to enhance its role in player education and vocational training. The scheme allows the players themselves to sample life outside football, and perhaps to consider what career opportunities might be available to them once their playing days are over (not everybody earns £25,000 a week). While some Community Officers regard the job as a stepping stone into coaching or management, others see the role as more akin to that of a social worker.

From the perspective of encouraging girls' participation in the game, Football in the Community's figures are impressive: 'The 1991–93 Football and the Community Development Programme Business and Action Plan had a target of 75,000 girls to be involved through coaching and other football involvement by the end of 1993 [Lopez, 1997, p 231].' In fact, over 200,000 girls were involved by that time. The schemes have been instrumental in providing girls with the opportunities to play in under-12, under-14, under-16 and women's teams. Given that the FA has been advised by FIFA of the need to develop the women's game, the role of the Football in the Community scheme is destined to become even more important in this regard.

But the fact remains that, despite the efforts that have been made to encouraging women's involvement and participation in some quarters, very few women presently hold full time, employed posts as coaches in Football in the Community schemes (the author discovered just three Assistant Community Officers in the Greater London area). None of these hold the exalted post of 'Community Officer'. This will come as no surprise, considering the dearth of women in employment as stewards, administrators, 'front of house' staff or in any other capacity in the professional game.

THE LIFE AND HARD TIMES OF THE PROFESSIONAL FEMALE COACH

The experiences of those three female Assistant Community Officers were markedly similar. They all started playing in primary school. One took it upon herself to organise after-school clubs once she reached secondary school (the school not being obliged to let them play with boys, following the decision in *Bennett* (1978)) and was fortunate to live near a club that had a women's team. The others had played in boys' sides until the age of 10 or 11, were then banned from doing so but were recruited by local women's teams who heard about their plight in local newspapers. As 13 year olds, these women were playing with and against women who were more than twice their age, which doubtless led to a lot of young female footballers giving up the game. *Bennett* had led to the bizarre situation where, at the age of 11, girls were banned from playing against boys of the same age but could play against 30 year old women.

Their role with Football in the Community involves organising girls' football teams and coaching courses and, it seems, doing more than their fair share of administration. But they all work with clubs that have developed innovative programmes which use football as a vehicle to challenge racism and to promote equal opportunities and work within the wider community. Two of the women work with young offenders, people with learning difficulties and the over 50s; the other runs literacy programmes and collaborates with local colleges to offer qualifications in the sport and leisure industry.

One does not need to be a former or aspiring professional footballer to make a worthwhile contribution to programmes like these, but, while not wishing to denigrate the value of such initiatives, it seems that the women who are involved in them have been deprived of football-specific opportunities as a consequence. The experience of one of those women tells its own story:

> While working here I've applied for three Head Community Officer posts at London clubs and I didn't get any of them. Now, that can be for a number of reasons, but I was told by a member of the panel that he wouldn't ever employ a woman. He's the Area Officer and, as such, he has sat on each of those three panels. He recommended that I stick to girls' football and community development work.

In the near future, a female coach, mindful of the decision in *Hardwick* (1997) and how it affects her own employment, will be able to bring an action against a club that fails to appoint her to a Head Community Officer post. Evidence that a member of the interview panel has freely admitted that he would never employ a woman in such a post would be of considerable interest to tribunal members and, as *prima facie* evidence of discrimination, would be rather difficult to rebut. Section 44 of the Sex Discrimination Act 1975 would provide no more of a defence than was the case in *Petty* (1981) or *Hardwick* (1997). The continuing prohibition on these women attending PFA's annual awards dinner hardly gives the right impression from an organisation that purports to support equal opportunities.

In fact, given the continued growth of girls' football, there are certain areas of the Community Officer's remit that are, if anything, more suited to women than to men. The FA has put funding forward for clubs to run girls' and women's Schools of Excellence as it seeks to convince FIFA that it takes the women's game seriously. Grants of £5,000 are available to the successful applicants, which is not a princely sum – some male players earn that much in a day – but, as community schemes only get £6,000 a year each from PFA, they have to find most of their money from other sources and an extra £5,000 is not a sum to be trifled with. Of course, the best coaches are men and, if excellence is to be achieved, the best coaches have to be used. But one would hope that any club that successfully bid for Women's Centre of Excellence funding would actually employ some women to work on it as well.

In time, more women and girls will become involved in football, there will be more coaching courses for them (presuming that the FA learns from the mistakes it made in *Hardwick*) and there will be a marked increase in the number of women with the highest coaching qualifications. If the prejudices that pervade football for too long can be overcome, and if more women are given the opportunity to earn a living from it, genuine gender equity may eventually prevail in other sports, too. The alternative is the imposition of affirmative action schemes along the lines of Title IX, which really would give the game something to worry about.

CHAPTER 11

BLOWING THE WHISTLE: TAKING THE LEAD IN PARTICIPANT PROTECTION

INTRODUCTION

This book contains some criticisms of the football industry and of the people who run it. While not all of these criticisms will be regarded as valid by everyone who takes the trouble to read it, one fervently hopes that they will be accepted in the spirit in which they are intended – as a contribution to a constructive debate on what the game has become and where it goes from here. The aim of this last chapter is to redress the balance somewhat by acknowledging the value of some thoroughly worthwhile initiatives in which football has taken the lead in recent years, and to suggest ways in which those efforts could be built upon. Some of the issues discussed here are practices that many sports organisations would prefer the general public not to know about, because they have failed to deal with them effectively, but they are areas where 'football people' have made their presence felt.

This chapter raises the spectre of sexual abuse in sport. Football's governing bodies, and some high profile clubs and players, have given their time to support the NSPCC's 'Full Stop' campaign, and this is another area in which the employees of Football in the Community have done some terrific work. This chapter tries to follow their lead by suggesting steps that could be taken to prevent abusers from gaining positions of trust within sport itself. In the wake of *R v Hickson* (1997), sports organisations can no longer pretend that abuse does not occur in sport; it is an issue that is not going to go away. Additionally, brief consideration is given to the Lyme Bay canoe tragedy as an example of a situation where former employees' concerns about safety went unheeded. It will be argued that, if proper provision had been made for employees to raise their concerns with individuals who did not have a vested interest in the running of the centre, the Lyme Bay tragedy could have been avoided. The conclusion calls upon the football industry to respond to these tragedies, and also to learn from its own mistakes in *Hardwick v FA* (1997), *Hussaney v Chester City FC* (1997) and other discrimination cases, by giving the lead to other sports. In particular, it advocates the introduction of proper reporting mechanisms through which employees and participants can raise their concerns about discrimination and malpractice without going to law or 'blowing the whistle' externally.

While the emphasis is on the law of England and Wales and the practices of sports bodies within that jurisdiction, examples from the US will be used to illustrate how recent Supreme Court rulings have obliged sports organisations there to take discrimination and harassment seriously. In an attempt to avoid liability for the discriminatory conduct of their employees, US sports organisations are making increased use of internal reporting mechanisms and employee codes of conduct. The steps that those organisations have taken in response to legal intervention would provide an invaluable starting point if the football industry decided to take issues seriously.

REPORTING WORKPLACE CONCERNS

The discriminatory practices of which Hardwick and Hussaney complained are so much a part of the culture of the football industry that it is difficult to believe that they would ever have been changed had it not been for the intervention of the law. Procedures which allowed employees, spectators and other 'participants', in the broad sense of the word, to report concerns will do little to effect change in the face of well established intransigence and the presence of systemic discriminatory practices. But the potential benefits of ensuring that employees are aware of their rights and obligations, and of providing individuals with an opportunity to raise their concerns about workplace malpractice, were apparent in *Cummins v Kingstonian FC* (1998), *Hussaney* and many of the other cases that have been discussed in this book. Individual clubs, governing bodies, trade unions and other interested organisations should be working together to create a viable reporting structure and a meaningful code of conduct which would avoid the need for individuals such as Cummins to seek recourse to the law in order to gain redress. At the very least, the creation of a written code of practice, disseminated to all staff regardless of the capacity in which they are employed and underpinned by a written guarantee that each signatory will adhere to the code's terms, would represent a worthwhile starting point.

A code of practice should outline employees' rights and obligations in respect of, *inter alia*, equal opportunities, creating a workplace environment that is free from harassment and which maintains health and safety at work. The next step would be the provision of a framework through which employees can report their legitimate concerns; however, this framework must be formulated in a manner which allows the employee to bypass the individual who is the subject of their concerns – a provision which was noticeably absent in *Cummins*. The existence of such a scheme, and its proper implementation, could help to persuade an employment tribunal that equal opportunities are being taken seriously in the particular workplace. It would also reassure employees that their workplace rights are being taken seriously.

There are two potential sources of information that sports organisations which are interested in supporting those who wish to raise concerns could look to for guidance. The first is the UK's own laws on whistleblowing, as contained in the Public Interest Disclosure Act 1998. The second is the practices of sports bodies in the US, which are presently dealing with changes to the law that have had a fundamental impact on their potential liability for harassing behaviour. The next two sections of this chapter will look at each of these developments in turn.

BLOWING THE WHISTLE

'Whistleblowing' is commonly understood to occur when workers express a concern externally about malpractice or wrongdoing within their organisation because they do not feel able to raise the matter internally, or where they have already raised the matter internally but it has not been satisfactorily dealt with. Although there is still a tendency to view whistleblowers as disloyal troublemakers, an alternative management approach is to treat them as dedicated individuals who provide an alternative to legal intervention when management structures fail (Lewis, 1995). Whistleblowers – and, crucially, the implementation of a worthwhile internal reporting mechanism to support them – give employers the opportunity to address problems before matters escalate to the extent that they did in *Cummins* and *Hussaney*. If employees are not given the opportunity to have their concerns addressed internally, then the likelihood is that legal action will ensue – which invariably results in expense, adverse publicity and the irretrievable breakdown of the parties' working relationship. The alternative, of course, is that the matter will not be dealt with at all and the harm or wrong will continue, unexposed. 'Whistleblowing is in the interests of wider society [and] proper protection must be provided for those who are driven to it [Lewis, 1995, p 209].'

Whistleblowers need the protection of the law and the security of internal codes of conduct and reporting mechanisms, because whistleblowing amounts to a *prima facie* breach of an employee's terms and conditions of employment. As such, blowing the whistle can result in dismissal or other disciplinary action. Ordinarily, there is an implied duty of fidelity that prevents an employee from disclosing information that has been acquired in confidence. Although, since *Initial Services v Putterill* (1968), it has been possible for employees to argue that the alleged misconduct was so serious that disclosure was in the public interest, disclosure had to be to someone who had an interest in receiving it. In *Lion Laboratories v Evans* (1985), the Court of Appeal indicated that disclosure to the press might not always be appropriate. This meant that, before the 1998 Act came into force, the only external bodies to whom one could safely report one's concerns were those regulatory bodies which had been established specifically to investigate breaches of statutory duty. These would include the Inland Revenue and the Health and Safety

Executive (Lewis, 1995). In fact, s 7 of the Health and Safety at Work Act 1974 places an express statutory duty on every employee 'to take reasonable care for the health and safety of himself and of other persons who may be affected by his acts or omissions'. This obliges employees to report any concerns internally and, if their representations are ignored, to report them to the Health and Safety Executive, regardless of any implied contractual duty of confidentiality they may owe to the employer. This provision could be used, for example, by football club employees who have concerns about the inadequate training undertaken by many of the stewards who are hired from stewarding agencies but whom the clubs continue to use for want of an alternative.

The Public Interest Disclosure Act 1998 amends the Employment Rights Act 1996 by inserting a new s 43 into that Act. It protects employees who disclose information which, *inter alia*, tends to show that a criminal offence has been committed; that a person has failed to comply with any legal obligation; that an individual's health and safety has been infringed; or that the environment has been damaged (s 43B). It covers workers who raise genuine concerns about mistreatment, financial malpractice, dangers to health and safety or the environment and 'cover-ups' by protecting so called 'public interest' whistleblowing to regulators, the media and Members of Parliament. It guarantees full compensation, with the promise of penalty awards if the whistleblower is sacked. It applies whether or not the information is confidential and whether the malpractice is occurring in the UK or overseas. It covers trainees (such as James Hussaney), agency staff (which would include agency stewards), contractors and those who work from home (s 43K). There are neither restrictions on the basis of age nor minimum qualifying periods, but the Act does not cover the genuinely self-employed or volunteers – a crucial and regrettable omission, bearing in mind the extent to which most sports organisations rely on volunteer workers.

The 1996 Act, as amended, provides that disclosure to a manager will be protected so long as the disclosure is made 'in good faith' (s 43H(1)(a)). Disclosure to a 'prescribed regulator' (s 43F) will similarly be protected, as will disclosure to a 'responsible person', if disclosure to that person has been authorised by the employer (s 43C). However, disclosures to 'outsiders' (such as the police, the media and those who are not prescribed regulators) will only be protected if they are reasonable in all the circumstances. Such disclosures will never be protected if they have been made for personal gain (s 43G).

Unless the whistleblower reasonably believed that he would be victimised, the concern must have first been raised with the employer, or with a prescribed regulator, if applicable. This provision does not apply if the matter is exceptionally serious, if there is no prescribed regulator *and* the whistleblower reasonably believed that evidence of the matter would be 'concealed or destroyed' if he first reported it internally (s 43G(2)). If the whistleblower is victimised or dismissed in breach of the Act, he can bring a claim to an employment tribunal for compensation and, if appropriate, may apply for an interim order prohibiting the employer from dismissing him (ss 4–16 of the 1998 Act). In assessing whether a disclosure that has occurred under these circumstances was reasonable, the employment tribunal will consider the identity of the person that it was made to, the seriousness of the concern, whether the risk or danger remains and whether it breached any duty of confidence that the employer owed a third party. If the concern has been raised with the employer or a prescribed regulator, the tribunal will also consider the reasonableness of their response. Contractual duties of confidentiality, or 'gagging clauses', in employment contracts and severance agreements are void if they conflict with the 1996 Act (s 43J of the 1996 Act).

Although the provisions of the Public Interest Disclosure Act 1998 have been broadly welcomed, whistleblowers are still vulnerable. In any event, the ultimate goal should be to prevent the necessity of the juridical field encroaching onto the sports field altogether, unless involvement of the law is a necessary and appropriate response to the sports industry's inertia. In order to explore the most efficacious ways of achieving that, it is necessary to examine the alternatives to legal intervention that may exist, through which it may be possible to protect those who are involved in sport and who have concerns that they seek to raise.

THE US EXPERIENCE

In the US, the law on sexual harassment in employment is governed by Title VII of the Civil Rights Act 1964. This provides that it is unlawful employment practice for an employer to discriminate against any individual with respect to his compensation, terms, conditions or privileges of employment, because of such individuals' race, colour, religion, sex or national origin. Sexual harassment within the field of education is covered by Title IX of the Education Amendments 1972, which similarly prohibits, *inter alia*, sexual harassment and discrimination in educational institutions which receive Federal financial assistance.

There is a broad range of behaviour that amounts to sexual harassment under US law, including unwelcome verbal banter or jokes of a sexual nature; unnecessary patting and touching; verbal harassment; and subtle pressure for sex. But, in the late 1990s, three Supreme Court decisions substantially extended the ramifications for companies whose employees engaged in behaviour that contravened those provisions. The first case, *Oncale v Sundowner Offshore Services* (1997), concerned a male employee who had been harassed by male co-workers and whose employer dismissed the incidents as 'horseplay'. The Supreme Court ruled that the sexual harassment provisions of Title VII apply to same-sex harassment. In *Burlington Industries v Ellerth*

(1998), the Supreme Court held that that an employee has a cause of action under the provisions of Title VII of the Civil Rights Act 1964 even if the harasser's threats have not been carried out. In this case, a sales representative who repeatedly rebuffed the amorous advances of a middle manager suffered no adverse consequences and was, in fact, promoted. She had been familiar with the company's sexual harassment policy but, rather than use that procedure, she filed a lawsuit. The Supreme Court was asked to rule on whether the employer could be liable for the harasser's behaviour when there had been no detrimental effect on the plaintiff's employment status.

The court held that the absence of tangible negative consequences did not prevent an employee from bringing a claim. However, it went on to say that employers can use the 'affirmative defense' and limit potential liability if they can show that they took reasonable steps to prevent and remedy sexual harassment. Employers may also avoid liability if they can show that an employee unreasonably failed to take advantage of corrective opportunities provided by the employer.

Finally, and most significantly, in *Faragher v City of Boca Raton* (1998), the plaintiff, a female lifeguard, had suffered sexual harassment by her supervisors. They had subjected her (and other female lifeguards) to uninvited and offensive touching and lewd remarks. Although she told another supervisor about the others' behaviour, the supervisor failed to report the misconduct to his superiors. The plaintiff had not taken steps to report the harassment to the city authorities and neither she nor her harassers had been aware of the city council's written policy against sexual harassment. Shortly before the plaintiff resigned, another female lifeguard wrote to the city council's personnel director and complained about the harassment. The plaintiff subsequently discovered that at least five other female lifeguards had made complaints about the conduct of the same supervisors. The council investigated the complaint and reprimanded the harassers. Subsequently, the plaintiff filed suit, claiming that the city was liable for the harassment she had suffered. The case turned on whether, in the circumstances, the council could be held liable for a first-line supervisor's sexually harassing behaviour.

The Supreme Court ruled in the affirmative: an employer will normally be liable for a pervasive, hostile environment of harassment – and is liable for the misconduct of its employees – regardless of whether it had been aware of the harassment. The court's reasoning was based on the fact that employers have the opportunity to screen, train and monitor staff members who carry out supervisory roles. However, the court also said that an employer would have a defence if it could establish that it exercised reasonable care to prevent and correct harassment, and that the complaining employee unreasonably failed to use the existing complaint procedures. In this case, the city's sexual harassment policy had never been disseminated effectively among the beach employees and the internal complaints procedure did not provide a mechanism for bypassing the offending supervisors.

US EMPLOYERS' LIABILITY:
THE NEW PLAYING FIELD

Oncale (1997), *Ellerth* (1998) and *Faragher* (1998) have substantially expanded US laws on employers' liability for acts of sexual harassment by their employees, especially in circumstances where the victim is a subordinate of the harasser. These changes to the law have provoked consternation among employers, not least within organisations that are concerned with the provision of sports and recreation and within university athletics departments, all of which have well documented histories of sexual harassment and abuse being dealt with ineffectually (Messner and Sabo, 1994). The most important development is that an employer is liable to an employee for a hostile environment created by a supervisor who has immediate (or successively higher) authority over the employee. In some circumstances, employers can avoid liability if they can show that they exercised reasonable care to prevent and promptly correct any sexually harassing behaviour (*Faragher*). The employee need only prove that a direct line supervisor engaged in actionable sexual harassment. If the harassment culminated in a tangible employment action (for example, if the harassed employee was demoted, dismissed or otherwise saw the circumstances of her employment change), the employer has no defence and is liable for damages.

The difficulty for employers is that a supervisor may engage in conduct that is so severe that a single incident amounts to sexual harassment (indecent assault or false imprisonment, for example). Consequently, all employees are now under pressure to maintain, and be able to prove that they disseminated to all employees, an anti-harassment policy that includes what the court in *Faragher* termed 'a sensible complaint procedure'. An employer which (a) had no policy; or (b) failed to disseminate its policy; or (c) failed to include a means of bypassing the harassing supervisor to register the complaint, would have no defence.

However, the court also stressed that employers must take reasonable care to *prevent*, as well as correct, any sexually harassing behaviour. Maintaining an anti-harassment policy alone is not enough to avoid liability and prudent employees will put all their supervisory personnel through rigorous training on an ongoing basis. Other means of prevention can be addressed through the specific contents of the harassment policy itself and through the dissemination and reaffirmation of that policy.

LEARNING FROM THE US EXPERIENCE

After *Faragher v City of Boca Raton* (1998), the steps that sports bodies in the US have been advised to take in order to comply with the law by preventing harassment or abuse in the workplace (and, failing that, to avoid liability should incidents occur) seem onerous. The recommended measures, which go far beyond the written equal opportunities policies that one occasionally encounters in sports organisations within the UK, include the following (www.jacksonlewis.com):

- Each company should carry out an immediate review of its sexual harassment and anti-retaliation policy to ensure that the company (*inter alia*):

  o provides employees with convenient and reliable mechanisms for reporting incidents;

  o posts the name, work location and telephone number of the person to whom employees may raise their concerns;

  o encourages employees to report incidents promptly, either verbally or in writing;

  o maintains a 24 hour complaint hotline.

- The company should identify all supervisors and make them accountable for compliance with the company's anti-harassment and anti-retaliation policy.

- The company should train all supervisors on sexual harassment prevention, and make attendance at these sessions mandatory.

- The company should make all its non-supervisory employees aware of the sexual harassment policy and the procedures to follow if they experience sexual harassment.

- In order to remove any doubt about dissemination of the sexual harassment policy, the company should obtain signed receipts from all employees when distributing it.

- The company should redistribute the policy periodically – at least annually – and obtain new receipts.

- The company should instruct appropriate managers on the guidelines for conducting investigations into allegations of harassment.

- The company should incorporate the anti-harassment policy into its training programmes for new employees.

- The company should document the attempts that it makes to prevent and correct harassment, and record any employee's failure to participate in the training programmes that it provides.

The benefits of employers operating a 24 hour hotline could be equally well achieved, at markedly less expense, by proper implementation of the other reporting mechanisms. However, proper risk management would involve extending all aspects of the training programme to all employees, rather than limiting some aspects of it to those who operate in a supervisory capacity. So far as the others are concerned, however onerous they may be, the reality is that they represent little more than good practice from a risk management perspective. Sports organisations in the UK would do well to consider whether there is anything they could learn from the US experience, for the Lyme Bay tragedy and the *Hickson* case (see below) illustrate what can happen when people's genuine concerns go unheeded.

SEXUAL ABUSE IN SPORT

Paul Hickson was a swimming coach who worked primarily with 13 and 14 year old girls. In the early 1990s, he was investigated in connection with allegations of indecent assault which were made by a number of girls whom he had coached in South Wales between 1983 and 1988. He was subsequently charged and was due to stand trial in 1992, but absconded before the trial started. However, publicity over his disappearance resulted in four other women, hitherto uninvolved in the case, coming forward to make complaints that they had been raped, buggered and sexually assaulted by Hickson when he worked in Norfolk between 1976 and 1981. Their evidence suggested that Hickson had used the same *modus operandi* in respect of all of his victims over the whole period of 1976–88. Consequently, when he finally stood trial, he was confronted by new charges, including two of rape, that arose out of the allegations from that earlier period – allegations that would probably have never come to light had Hickson not absconded. Hickson was duly convicted on 11 counts, including the rape charges, relating to young women aged between 13 and 20 ((1995) *The Times*, 28 September, p 1). He was sentenced to 17 years' imprisonment.

R v Hickson (1997) is a significant criminal evidence case. Hickson appealed against conviction on the ground, *inter alia*, that, in summing up, the judge had failed to comment on the fact that the most serious counts – those concerning the allegations of rape – dated from 1976–77. No complaint had been made against Hickson at the time and the judge might have said that, given the absence of complaint in 1976–77, Hickson could not be expected to provide alibi evidence for those dates nearly 20 years later. However, the appeal was dismissed. The Court of Appeal ruled that the absence of a direction on those issues had not rendered the verdict unsafe or unsatisfactory. It is unusual for a conviction to be upheld in the absence of a direction on the difficulties that the defence faces when there has been a delay in the making of allegations. However, in reaching its decision, the Court of Appeal was particularly swayed by the striking similarities in the evidence of the two, entirely independent, groups of young women.

There is little quantitative evidence of the prevalence of sexual abuse in sport; given the sensitive nature of the topic and the fact that a lot of people involved in sport have a vested interest in denying its existence at all, this is of little surprise. Brackenridge has documentary evidence of 'almost 90' cases in the UK, and research suggests that approximately one in four girls and one in nine boys experience sexual abuse before the age of 16 (Brackenridge, 1997). If these figures are accurate, 'then it must be accepted that a large proportion of participants go through the traumatic experience of sexual abuse before their introduction to sport' (Brackenridge, 1997, p 118). Given that the victims of sexual abuse are quite likely to be victims on more than one occasion, one has to confront the likelihood that, where sexual abuse does occur in sport, abusers are probably building upon vulnerabilities that have already been established. The process of 'grooming' by an abuser – building trust, pushing back boundaries and making ever increasing use of verbal and physical familiarity – is easier to achieve when the 'target' displays guilt, depression or low self-esteem, or manifests the other forms of behaviour that are associated with abuse victims.

In sports, abusers may come in the guise of 'coaches, instructors, chaperones, parent-helpers, bus drivers, other athletes' or anyone else who has access to persons who are potentially at risk (Brackenridge, 1997, p 115). The 'classic' sexual abuse scenario often involves a period of grooming or coercion on the part of the abuser, and the dividing line between sexual abuse and sexual harassment is often blurred. Brackenridge provides examples of the range of behaviour which amounts to harassment but which falls short of abuse, and her examples closely reflect what employers in the US have, in the wake of *Faragher* (1998), come to understand as 'hostile environment' harassment. More controversially (but, it is submitted, correctly), she identifies 'exchange of reward or privilege for sexual favours' as sexual *abuse* rather than 'mere' harassment. Such behaviour would probably need a sufficiently strong aura of consent to avoid attracting the attention of the criminal law (unless, of course, the victim is under age). Many of the other forms of abuse that Brackenridge mentions (rape, forced sexual activity, sexual assault and physical/sexual violence) are all criminal offences. But Brackenridge recognises that sports lend themselves particularly well to coercive behaviour, where abusers can spend months, or even years, gaining the trust and adulation of their victims, culminating in the creation of an environment where the distinction between coercive sex and consensual relationships between adults becomes blurred. As Brackenridge infers, abuse is abuse, regardless of the age of the victim and abuser, and this does not change simply because the abuse can be passed off as a consensual relationship.

Once again, much can be learned from the US experience. In collegiate sport, coaches having sex with student-athletes is regarded as unacceptable conduct which strikes at the heart of the employment relationship, especially in the wake of *Faragher*. No university has attempted to impose a blanket prohibition on consensual sexual relationships between coaches and athletes, but the sexual harassment policies at all these institutions make it clear that, in some circumstances, even consensual relationships can lead to discipline or dismissal (see, for example, the University of Nebraska's harassment policy at www.uneb.edu/employees). Most universities' harassment policies stress that the institution may refuse to support the coach if a student-athlete with whom he had a consensual relationship subsequently makes allegations of harassment against him. In the UK, the view that sexual relationships between coaches and athletes are unprofessional is less widely held and would not result in disciplinary action, unless, of course, the matter attracts the attention of the criminal law, as in *Hickson* (1997). One can envisage situations where discipline or dismissal would be an appropriate response to these relationships (if, for example, a coach's lover were selected ahead of better athletes). However, the view that these relationships are no concern of the club, governing body or other employing institution remains the norm. Organisations and individuals need to accept that having sex with athletes is not a 'perk of the job' and that the question of whether the athlete is over the age of 15 is largely irrelevant. Sexual relationships with athletes are always unprofessional and should not ever be condoned.

THE LYME BAY TRAGEDY

In the late 1980s and early 1990s, several disaster inquiries revealed situations where employees had been aware of risks but had not said anything (see, for example, the Bingham Inquiry, 1992) or did not want to 'rock the boat' (the Hidden Inquiry, 1988). In other cases, employees had voiced concern but either nothing was done (the Sheen Inquiry, 1987) or they were victimised for speaking up (the Blom-Cooper Inquiry, 1992). Within the context of sport, the Lyme Bay canoe disaster of March 1993 did much to raise awareness of the difficulties facing those who have concerns about the industry.

The four teenagers who died at Lyme Bay were in a party of 11 that had tried to canoe its way across Lyme Bay in Dorset. They died of hypothermia after heavy seas forced their canoes away from the coast and they capsized in strong winds. Their first aid and safety equipment was inadequate – some canoes were not equipped with spray decks, some lifejackets had no whistles and no distress flares were carried. Although the weather forecast was for maximum temperatures of 10°c with a force five wind, the party had been told to wear only swimming costumes under their wetsuits. A safety boat that was supposed to be in attendance was several miles away and the local coastguard had not been informed of the trip. The centre manager did not report the party's failure to return to the centre until three hours after their estimated time of arrival, and the children spent another three hours in the water before the coastguard spotted them.

Less than a year before the disaster, two leisure centre employees had voiced their concerns about practices at the centre and had resigned over the inadequate safety and levels of training that they and other staff members had received. The two had written to Peter Kite, the managing director of the company which ran the centre, complaining of the £50 per week wages paid to instructors and stating that 'not one person here is technically qualified to instruct children ... We are walking a very fine line between getting away with it and having a serious incident'. Their letter concluded by recommending that 'you should have a very careful look at your standards of safety, otherwise you might find yourself trying to explain why someone's son or daughter will not be coming home'. Their concerns had been ignored.

Kite and the manager of the activity centre, one Joseph Stoddart MBE, were subsequently charged with four counts of unlawful killing. At the trial, one of the instructors said that, although he had been canoeing since the age of 14, he had received no training in taking people out to sea. An official from the British Canoe Union said that the training course that the two instructors had attended was 'absolutely inappropriate' for sea canoeing instructors. He went on to say, 'I cannot believe anyone would contemplate taking a group of absolute and complete beginners on a trip like this' ((1994) *The Guardian*, 24 November, p 13). The single biggest contributory factor to the tragedy was that neither the instructors nor the members of their party knew how to inflate their lifejackets properly. Kite was convicted of corporate manslaughter after a three week trial – the first successful prosecution for that offence in the UK. His company, OLL Ltd, was fined £60,000. The jury failed to reach a verdict in respect of Stoddart and he was formally acquitted. Sentencing him to three years' imprisonment (reduced to two on appeal), the judge commented that Kite was 'more interested in sales than in safety' and had ignored the 'chillingly clear' warning letter he had received from the two former employees. In July 1996, a report by John Reeder QC absolved the coastguards from any responsibility for the youngsters' deaths, although he did say that there had been 'some complacency' on the part of the coastguards who had been on duty that day ((1996) *The Guardian*, 18 July, p 6).

At the end of the trial, Ognall J criticised the Government for its approach towards outdoor activity centres and, in particular, for its failure to introduce statutory registration of outdoor activity centres and their mandatory accreditation and inspection. In January 1996, the Government announced that it would support a Private Members' Bill introduced by David Jamieson MP, which provided for the compulsory registration of activity centres and the introduction of a complaints procedure through which centre users (but not employees) could voice their concerns. The Activity Centres (Young Persons' Safety) Act 1995 accordingly requires centres which offer activity holidays in caving, climbing, trekking or watersports for persons under the age of 18 to register with the Adventure Activities Licensing Authority. Leisure centres which do not offer any of these activities are simply required to comply with the provisions of the Health and Safety at Work Act 1974, as extended by various pieces of European Union health and safety legislation.

CONCLUSION AND RECOMMENDATIONS

Sports organisations' role in preventing abuse rests in placing effective 'external inhibitors' in the path of potential abusers. Reporting mechanisms and codes of conduct go hand in hand with taking steps to help children, in particular, to understand that it is fine to say 'no' and with providing a supportive environment in which participants, co-workers and others can concerns about inappropriate behaviour. Codes of practice should stress that reporting concerns internally (that is, to one's employer) in the first instance is preferable to 'blowing the whistle' externally, which is likely to place an intolerable strain on the employment relationship.

The importance of communicating this policy to employees in writing, and in advance of any concerns arising, is that employees need to know beforehand what to expect. If an aggrieved employee attempts to raise an allegation of harassment with (for example) the governing body and is told for the first time that concerns should first be raised with their employer, there is a strong possibility that the employee will either keep silent or talk to the media. This is particularly the case if the employee has no confidence in the employer's taking the matter seriously. Consequently, the code of practice should also clearly outline a recommended course of action for employees who feel unable to report their concerns internally or who are dissatisfied with the action that results from it. In order to comply with the Public Interest Disclosure Act 1998, the code must stress that, although confidentiality will be respected, guarantees of anonymity can never be given. While the main argument in favour of anonymity is that it acknowledges whistleblowers' vulnerability and tries to accommodate it, the US experience shows that giving an undertaking of anonymity that should have never been given can prevent proper consideration of the issue. If an investigation results, the identity of the person concerned will quite possibly be revealed during that process.

The code should emphasise that the subsequent victimisation of employees who make a complaint of race or sex discrimination is an offence under s 4(1) of the Race Relations Act 1976 or s 291 of the Sex Discrimination Act 1975 respectively; and would, in addition, result in the governing body taking appropriate disciplinary action. Similarly, victimising employees who report concerns is unlawful under s 47B of the Public Interest Disclosure Act 1998. Once again, the code should stress that such conduct, and seeking to deter employees from raising concerns in the first place, amounts to a serious breach of the code and will be treated accordingly – meaning that, if circumstances demand, the governing body will levy financial or other penalties. Similarly, the code should stress that the making of false allegations, or allegations that are financially motivated, also amounts to a serious breach. If phrases such as 'malpractice,' 'wrongdoing', 'reasonable' and 'in good faith' are used, they should be defined accurately but in terms that a layperson can understand.

The circumstances in which employees can refer their concern to the governing body rather than to their employer in the first instance should be stipulated. Likewise, provision should be made for employees to reveal their concerns to outside agencies, such as the police or the media, if such a revelation would be 'in the public interest'. The code should also provide guidance on the meaning of this latter phrase. While this would undoubtedly present difficulties of definition, a satisfactory solution might be to state that disclosing unlawful acts or activities that would tend to bring the sport into disrepute would necessarily be 'in the public interest'.

Finally, the necessity of sports bodies ensuring that they take up references and carry out criminal conviction checks on potential employees needs to be emphasised. Failing to do so lays the organisation open to an action in negligence if participants suffer harm at the hands of an employee whose *bona fides* have not been established. Taking these steps also suggests that an organisation is committed to best practice. Until recently, providing a reference that was unfavourable and/or inaccurate did not provide the employee with a course of action unless that reference was defamatory. But, in *Spring v Guardian Assurance* (1994), the House of Lords ruled that an employer does owe a duty of care to an employee in respect of the preparation of a reference. This means that the employer would be liable in damages for any economic loss suffered by the employee if the reference was negligently prepared. The case extends the law on professional references because the employee no longer has to prove that the reference was defamatory *and* was motivated by malice. Consequently, employers now have to be careful that the opinions expressed in references are accurate. In the US, new employers have sued previous employers who have provided inaccurate references. An 'overblown' reference, over-accentuating the positive in order to get rid of an employee, could see the new employer bringing a negligence action if the employee's competences or *bona fides* are at odds with the previous employer's assertions (Wallace-Bruce, 1997). Employers also need to keep full and accurate written records, making sure that anything said in a reference can be substantiated. And, once again, the desirability of providing properly thought out and implemented reporting mechanism through which any concerns that may arise can be dealt with becomes apparent. The alternative is the maintenance of a culture of silence, in which the only winners are those who have something to hide.

PROFESSIONAL CLUBS' RESPONSES TO THE KICK-IT CAMPAIGN[1]

EXECUTIVE SUMMARY

- In mid-June 1997, a confidential questionnaire was sent to the 91 professional football clubs who played in the FA Premier League or the Nationwide League in both the 1996/97 and 1997/98 seasons. By the end of July 1997, 65 clubs had completed and returned the questionnaire, giving a participation rate of 71%.

- Sixty clubs (92% of all participants) stated that they had complied, in whole or in part, with the Commission for Racial Equality's request that they introduce three fundamental anti-racism strategies in support of the 'Kick Racism Out of Football' campaign. These strategies are: the insertion of anti-racism messages in match day programmes; the broadcasting of similar messages over the public address system; and the use of perimeter advertising to indicate clubs' support for the campaign.

- Of the 65 clubs responding, 10 (15% of all participants) had implemented all three of the 'Kick-It' strategies. Twenty one clubs (32%) had introduced two of them and 29 (45%) had introduced one. Only five (8%) had not introduced any.

- Of the 29 clubs who had implemented only one of the three anti-racism strategies, 27 indicated that 'statements in match day programmes' were their sole means of communicating their support for the campaign.

- In the 1996/97 season, two of the clubs had dedicated telephone 'hotlines' which fans could use to report incidents of alleged racial abuse. Four other clubs said that they were introducing hotlines for the 1997/98 season.

- Twenty seven clubs (41% of all respondents) stated that they used other methods of discouraging racially abusive behaviour, either in addition to or instead of hotlines or the 'Kick-It' campaign's three strategies.

- Of the five clubs who had not implemented any of the three strategies, three said that they used other methods to discourage racist behaviour instead. Only two of the 65 respondents had neither implemented any of the Kick-It strategies nor used other means of discouraging racism.

---

1   This report was written by Professor David Lewis and David McArdle in 1998 and was published by the Centre for Research in Industrial and Commercial Law, Middlesex University Business School.

- The authors conclude that, while a number of clubs are doing a great deal, both in terms of implementing Kick-It and developing their own anti-racism initiatives, the efforts of the country's top teams outside London have not really matched those of clubs within the capital. It would appear that a club's decision as to whether or not to actively participate in the Kick-It campaign depended primarily on whether influential individuals felt that it was something they wanted to get involved in.

- During the next year, the authors will be conducting follow-up interviews to discuss aspects of the clubs' anti-racism and broader 'Football in the Community' programmes.

INTRODUCTION

1 The Kick-It campaign

The 'Kick Racism Out of Football' campaign ('Kick-It') was launched by the Commission for Racial Equality (CRE) and the Professional Footballers' Association (PFA) in August 1993. Although there had been anti-racism initiatives in the game before (mostly instigated by the fans themselves), this was the first campaign to get the backing of the PFA, the Football Association and most of the clubs. At the time of the launch, around 75% of all clubs agreed to display anti-racist posters around their grounds and to print in their match day programmes a joint statement from the PFA Chief Executive and the CRE Chairman. That statement condemned both those who are responsible for racist behaviour at football grounds and those who condone it by doing or saying nothing. The campaign also called upon clubs to take the following steps to help to tackle racism:

- issue a statement that the club will not tolerate racism, spelling out the action that it will take against those engaged in indecent or racist chanting. The statement should be printed in all match programmes and displayed permanently and prominently around the ground;

- make public address (PA) announcements condemning racist chanting at matches;

- make it a condition for season ticket holders that they do not take part in this or other forms of offensive behaviour;

- take action to prevent the sale of racist literature inside and around the ground;

- take disciplinary action against players who engage in racial abuse;

- contact other clubs to make sure that they understand the club's policy on racism;
- encourage a common strategy between stewards and police for dealing with abusive behaviour;
- remove all racist graffiti from the ground as a matter of urgency;
- adopt an equal opportunities policy in relation to employment and service provision.

2 The scope of the survey and the reasons for it

The research team was interested in the relationship between attempts by the football community to maintain control of its own affairs and the efforts made by governments to impose control over the game. The introduction of new legislation in the wake of the Hillsborough and Bradford disasters, the Heysel riot and the well publicised incidents of racist chanting and racially motivated violence epitomises the increased use of the ordinary 'law of the land' in a sport which has traditionally been self-policing. We wanted to see how the game has responded to this changing pattern of legislative intervention.

Furthermore, our own recent experiences of watching professional football had made us aware that there were wide differences in clubs' support for Kick-It. We were aware that some clubs were taking racism very seriously: in addition to pledging their support for the campaign, they were organising open days and 'Football in the Community' projects, where the issue was high on the agenda. Other clubs seemed to be doing very little, and often there were no obvious reasons for these different approaches. For example, it did not appear to us that clubs situated in racially homogenous areas of the country were 'doing less' about racism than those situated in the multi-racial cities of London or the North West. We were therefore anxious to ascertain whether there were any patterns which characterised the level of clubs' involvement and, if possible, to make tentative conclusions about the level of support that Kick-It was enjoying four seasons after its introduction.

We were particularly interested in the extent to which the clubs had implemented a number of low cost (or no cost) anti-racism strategies which the CRE had asked clubs to introduce back in August 1993. These were: relevant slogans on perimeter advertising boards; statements inserted in match day programmes; and the use of PA announcements. We also wanted to give clubs the opportunity to outline other methods which they may have decided to use, such as posters displayed around the ground. In addition, we were aware that at least one club had introduced a telephone 'hotline', which fans could use to report instances of racist behaviour, and we were interested in whether other clubs intended to follow suit.

3 Methodology

On 11 June 1997, the questionnaire was sent to the chairmen of all the clubs who had played in the Premier League or the Football League in 1996/97 *and* who would be playing in one of those leagues in 1997/98.[2] In addition, clubs were invited to make comments about their anti-racism policies and to send us relevant literature. We also asked whether club personnel would be willing to participate in short follow-up interviews where some of the issues raised by this survey could be considered in more detail. By the end of July, a total of 65 clubs had responded, giving a participation rate of 71%. This includes 30 clubs (46% of respondents) who are willing to participate in follow-up interviews. We were delighted with this level of response and would like to take this opportunity to thank all the clubs who replied.

RESPONSES TO THE SURVEY

1 By division

There are 20 clubs in the Premier League and each division in the Nationwide League has 24 clubs. Of the 65 clubs who responded, 16 had played in the Premier League in 1996/97 (80% of clubs in that league), 18 in the First Division (75%), 16 in the Second Division (67%) and 15 in the Third (65%). Thus, there is a very small (and probably insignificant) decline in response rates as one goes down the league pyramid. However, since the clubs who are not actively involved in Kick-It were the ones least likely to participate in our survey, it could be argued that these responses provide *prima facie* evidence that the higher division clubs are more proactive. We have dealt with this in more detail below.

2 By average crowd size

All league clubs were divided into one of six categories, corresponding to their average attendance in the 1995/96 season:

Category A: *average less than 3,000*: 14 clubs (15% of all clubs).

Category B: *average 3,001–6,000*: 29 clubs (32% of all clubs).

Category C: *average 6,001–12,000*: 16 clubs (18% of all clubs).

Category D: *average 12,001–18,000*: 13 clubs (15% of all clubs).

---

2 Thus, only 23 Third Division sides were sent a questionnaire.

Category E: *average 18,001–24,000*: 5 clubs (4% of all clubs).

Category F: *average more than 24,001*: 14 clubs (15% of all clubs).

(*Rothman's Football Yearbook 1996/97*.)

From those clubs whose average crowd was no more than 3,000 in the 1995/96 season, nine replies were received (64% of clubs in that category). Nineteen of the clubs with gates of between 3,001 and 6,000 replied (66%) and 13 clubs averaging 6,001–12,000 replied (84%). Responses were received from eight of the clubs with average attendances of 12,001–18,000 (57%). All five clubs with averages of 18,00–24,000 replied (100%), as did 11 of the clubs whose average attendance was over 24,000 (87%). The disparate nature of these figures suggests that size isn't everything. There was no more of a relationship between the level of a club's support (as measured by attendance figures) and participation in our survey than there was between response rates and clubs' position in the league pyramid.

3 By region

England and Wales was divided into a number of geographical regions, and the league clubs located accordingly:

London: 13 league clubs (14.3% of total clubs).

South East: 12 clubs (13.2%).

South and South West: 13 (14.3%).

West Midlands: 9 (9.9%).

North West: 19 (20.8%).

North East, North and West Yorkshire: 14 (15.4%).

South Yorkshire and East Midlands: 11 (12%).

Replies were received from 10 London clubs (79% of those in this category); 10 located in the rest of the South East (92%); seven located in the South and South West (46%); six from the West Midlands (66%); 14 from the North West (73%); 10 from the North East, North and West Yorkshire (71%); and 8 located in South Yorkshire and the East Midlands (73%).

Given the racial diversity of city populations, it might be expected that clubs based in the large urban areas would have sophisticated anti-racism policies in place and would be willing to publicise them. Thus, the high response rate from the London, the North West and other urban conurbations did not really come as a surprise. What was noticeable was the exceptionally high response rate from the rest of South East England, where many of the clubs are based in towns characterised by such a high degree of racial homogeneity that one would not necessarily expect clubs to be aware of a racism problem. Indeed, one might expect that racists would feel more comfortable in targeting visiting black players or fans at these clubs than they would do elsewhere. If this is the case, it might account for the willingness of these clubs to support Kick-It. However, when the survey results were analysed in detail, alternative explanations presented themselves. We have dealt with these in greater depth below.

SURVEY RESULTS

1 The extent of clubs' participation in Kick-It

A Generally

Sixty of the 65 clubs who responded (92% of participants) stated that they had implemented, in whole or in part, the anti-racism strategies outlined above. Of those 65 clubs, 10 (15% of participants) had implemented all three aspects of the campaign – the programme statements, the perimeter adverts and the PA announcements. Twenty one (32%) had introduced two of the three, and 29 (43%) had introduced one. Five respondents (11%) had not implemented any of the three elements (but see our comments on the use of alternative anti-racism strategies by some of these clubs, below).

Given that 75% of all league clubs had pledged their support for the Kick-It campaign back in August 1993, it is disappointing that only 10 used all three of the Kick-It strategies in 1996/97. We were particularly surprised to find that very few Premiership or other 'big name' clubs were leading the way in this respect. With two exceptions, the clubs implementing all three strategies were in the First Division (five clubs) or the Second (three clubs) and had average gates of between 6,000 and 12,000. The two exceptions were both London Premier League clubs. In all, five out of the 10 clubs using all three strategies came from London. Of the other five, only one could really be considered to be based in a multi-racial community, and none could be regarded as a 'big club'. Two of the five were based in the South Yorkshire and East Midlands region, two were based in the South/South West and one came from the South East.

All 21 clubs who had introduced two elements were using programme inserts, but 17 (82% of this group) of those used them in conjunction with PA announcements. Four (18%) were using programme inserts in conjunction with perimeter advertising. Of the 29 who had introduced one element, 27 had chosen 'inserts in match day programme' as their sole way of supporting Kick-It. The other two (a Premier League club and a Second Division side) used PA announcements alone.

We received letters from three clubs explaining that they had a policy of not answering surveys and/or did not have the time to complete ours. A number of those who did respond and had either implemented none of the Kick-It strategies or relied on programme inserts alone, made comments which illustrated they had at least given careful consideration as to whether and to what extent they ought to participate in the campaign. One club initially refused to complete the questionnaire on the ground that 'the incidence of abusive behaviour towards the ethnic minorities is virtually non-existent ... vigorously pursuing a policy ... may be counter-productive by creating a problem that is not there'. Similar suggestions were made by seven other clubs:

- 'There is a danger of promoting a problem that (at this ground) is not a big one at all.'

- 'The home support has no record of racist action. We monitor away fans but, thankfully, have found few problems of overt racism.'

- '[The club] has no "racist problem" to speak of. Nevertheless, we have been quick to act should a problem occur.'

- 'We have no problem so feel we should keep a low profile and not instigate something which at the present time is not there.'

It is noteworthy that five of the eight clubs who were using one or no strategies and who made comments along these lines were based in the South East of England. This may help to explain the high response rate from that region which we mentioned earlier. Although 10 of this region's clubs replied, seven were using one strategy at most and, of these, five were keen to point out that their relatively low level of participation was motivated by their perception that racism simply was not a problem at their club.

Of course, there is a powerful commonsense argument at work here – that highlighting a non-existent problem might actually lead to the emergence of that problem. A future aspect of this research will be to look at existing studies on whether publicising violent or anti-social actions can actually lead to the creation of the problem that one is seeking to avoid. Another possibility is that this is just another example of hegemonic discourse which has been repeated so frequently that its truth is generally, but erroneously, accepted. In any event, we received responses from a number of clubs from similarly racially homogenous areas who were more actively involved. A couple of these were not aware of overt racism but felt that they had a duty to actively support a campaign which has the backing of the Football Association, the Football League and the players' trade union:

We don't feel a 'hotline is necessary here as we have had very few incidents ... but we will always oblige with posters or artwork in the match programme. We are avid supporters of Kick Racism Out of Football.

B By division

Of the 16 clubs using PA and programme together, three came from each of the Premiership and Nationwide Leagues One and Two and seven were in Nationwide League Three. Of the eight other Third Division sides who responded to the survey, seven used programme inserts alone and one had not implemented any of the Kick-It strategies. Of the five clubs using programmes in conjunction with perimeter adverts, three were Premier League sides and the other two were First Division teams.

These figures suggest that, although there was a slight tendency for the Premier League and First Division clubs to do more, league position is largely immaterial so far as the extent of clubs' participation in Kick-It is concerned. This perception is reinforced by the fact that, of the 10 clubs who had implemented all three of the anti-racist strategies outlined above, only two were Premier League clubs. Five were in Nationwide League One and three were in Nationwide League Two in 1996/97. There was no significant divisional variation between the 29 clubs implementing only one strategy: seven were in the Premier League (44% of that division's respondents), eight were in Nationwide One (46%), seven were in Nationwide Two (42%) and seven were in Nationwide Three (46%).

C By average attendance

As indicated above, respondents were assigned to one of six categories according to their average league attendance in 1995/96. Of the nine respondents with an average attendance of under 3,000, four clubs had implemented one anti-racism strategy (programme inserts in every instance) and four had implemented two (each one of these being a combination of programme inserts and PA announcements). The other respondent neither implemented any of the three strategies nor used any other means of indicating opposition to racism. None of the clubs in this category used perimeter advertising to show their support for the campaign.

Of the 19 respondents whose attendance averaged 3,000–6,000, two had implemented all three strategies and one had implemented none of them (although this club said that it used other methods). Nine clubs had programme inserts alone, and one of the two clubs to use PA systems alone also fell into this category. A further six clubs had implemented two strategies – programme and PA – on each occasion.

The data received from the clubs revealed that, of the 28 respondents with average crowds of less than 6,000, only two (both of whom had implemented all three strategies) used perimeter adverts to show their support for the campaign in the 1996/97 season. It could be inferred that, although the creation of a suitable perimeter advert is a relatively low cost measure, the smallest clubs are unwilling to 'lose money' by using advertising space in this way. It is hoped that the follow-up interviews will shed more light on the matter.

Although five of the clubs who had implemented all three strategies had attendances of between 6,000 and 12,000, this group also contained two of the sides who had not implemented any of those measures. Four clubs were using programme inserts alone, one was using PA and programme and another was using perimeter adverts in conjunction with programme inserts.

Of those clubs with average attendances of between 12,000 and 18,000, one club had implemented all three strategies and one club had implemented none.[3] Three were using programme inserts alone, two used programme and PA and one used programme and perimeter adverts.

Of the five respondents from clubs with between 18,000 and 24,000 fans on average, one had implemented all three strategies, one was using programme notes alone, one used programme and PA and the other used programme and perimeter advertising.

Only one of the 11 respondents averaging 24,000 and over – a London Premiership side – had implemented all three strategies. Four of these clubs used programme notes alone and one relied solely on PA announcements. Four others used the combination of PA and programme, and one used programme and perimeter adverts.

D By region

Of the 10 *London* clubs to respond, five had implemented all three anti-racism strategies. Two were using PA/programme, one was using perimeter advertising/programme and two relied on programme inserts.

Only one of the 10 *South East* clubs who responded was using all three strategies. Two of them had implemented none and five relied on programme inserts alone. Two used a combination of programme/PA.

Seven teams responded from the *South and South West*, two of which had implemented all three strategies. Three relied on programme inserts and two used PA/programme.

In the *West Midlands*, three of the six respondents used programme notes alone: two used programme/PA and one used programme/perimeter adverts.

Of the *North West's* 14 respondents, two had not implemented any of the strategies and six relied on programme notes alone: four used programme/PA and two used programme/perimeter adverts.

---

3   Interestingly, both of these now have anti-racism 'hotlines'.

In the *North East, North and West Yorkshire* region, six clubs used only programme inserts and three others used programme/PA. One club used PA alone.

South Yorkshire and East Midlands includes two clubs who have implemented all three strategies and one club which has not implemented any.[4] Two used programme/PA, two relied on programme alone and one other used PA alone.

2 Anti-racism hotlines

Our decision to look at 'hotlines' in the context of football stemmed from our research into the use of hotlines in other industries – especially the health service and local government – and their use by trade unions.[5] We were aware from our own experiences of attending games in 1996/97 that one club had a hotline, but we had no reason to believe that others existed or that clubs were considering introducing them. Indeed, they were not something that the CRE/PFA had asked clubs to consider introducing as part of the campaign.

Of those clubs who gave reasons for not having hotlines, 33 (51% of respondents) indicated that they did not believe that hotlines were necessary at their club. This was either because they had no history of racial abuse or because existing methods for enabling fans to complain about abusive behaviour were regarded as adequate. Sixteen clubs (25%) did not give reasons for not introducing a hotline, two clubs cited lack of resources and two gave other reasons. Six clubs were interested in the concept of hotlines but felt that they needed more information about their cost and effectiveness before deciding whether to introduce one.

Of the two clubs who had operated hotlines in the 1996/97 season, one was a Second Division side based in the West Midlands and the other a First Division London club. The London side had introduced their hotline at the beginning of the 1996/97 season and its existence was made known to fans by way of a message in the match day programme. It had been used more than a dozen times during the season[6] and, as a result, some fans had been informally warned about their future behaviour. The club intends to retain the system for the 1997/98 season.

By way of contrast, the West Midlands club introduced their hotline after the season had started. It invited fans to telephone the club's main switchboard during office hours and used a number of means to advertise its

---

4   Although that club has introduced a 'hotline' for the 1997/98 season.
5   Eg, the Transport and General Workers' Union and the National Association of Teachers in Further and Higher Education.
6   The number being an internal extension, staffed during normal office hours and reached via the main switchboard.

existence – PA announcements, messages in the programme, adverts in the local newspaper and perimeter advertising. By the end of the season, fans had used this hotline (sometimes anonymously) on between three and six occasions. As a result of those calls, some fans had been informally warned as to their future behaviour, but others had been permanently banned from the ground and/or reported to the police. This club also intended to keep the hotline for the new season, stating that they considered it important 'to involve supporters in ridding the club of spectators involved in anti-social behaviour'.

Although both those sides are 'big city' clubs, neither would be regarded as being a 'big club' in terms of history or present league position. However, both have had problems with racism in the recent past – one of them being particularly notorious for the ease with which it has been possible to buy far-Right publications within the environs of the ground on match days.[7] Similarly the four clubs who are introducing hotlines in the 1997/98 season are all based in cities with large black and Asian populations and two of them were notorious hotbeds of racism and hooliganism in the 1970s and 1980s. Three of them are Premiership sides while the fourth is in the Second Division but attracts large crowds.

All six clubs with a hotline said that their decision to introduce one reflected their 'determination to eradicate racism from our club', yet the implementation of the Kick-It strategies by these clubs has been varied. One of the clubs with a hotline had implemented all three strategies, while another had done everything except use perimeter advertising. The two with notorious histories of hooliganism similarly used PA and programme announcements. However, the other two who have just introduced hotlines were among the five clubs who had not introduced any of the Kick-It campaign's strategies.

3 Clubs using other methods of combating racism

Of the 65 clubs surveyed, 27 (41%) said that they used other methods of discouraging racially abusive behaviour, either in addition to or instead of hotlines or the campaign's three strategies. Sixteen identified their 'other means' as involving the local media, the use of stewards and/or the displaying of relevant posters around the ground. These clubs did not reveal much detail about how those systems operated or whether they considered them effective. However, as some of them have expressed a willingness to take part in the follow-up survey, we hope to be able to glean more information as this research progresses.

---

7   This being something which Kick-It specifically requested clubs to deal with.

The other 11 members of this group have developed highly sophisticated anti-racism or 'Football in the Community' programmes, which appear to represent models of 'best practice' so far as community initiatives are concerned. Northampton Town[8] has worked closely with the CRE and the local authority to devise the game's first comprehensive equal opportunities policy for all its employees.[9] Millwall, Leyton Orient and the supporters' club at Charlton Athletic have worked closely with their respective local authorities and are heavily involved in a wide range of anti-racism initiatives which extend beyond football.[10] Blackburn has also worked closely with local community leaders and employs Asian stewards as part of a policy designed 'to educate our younger supporters, and to eliminate such abuse'. Manchester City, which undertakes community-based projects in Moss Side, launched 'Kicking Out' on its national tour and Leicester City's Football in the Community department is heavily involved in LASI – the city council's Asian Sport Initiative.

Such clubs are worthy of further study – not least because the various approaches to racism and community initiatives represent another example of the contradiction between the high profile, commercialised, globalised game, as played by a handful of élite superclubs and the community oriented, localised sport in which other clubs are participating. The contradiction is particularly strong in the case of clubs like Manchester City and Blackburn, who endeavour to have a foot in both camps.

SUMMARY AND CONCLUSION

A number of clubs are doing a great deal, both in terms of implementing Kick-It and developing their own anti-racism community initiatives, usually in conjunction with local authorities, schools and trade unions. The London clubs seem to be taking the lead in this respect – through their implementation of the Kick-It strategies, the use of hotlines and some imaginative community initiatives. However, even here some clubs could be doing a lot more – if only to acknowledge that they are the representatives of a multi-racial community. In the other urban centres, the response to the Kick-It campaign has been

---

8 We have departed from the principle of confidentiality here because we felt that these initiatives ought to be publicised. All of these clubs have given permission for the details of their projects to be made public and have stated that they would welcome anything which draws attention to their efforts.

9 The club has also dedicated part of its new ground to Walter Tull – a black professional player who died in action in the Somme in 1918.

10 Leyton commissioned 'Kicking Out', an anti-racist play which has been performed in schools and youth centres throughout the UK, while Charlton are at the forefront of the 'Red, White and Black in the Community' project in Greenwich.

disappointing in some respects. This is particularly so in the North West, where one would have hoped to see more of a lead from some of the country's biggest clubs. Indeed, the efforts of the country's top teams have generally been less than wholehearted. We did not find many examples of élite Premiership sides with highly developed community initiatives or a willingness to engage in wholehearted support of Kick-It, certainly so far as the clubs outside London were concerned. Perhaps this lends support to the idea that, in the contemporary game, clubs are either local community-based or participants in a globalised industry. Few clubs appear able or willing to adopt both roles. In some regions there appears to be a definite split: there are examples where less successful clubs in particular regions have developed a strong community role, apparently in response (conscious or otherwise) to a nearby club's success in chasing on-field glory. This is something we will be looking at over the next year or so, both from the perspective of how football contributes to 'community policing', and from the perspective of what such developments might tell us about the future of clubs outside the Premiership.

The overriding impression we have formed is that, with the exception of most London sides (who often appear to be galvanised by supporters' involvement or local authority initiatives), a club's decision as to whether or not to participate actively in the Kick-It campaign appears to depend primarily on whether influential individuals (both within and outside the club) felt that it was something they wanted to get involved in. If, for whatever reason, a chairman, prominent employee or board member decided that it was important for their club to support the campaign, then they would do so. Geographical location, on-field success, level of support and a history of racism were far less significant than whether individuals within the club were willing to make the effort.

It also seemed that most clubs where Kick-It and/or community programmes had been implemented were working closely with local authorities and schools. If this is the case, then in opens up another interesting aspect of this research. Can one say that the football community's response to Kick-It and community issues has generally been the result of overtures from outside the game, rather than a post-Hillsborough desire among clubs to take more responsibility for what goes on within it? Will the recently instigated 'Football Taskforce' result in an increase in these collaborative projects? If the clubs who say that racism and hooliganism (at least off the pitch) aren't a problem any more are right – and there is evidence which suggests that they may be – then is there a future role for the Kick-It and Football in the Community projects?

We are not in a position to say whether Kick-It and other community initiatives have played any part in the reduction of racist behaviour at football matches which we have seen over recent years. However, our research has raised a number of issues which will be worthy of further study. For example, we will be looking closely at the role of hotlines and methods used by the clubs to combat racism other than the Kick-It strategies that we have discussed here. The broader issue of race and sex discrimination within sports related employment merits further attention. While it is true to say that many clubs are doing far less than they agreed to do when they signed up to the Kick-It campaign in 1993, there are also many clubs who are taking the issue seriously and doing a lot of worthwhile work. As one of our respondents observed: 'the clever thing is to stress the real improvements which have been made.' We are happy to do that.

PROFESSIONAL CLUBS' COMPLIANCE WITH DATA PROTECTION LEGISLATION

The research into the Kick-It campaign gave rise to other evidence which suggested that football clubs are not taking discrimination and equality of opportunity as seriously as they ought to. The work on an equal opportunities code of conduct that clubs could use was not only concerned with effective disciplinary action against racially abusive managers and players; it sought to encourage the establishment of equal opportunities policies in other areas too, notably, the recruitment of administrative, clerical and 'front of house' staff.

A worthwhile equal opportunities code would, at the very least, require any employer to keep basic records of the sex and race of all job applicants for the purpose of monitoring the effectiveness or otherwise of their recruitment policies. This is not merely good practice. Registration of such information is a legal obligation on employers under the terms of the Data Protection Act 1998. The Act is derived from the Council of Europe Convention for the Protection of Individuals with regard to Automatic Processing of Personal Data, 1981. It replaces the Data Protection Act 1984 and brings domestic law into line with European Union law, as contained in the 1995 Data Protection Directive (95/46/EC). Information of this nature is classified as data relevant to 'the administration of prospective, current and past employees' and, accordingly, needs to be registered with the Data Protection Registrar so long as that information is held on a computer database.

Most clubs have progressed beyond the use of quill pen and parchment and it is a fair bet that, if they hold information of this nature at all, it is stored on a computer disk or hard drive. In any case, even those clubs that do not keep information of this specific nature should be registered with the Data Protection Registrar for other reasons. All clubs will keep such data as the names and addresses of shareholders, season ticket holders, participants in club lotteries, etc, and that data should similarly be registered if it is held on a computer. The research that is documented here was carried out when the 1984 Act was still in force. It is reported here in order to draw attention to many clubs' failure to comply with basic legal requirements.

THE SCOPE OF THE LEGISLATION

The Data Protection Act 1984 sought to strike a balance between the freedom to process information on the one hand and rights of privacy on the other. It provided that a data user who stores processed information on a computer relating to living, identifiable individuals is obliged to register that data, unless it is exempt. Those exemptions are strictly limited but extend to, for example, personal data held by unincorporated members' associations, personal data that the law requires to be made public and personal data which should be exempt in order to safeguard national security. Personal data that is used only for calculating and paying wages and pensions is also exempt, but the exemption lapses if the data is used for wider purposes – for example, as a personnel record or for marketing reasons. Data is not exempt merely because the data user thinks that it is routine, harmless or non-sensitive.

Registered data users must comply with the data protection principles established by the Data Protection Regulations 1985 (SI 1985/1463). These require that the personal data shall be:

- obtained and processed fairly and lawfully;
- held only for lawful purposes which are described in the register entry;
- used or disclosed only for those or compatible purposes;
- adequate, relevant and not excessive in relation to the purpose for which they are held;
- accurate and up to date;
- held no longer than the purpose for which they are necessary;
- surrounded by proper security.

To enforce compliance with those principles, the Registrar can serve three types of notice on registered data users:

- an enforcement notice, requiring the data user to take specified action to ensure that a particular principle is complied with;
- a de-registration notice, cancelling all or part of the user's entry. It would then be a criminal offence for the user to continue using the data as though they were still registered;
- a transfer prohibition notice, preventing the data user from transferring personal data overseas if the Registrar feels that the transfer is likely to lead to a principle being broken.

The principles provide for data subjects to have access to the data held about them and, where appropriate, to have that data corrected or deleted. On making a written request to the data user, the data subject is entitled to a copy of all the information that forms the personal data held about him. The data user may charge a fee of up to £10 for supplying this information, but must normally respond within 40 days. If the data is inaccurate, the data subject may complain to the Registrar or apply to the magistrates' court for correction or deletion of the data.

A data subject is entitled to seek compensation if damage has been caused by the loss, unauthorised destruction or unauthorised disclosure (that is, disclosure which has occurred without the authority of the data user) of their personal data. However, many organisations fail to appreciate that, provided that the principles and the registration requirements are complied with, the Act does not prevent a data user from disclosing information about an individual. There is no general right for the data subject to object to the commercial use of their data, but users need to be particularly mindful of the need to obtain and process information fairly and lawfully. This obliges the data user to ensure that they do not deceive or mislead subjects (even inadvertently) about the purposes for which information is to be held, used or disclosed. Compensation can be awarded for damage caused by inaccurate data; compensation for distress may also be awarded, provided that damage can be proved.

A data subject who considers that there has been a breach of one of the principles or any other provision of the Act is entitled to complain to the Registrar. The Registrar must consider the complaint if it: (a) raises a matter of substance; (b) is made without undue delay; and (c) directly affects the complainant. If the complaint is justified and cannot be resolved informally, then the Registrar may prosecute or serve one of the notices mentioned above.

Possible criminal sanctions against non-compliant clubs

In addition to the various offences applying to registered data users, their servants or agents and to computer bureaux, it is an offence to hold personal data 'without being registered or without having applied for registration'.

If the Registrar has reasonable grounds for suspecting that a criminal offence (such as non-registration) has been committed – or that a registered organisation has breached any of the data protection principles – he may apply to a circuit judge for a warrant to enter and search the company's premises. A successful application for a warrant authorises the Registrar's officers or servants to search the premises within the next seven days, to inspect and operate any automatic processing equipment found there. They may also seize any documents or other material that may be evidence of an offence or breach of the principles. It is a criminal offence to obstruct a person in the execution of a warrant or to fail, without reasonable excuse, to give anyone executing the warrant such help as they may reasonably require.

In England and Wales, proceedings for criminal offences under the Act can only be commenced by the Registrar, or by or with the consent of the Director of Public Prosecutions. The criminal convictions attract, in the magistrates' court, a fine not exceeding level five on the standard scale (a maximum of £5,000), as contained in the Criminal Justice Act 1982. Offences tried in the Crown Court can meet with an unlimited fine.

The offences of being an unregistered data user and of a registered data user failing to keep addresses up to date are offences of strict liability. A data user who did not register because of an honest but mistaken belief that the personal data was exempt has no defence to a charge of being an unregistered data user. On conviction, the court may order the forfeiture of any data material connected with the offence. If the offence is committed by a company, then any director, manager, secretary or similar officer is personally guilty of a criminal offence if he consented to or connived at the offence, or if the offence is attributable to any neglect on his part.

A club that was already registered would not have any particularly onerous obligations to fulfil if it decided to develop an equal opportunities code of conduct. It would merely have to amend its existing registration in order to give notice to data subjects (that is, the individuals whose data it holds) that information was stored on a computer database for equal opportunities purposes. Accordingly, another piece of research was undertaken in order to establish: (a) whether all clubs were properly registered in accordance with the 1984 Act; and (b) precisely what kinds of computer data football clubs held on computer, in addition to details held for the purpose of equal opportunities monitoring.

The Data Protection Register is a public document and, as such, one is entitled to limited access to the individual entries of those organisations that have registered. By accessing the Data Protection Registrar's website (www.dpr.gov.uk), it is possible to glean basic information about the entry of any organisation that has registered under the 1984 Act.

The Data Protection Registrar recommends a three stage approach to surveys of this nature in order to ensure that organisations' entries are not missed, and this recommendation was followed while searching for the entries of the 92 Premiership and Football League clubs in January 1998. The first stage was simply to key in the name of each club, but this suggested that only 49 of the 92 clubs were registered at all. The next was to write the phrase 'football club', which produced a list of all the English, Welsh and Scottish Association Football *and* Rugby Football Clubs who were registered. This list contained the same 49 English and Welsh clubs as before, but no new ones. The final step was to key in the postcodes of the 43 clubs who did not appear to be registered (the Rothman's Yearbook provides their full postal address). Again, this yielded nothing new.

The website survey confirmed that, in January 1998, almost half of the 92 professional clubs in England and Wales were not registered at all: a criminal offence under the 1984 Act (when this survey was repeated in January 1999, there were 15 new names on the register).

Before the Data Protection Act 1984 came into force, the Data Protection Registrar had embarked on a publicity drive, bringing the public's attention to the legislation and outlining the steps that companies and other organisations would have to take in order to comply with it. The lamentable registration rate among the clubs suggested that half of them were not aware of the need to comply and that the Data Protection Registrar's publicity campaign had failed miserably. The alternative explanation was that the clubs had known about the Act but, for whatever reason, had failed to comply with it. Before looking into that matter, the Football League was informed that the majority of their 72 members were breaking the law (17 Premiership sides had registered). The Football League replied within days, saying that the clubs had been informed and advised that they needed to register.

One week after receipt of the Football League's letter, a questionnaire about data protection compliance was despatched (along with a pre-paid envelope) to the secretaries of the 72 Football League clubs. In the middle of February, a reminder was sent to the 37 clubs who had not responded. By the end of March 1998, 47 of the 72 surveyed clubs had replied – a response rate of 66%.

Results

Twenty four of the 47 clubs who responded said that they had complied with the provisions of the Act (this was checked against the Data Protection Registrar's website, which confirmed that this was the case). When broken down by division, the responses confirm a marked decline in the number of clubs in compliance as one goes down the league pyramid. Well over half of the respondent clubs in the bottom two divisions in the league pyramid had failed to register.

Of the 24 clubs in compliance, 13 said that their awareness had been purely the result of information sent to them by the Data Protection Registrar. Of the others, six said that they knew of the need to register primarily because of newspaper coverage of the Act or because of solicitors' advice. Five clubs did not answer that question but, at all of these five, the club had registered before the club secretary who filled in the questionnaire commenced employment, so they were probably unable to give an answer. However, only one of the 24 clubs said that they had not used information from the Data Protection Registrar at all: it may not have been the main source of information for some of them, but virtually all had received it and had used it to some extent. All but one of the 24 were fairly sure that they had fulfilled their obligations under the Act.

Non-compliant clubs

All 23 secretaries in this category had received the Football League's letter and 17 of them confessed to having been aware of the Act's existence before they received that communication. Worse, eight of them admitted that they actually knew what the aims of the Act were – not in any great depth, but enough to know that they might have to register. Twenty two of the non-compliant clubs said that they held data which fell into one or more of the 16 data categories outlined above. Four of them held data that fell into six different categories.

These figures raise the strong possibility that many non-compliant clubs know about the Act but have weighed the cost of registration (£75) against the likelihood of prosecution for failure to register and have decided – not unreasonably – that it is a gamble worth taking. This gives rise to the fundamental issue of enforcement and the ramifications of the fact that the Data Protection Registrar does not have the statutory power to instigate prosecutions: it relies on data subjects discovering that their details have not been registered by a data user and notifying the Registrar. Only then can enforcement action be taken or (in the case of organisations that have not registered at all) a criminal prosecution be commenced.

Anderman, S, *Labour Law: Management Decisions and Workers' Rights*, 1993, Butterworths

Armstrong, G, 'Like that Desmond Morris?', in Hobbs, D and May, T (eds), *Interpreting the Field*, 1993, OUP

Armstrong, G and Hobbs, D, 'Tackled from behind', in Giulianotti, R *et al* (eds), *Football, Violence and Social Identity*, 1994, Routledge

Armstrong, G and Giulianotti, R (eds), *Entering the Field: New Perspectives on World Football*, 1997, Berg

Armstrong, G and Giulianotti, R, 'Avenues of contestation: football hooligans running and ruling urban spaces', 1997a, available: www.memphis.edu/wpslc

Armstrong, G and Young, M, 'Legislators and interpreters: the law and "football hooligans"', in Armstrong, G and Giulianotti, R (eds), *Entering the Field: New Perspectives on World Football*, 1997, Berg

Bale, J, 'Playing at home', in Williams, J and Wagg, S (eds), *British Football and Social Change: Getting into Europe*, 1994, Leicester UP

Bale, J, *Sport, Space and Society*, 1993, Routledge

Bale, J, *Landscapes of Modern Sport*, 1994, Leicester UP

Birley, D, *Sport and the Making of Britain*, 1993, Manchester UP

Birley, D, *Land of Sport and Glory*, 1995, Manchester UP

Bitel, N, 'Disciplinary procedures from the point of view of the individual' (1995) 3(3) Sport and LJ 7

Bloomfield, A, 'Muscular Christian or mystic? Charles Kingsley reappraised' (1994) J Sport History 107

Bourdieu, P, 'Sport and social class' (1978) 17 Social Science Information 819

Bourdieu, P, 'The force of law: towards a sociology of the juridical field' (1987) 38 Hastings LJ 814

Bourdieu, P, *Distinction: A Social Critique of the Judgment of Taste*, 1992, Routledge

Boutilier, S and San Giovanni, L, 'Politics, public policy and Title IX', in Birrell, S and Cole, C (ed), *Women, Sport and Culture*, 1994, Human Kinetics

Boyes, S, 'Salary caps in sport: objectives, problems and the law' (2000) 3(1) Sports Law Bulletin 12

Brackenridge, B, '"He owned me, basically ...": women's experience of sexual abuse in sport' (1997) 32(2) Int Rev Sociology of Sport 115

Brackenridge, C and Kirby, S, 'Playing safe. assessing the risk of sexual abuse to elite child athletes' (1997) 32(3) Int Rev Sociology of Sport 407

Brohm, J-M, *Sport – A Prison of Measured Time*, 1978, Ink Links

Bromberger, C *et al*, 'Fireworks and the ass', in Redhead, S (ed), *The Fashion and the Passion: Football Fandom in the New Europe*, 1993, Arena

Brown, A and Walsh, A, *Not for Sale*, 2000, Mainstream

Caiger, A and O'Leary, J, 'Whither the transfer system?' (2000) 3(1) Sports Law Bulletin 13

Chaudhary, V and Thomas, R, 'Door kept open for foreign players' (1999) *The Guardian*, 30 November, p 34

Clarke, A, 'Figuring a brighter future', in Dunning, E and Rojek, C (eds), *Sport and Leisure in the Civilising Process*, 1992, Toronto UP

Clarke, J, 'Football and working class fans: tradition and change', in Ingham, R (ed), *Football Hooliganism: the Wider Context*, 1978, Inter-Action

Cohen, S, *Folk Devils and Moral Panics*, 1980, Robertson

Collier, R, *Masculinity, Law and the Family*, 1996, Routledge

Connell, R, *Which Way is Up?*, 1987, Queensland UP

Cunningham, H, *Leisure in the Industrial Revolution*, 1980, Croom Helm

Davies, N, *Europe – A History*, 1996, OUP

Dunning, E (ed), *Sociology of Sport*, 1971, Frank Cass

Dunning, E, Murphy, P, Williams, J and Maguire, J, 'Football hooliganism in Britain before the First World War' (1984) 19 Int Rev Sociology of Sport 215

Dunning, E and Rojek, C (eds), *Sport and Leisure in the Civilising Process*, 1992, Toronto UP

Dunphy, E, *Only a Game*, 1991, Penguin

Dyer, K, *Catching Up The Men*, 1992, Queensland UP

Elias, N, *The Civilising Process, Volume 2: State Formation and Civilisation*, 1982, Blackwell

Elias, N and Dunning, E, *Quest for Excitement: Sport and Leisure in the Civilising Process*, 1986, Blackwell

Eraut, M, *Developing Professional Knowledge and Competence*, 1994, Falmer

Finn, G, 'Football violence: a societal psychological perspective', in Giulianotti, R *et al* (eds), *Football, Violence and Social Identity*, 1994, Routledge

Football Association, *Blueprint for Football*, 1991

Football Licensing Authority, *Guidance on Safety Certificates*, 1992

Football Taskforce, *Eliminating Racism from Football*, 1998

Foucault, M, *Power/Knowledge*, 1980, Harvester

Gardiner, S, 'Not playing the game: is it a crime?' (1993) 138 SJ 628

Gardiner, S and Felix, A, 'Juridification of the football field: strategies for giving law the elbow' (1995) 5(2) Marquette Sports LJ 189

Gardiner, S, 'World Cup 98 ticketing' (1998) 2(5) Sports Law Bulletin 13

Gardiner, S, Felix, A, James, M, Welch, R and O'Leary, J, *Sports Law*, 1998, Cavendish Publishing

Gardiner, S, 'Support for quotas in EU professional sport' (2000) 3(2) Sports Law Bulletin 1

Garland, J and Rowe, M, *Racism and Anti-Racism in British Football*, 2000, Macmillan

Giulianotti, R, Hepworth, N and Bonney, M (eds), *Football, Violence and Social Identity*, 1994, Routledge

Giulianotti, R, 'Taking liberties: Hibs Casuals and Scottish law', in Giulianotti, R *et al* (eds), *Football, Violence and Social Identity*, 1994, Routledge

Giulianotti, R, 'Football and the politics of carnival: an ethnographic study of Scottish fans in Sweden' (1995) 30(2) Int Rev Sociology of Sport 191

Grayson, E, *Sport and the Law*, 1994, Butterworths

Greenfield, S and Osborn, G (eds), *Sport and Law in Contemporary Society*, 2000, Frank Cass

Greenfield, S and Osborn, G, 'When the whites go marching in: racism and resistance in English football' (1996) Marquette Sports LJ

Greer, S, 'A guide to the Human Rights Act 1998' (1999) 24 EL Rev 3

Gunn, M and Ormerod, D, 'The legality of boxing' (1995) 15(2) LS 181

Hamil, S, Michie, J, Oughton, C and Warby, S (eds), *Football in the Digital Age*, 2000, Mainstream

Hammond, B and Hammond, J, *The Village Labourer*, 1911, London

Harding, J, *For the Good of the Game*, 1991, Robson

Hargreaves, Jennifer, *Sporting Females: Critical Issues in the History and Sociology of Women's Sports*, 1994, Routledge

Hargreaves, John, 'The body, sport and power relations', in Horne, J *et al* (eds), *Sport, Leisure and Social Relations*, 1986, Routledge

Harrington, J, *Soccer Hooliganism: A Preliminary Report*, 1968, John Wright

Hay, D, 'Property, authority and the criminal law', in Thomson, E (ed), *Albion's Fatal Tree*, 1974, Penguin

Hervey, T, 'Justification for indirect sex discrimination in employment: European Community and United Kingdom law compared' (1991) 40 ICLQ 807

Hobbs, D and May, T (eds), *Interpreting the Field*, 1993, OUP

Holt, R, *Sport and the British*, 1989, OUP

Hopcraft, A, *The Football Man*, 1988, Simon & Schuster

Horne, J, Jary, D and Tomlinson, A (eds), *Sport, Leisure and Social Relations*, 1986, Routledge

Hunt, A, 'The role of law in the civilising process and the reform of popular culture' (1995) 10(2) Can J Law and Society 5

Inglis, S, *Digest of Stadium Criteria*, 1992, Football Stadium Advisory Design Council

Ingham, R (ed), *Football Hooliganism: the Wider Context*, 1978, Inter-Action

James, M, 'Prosecuting sportsfield violence' (1997) 7(2) J Legal Aspects of Sport 81

Jessup, G, *Outcomes: NVQ and the Emerging Model of Education and Training*, 1991, Falmer

Johnson, J, 'Title IX and intercollegiate athletics: current judicial interpretation of the standard of compliance' (1994) 74 Boston UL Rev 553

Law Commission, *Consent in the Criminal Law*, 1995, Consultation Paper No 139

Law Commission, *Criminal Law, Consent and Offences Against the Person*, 1994, Consultation Paper No 134

Lester, A, 'Discrimination: what can lawyers learn from history?' [1994] PL 224

Lewis, J and Scarisbrick-Hauser, A, 'An analysis of football crowd safety reports using the *McPhail* categories', in Giulianotti, R *et al* (eds), *Football, Violence and Social Identity*, 1994, Routledge

Lewis, D and McArdle, D, *Reporting Concerns in the Public Interest: What Assistance do Unions Offer their Members?*, 1997, Centre for Research in Industrial and Commercial Law

Lewis, D, 'Whistleblowers and job security' (1995) 58 MLR 208

Lopez, S, *Women on the Ball*, 1997, Scarlet

Malcolmson, R, *Popular Recreations in English Society 1700–1850*, 1973, CUP

Mangan, J and Walvin, J, *Manliness and Morality: Masculinity in Britain and America 1800–1940*, 1987, Manchester UP

Marsh, P, Rosser, E and Harré, R, *The Rules of Disorder*, 1978, Routledge and Kegan Paul

Martin, J, 'Scoring points for women' (1981) 8 Ohio Northern L Rev 481

Mason, A, *Association Football and English Society*, 1980, Harvester

McArdle, D, 'A few hard cases? Sport, sadomasochism and public policy in the English courts' (1995) 10(2) Can J Law and Society 109

McArdle, D, 'Elite athletes' perceptions of the use and regulation of performance enhancing drugs' (1999a) 9(1) J Legal Aspects of Sport 43

McArdle, D, 'Full yellow jacket: stadium safety a decade after Hillsborough' (1999c) 6 Euro J Sport Management 113

McArdle, D, 'Judicial review, "public authorities" and the disciplinary powers of sports governing bodies' (1999b) Cambrian LR 31

McCormick, P, 'The *Bosman* case: the contractual nightmare' (1999) 2(6) Sports Law Bulletin 2

McCrudden, C, 'Rethinking positive action' (1986) 15 Industrial LJ 219

McCutcheon, P, 'Negative enforcement of employment contracts in the sports industries' (1997) 17(1) LS 65

McCutcheon, P, 'Sports discipline, natural justice and strict liability' [1999] Anglo-Am L Rev 37

Messner, M and Sabo, D, *Sex, Violence and Power in Men's Sports*, 1994, Crossing

Miller, F, 'Beyond *Bosman*' (1996) Sport and LJ 45

Miller, F, 'Free market football' (1993) 1(1) Sport and LJ 13

Miller, F, 'Profession: UK footballer; nationality: unclear' (1994) 2(1) Sport and LJ 10

Moran, L, 'Violence and the law: the case of sadomasochism' (1995) 4(2) JSLS 225

Morris, P and Little, N, 'Challenging sports bodies' determinations' (1998) 17 CJQ 128

Morris, P, Morrow, S and Spink, P, 'EC law and professional football: *Bosman* and its implications' (1996) 59 MLR 893

Mullin, J, 'This is the modern world in the penalty area' (1996) *The Guardian (Weekend)*, 20 January, p 5

Murphy, P, Williams, J and Dunning, E, *Football on Trial: Spectator Violence and Development in the Football World*, 1990, Blackwell

National Coaching Foundation, *Protecting Children: a Guide for Sportspeople*, 1998

National Council for Vocational Qualifications, *NVQ: National Targets*, 1990

Neeson, J, 'The opponents of enclosure in 18th century Northamptonshire' (1984) 105 Past and Present 114

Nelson, MB, *The Stronger Women Get, the More Men Love Football*, 1994, Harcourt Brace

O'Leary, S and Caiger, A, 'Footballers' contracts' (2000) 3(2) Sports Law Bulletin 2

Osborn, G and Greenfield, S, *Contract and Control in the Entertainment Industry*, 1998, Ashgate

Pannick, D, *Sex Discrimination in Sport*, 1983, EOC

Parker, B, 'Disciplinary proceedings from the governing body point of view' (1995) 3(3) Sport and LJ 3

Parpworth, N, *Judicial Review of Sports Governing Bodies*, 1995, Manchester Metropolitan University Working Papers in Law and Popular Culture

Parrish, R, 'Who does what in the European Union? Accessing information on sport' (1998) 1(2) Sports Law Bulletin 9

Pearson, G, 'Legitimate targets? The civil liberties of football fans' (1999) 4(1) J Civ Lib 28

Pearson, G, 'Legislating for the football hooligan and the case for reform', in Greenfield, S and Osborn, G (eds), *Sport and Law in Contemporary Society,* 2000, Frank Cass

Pitt, G, *Employment Law,* 1994, Sweet & Maxwell

Pons, J-F, 'Sport and European competition policy', 1999, available: www.europa.eu.int/comm/dg04/speech/1999/en/sp99019.pdf

Potter, M and Regan, E, 'The legal limits of affirmative action in redundancy selection' (1997) 147 NLJ 735

Power, P, 'Kick Racism Out of Football', in Hamil, S *et al* (eds), *Football in the Digital Age,* 2000, Mainstream

Redhead, S, *The Fashion and the Passion: Football Fandom in the New Europe,* 1993, Arena

Redhead, S, *Unpopular Cultures: the Birth of Law and Popular Culture,* 1995, Manchester UP

Robins, D, 'Review of Giulianotti *et al*' (1994) 43(1) Sociological Rev 215

Robson, C, *Real World Research,* 1993, Blackwell

Ross, J, 'Equal pay and sex discrimination law in the UK and Europe: the need for coherence' (1997) 18 J Social Welfare and Family Law 147

Russell, D, *Football and the English,* 1997, Carnegie

Salter, M, 'The judges v the football fan: a sporting contest?' (1985) 36(4) NILQ 351

Salter, M, 'Judicial responses to football hooliganism' (1986) 37(3) NILQ 280

Sanger, J, *The Compleat Observer: A Field Research Guide to Observation,* 1996, Falmer

Sassoon, S, *The Complete Memoirs of George Sherston,* 1972, Penguin

Scraton, P, Jemphrey, A and Coleman, S, *No Last Rights: The Denial of Justice and the Promotion of Myth in the Aftermath of the Hillsborough Disaster,* 1995, Alden

Scraton, P, *Hillsborough – The Truth,* 1999, Mainstream

Simon, R, *Fair Play: Sports Values and Society,* 1991, Westview

Spink, P, 'Post-*Bosman* legal issues' (1997) 42(3) J Law Society of Scotland 108

Stanko, E and Newburn, T (eds), *Just Boys doing Business,* 1994, Routledge

Taylor, I, 'Football mad: a speculative sociology of soccer hooliganism', in Dunning, E (ed), *Sociology of Sport*, 1971, Frank Cass

Terdiman, R, 'The force of law: towards a sociology of the juridical field' (1987) 38 Hastings LJ 805

Thompson, B, *Sadomasochism*, 1995, Cassell

Thompson, E, *Whigs and Hunters*, 1980, Penguin

Thomson, E, *Albion's Fatal Tree*, 1974, Penguin

Thorpe, M, 'Seeing red when the air turns blue' (1995) *The Guardian*, 28 January, p 19

Trivizas, E, 'Offences and offenders in football crowd disorders' (1980) 20(3) Br J Crim 276

Trivizas, E, 'Sentencing the "football hooligan"' (1981) 21(4) Br J Crim 342

Trivizas, E, 'Disturbances associated with football matches: types of incidents and selection of charges' (1984) 24(4) Br J Crim 361

Turner, B, *The Body and Social Theory*, 1984, Sage

Vamplew, W, *Pay Up and Play the Game*, 1988, CUP

Velasquez, B, 'Recent US Supreme Court cases in sexual harassment' (1999) 9(1) J Legal Aspects of Sport 26

Vertinsky, P, *The Eternally Wounded Woman: Women, Sport and Exercise in the 19th Century*, 1990, Manchester UP

Wallace-Bruce, N, 'Employers beware! The necessity of providing an employment reference' (1997) J Bus Law 456

Walvin, J, *The People's Game: The History of Football Revisited*, 1994, Edinburgh UP

Weatherill, S, 'Discrimination on the grounds of nationality in sport' (1989) EL Yearbook

Weatherill, S and Beaumont, P, *EC Law*, 1995, Penguin

Weatherill, S, *Cases and Materials on EC Law*, 1996, Penguin

Welch, R, 'Swamping the British game? Foreign football players and the new Work Permit Regulations' (2000) 3(2) Sports Law Bulletin 6

Williams, D, 'The law relating to public disorder and sporting events', in *Public Disorder and Sporting Events*, 1978, Sports Council/Social Science Research Council

Williams, J and Wagg, S (eds), *British Football and Social Change: Getting into Europe*, 1994, Leicester UP

Williams, J and Taylor, R, 'Boys keep swinging', in Stanko, E and Newburn, T (eds), *Just Boys doing Business*, 1994, Routledge

Government inquiries and reports

Bingham Inquiry into the BCCI Affair, 1992, HMSO, Cmnd 198

Blom-Cooper Inquiry into Ashworth Special Hospital, 1992, HMSO, Cmnd 2028

Chester Report of the Committee on Football, 1967, HMSO

Coopers and Lybrand Final Report on the Impact of EC Activities on Sport, 1993, European Commission

Cullen Inquiry into the Shootings at Dunblane Primary School, 13 March 1996, 1996, Scottish Office, Cmnd 3386

Hidden Inquiry into the Clapham Rail Crash, 1988, HMSO, Cmnd 820

Hughes Inquiry into the Disaster at Bolton Wanderers Football Ground on 6 March 1946, 1946, HMSO, Cmd 6846

McElhone Report into Football Crowd Behaviour, 1978, Scottish Education Department

Popplewell Inquiry into Crowd Safety and Safety at Sports Grounds – Interim Report, 1985, HMSO, Cmnd 9585

Popplewell Inquiry into Crowd Safety and Safety at Sports Grounds – Final Report, 1986, HMSO, Cmnd 9710

Sheen Inquiry into the Zeebrugge Ferry Disaster, 1987, HMSO, Cmnd 8074

Shortt Report on the 1923 FA Cup Final, 1924, HMSO

Street Report on Anti-Discrimination Legislation, 1967, HMSO

Taylor Report on the Hillsborough Disaster – Preliminary Inquiry, 1989, HMSO, Cmnd 765

Taylor Report on the Hillsborough Disaster – Final Report, 1990, HMSO, Cmnd 962

Van Raay Report on the Free Movement of Professional Footballers, 1989, European Parliament Committee on Legal Affairs and Citizens' Rights, Doc A-0415/88

Wheatley Report into Crowd Safety at Sports Grounds, 1972, HMSO, Cmnd 4952

INDEX